THE LEGACY OF JOHN CALVIN

Papers Presented at the 12th Colloquium of the Calvin Studies Society
April 22-24, 1999

Union Theological Seminary and
Presbyterian School of Christian Education
Richmond, Virginia

Edited by David Foxgrover

Published for the Calvin Studies Society by
CRC Product Services
Grand Rapids, Michigan
2000

Cover: Calvin's letter to Edward VI, facsimile in *Letters of Calvin*, trans. Jules Bonnet (Philadelphia: Presbyterian Board of Publication, 1858), vol. 1, title page.

The image of Calvin is from Emile Doumergue, *Iconographie Calvinienne* (Lausanne: Georges Bridel & Cie Editeurs, 1909), plate V, 34.

Copyright © Calvin Studies Society, 2000

Library of Congress Card Number: 00-105929

ISBN 0-9700028-0-7

Contents

Preface

The topic of Calvin's legacy may at first appear predictable or pedestrian; however, readers of these essays will quickly realize that "legacy" is a provocative term that gives rise to important questions about Calvin's writings and his activities in Geneva, as well as how his legacy was appropriated.

Our authors approached their topic with different understandings of "legacy" and, for the most part, focused on the legacy that Calvin bequeathed rather than the one he himself received. Children may spend an inheritance in ways that their parents might reject, and our writers found that Calvin's legacy, in some instances, has been modified and misrepresented and, in others, ignored or rejected.

No doubt the contributors felt at times that the topic of Calvin's legacy was so broad as to be unmanageable; however, that breadth gave each scholar an opportunity to find an approach that would shed new light on Calvin's own thought and ministry, as well as on those who followed him. Moreover, from their various backgrounds as historians and as historians of biblical exegesis and Christian thought, the authors consider issues and theologians from a broad range of periods, from the 16th to the 20th centuries.

We extend our thanks to the members of the Calvin Studies Society whose thoughtful responses and carefully posed questions led to lively discussions among those attending the colloquium.

The Calvin Studies Society expresses its thanks to Louis Weeks, the President of Union Theological Seminary and the Presbyterian School of Christian Education, and to the staff and faculty who made our conference so delightful.

David Foxgrover

Contributors

Philip W. Butin, Pastor, Shepherd of the Valley Presbyterian Church; Instructor, Ecumenical Institute for Ministry, Albuquerque, New Mexico.

Thomas J. Davis, Associate Professor of Religious Studies, Indiana University-Purdue University at Indianapolis; Managing Editor, *Religion and American Culture.*

B. A. Gerrish, John Nuveen Professor, *Emeritus,* University of Chicago Divinity School; Distinguished Service Professor of Theology, Union Theological Seminary and Presbyterian School of Christian Education, Richmond, Virginia.

W. Fred Graham, Professor of Religious Studies, *Emeritus,* Michigan State University, East Lansing, Michigan.

R. Ward Holder, Assistant Professor of Religious Studies, Stonehill College, North Easton, Massachusetts.

Merwyn S. Johnson, Professor of Historical and Systematic Theology, Erskine Theological Seminary, Due West, South Carolina.

Robert M. Kingdon, Hilldale Professor of History, *Emeritus,* Humanities Institute, University of Wisconsin-Madison.

Karin Maag, Director, H. Henry Meeter Center for Calvin Studies, Calvin College and Seminary, Grand Rapids, Michigan.

Jeannine E. Olson, Professor of History, Rhode Island College, Providence, Rhode Island.

Barbara Pitkin, Assistant Professor of Religious Studies, Stanford University, Palo Alto, California.

John L. Thompson, Associate Professor of Historical Theology, Fuller Theological Seminary, Pasadena, California.

John D. Witvliet, Director, Calvin Institute of Christian Worship, Calvin College and Seminary, Grand Rapids, Michigan.

Randall C. Zachman, Associate Professor of Reformation Studies, University of Notre Dame, Notre Dame, Indiana.

Abbreviations

CHB   *Cambridge History of the Bible*. 3 vols. Cambridge: Cambridge University Press, 1963-1970.

CNTC   *Calvin's New Testament Commentaries*. 12 vols. Eds. D. W. and T. F. Torrance. Grand Rapids: Eerdmans, 1959-1972.

CO   *Ioannis Calvini Opera Omnia Quae Supersunt*, ed. G. Baum, E. Cunitz and E. Reuss. 59 vols. Brunsvigae: C. A. Schwetschhke, 1863-1900.

CR   *Corpus Reformatorum*, ed. C. G. Bretschneider. Halis, Saxoum: C. A. Schwetschke and Sons, 1842.

CTS   Calvin Translation Society edition of various works by Calvin. 46 volumes. Edinburgh, 1843-1855.

FC   *The Fathers of the Church*. 92 vols. Washington: Catholic University of America Press, 1947-

LCC   *Calvin: Institutes of the Christian Religion*, ed. John T. McNeill, trans. Ford Lewis Battles. Library of Christian Classics, vols. 20-21. Philadelphia: The Westminster Press, 1960.

OER   *Oxford Encyclopedia of the Reformation*. Ed. Hans J. Hillerbrand. 4 vols. New York: Oxford University Press, 1996.

OODR   *Ioannis Calvini Opera Omnia Denuo Recognita*. Geneva: Librarie E. Droz, 1992- .

OS   *Ioannis Calvini Opera Selecta*. Ed. P. Barth, W. Niesel and D. Scheuner. 5 vols. Monachii in Adeibus: Chr. Kaiser Verlag, 1926-1952.

SC   *Supplementa Calviniana*. Ed. Erwin Mülhaupt. 8 vols. Neukirchen: Neukirchener Verlag, 1936-1961.

Calvin's Academic and Educational Legacy

Karin Maag

My topic raises some of the questions which surely need to be debated and discussed when dealing with the theme of Calvin and his legacy. As a historian with strong interests in early modern higher education and the relations between civil and ecclesiastical authorities in early modern cities, I must observe that my topic raises more questions than answers. How can one speak about *John Calvin*'s educational legacy without wrenching him from his historical context, making it sound as though he, and he alone of the Genevans has a legacy in education which we ought to study and analyze? Calvin himself did not create educational systems, structures, or approaches *ex nihilo*. Indeed, this study will argue that the Genevans were less creators than adaptors, and instead built upon the educational models of their predecessors and contemporaries. Furthermore, it would be historically inaccurate to ascribe the Genevan approach to education entirely to Calvin himself. Indeed, the Genevan Academy, long considered the pinnacle of Genevan education, was only formally established in 1559, five years before Calvin's death in 1564. To try to tie all academic developments in Geneva to Calvin himself would be both short-sighted and unhelpful, and would obscure the fact that the enduring strength of the Genevan educational system lay precisely in the collaborative efforts of the Genevan pastors and magistrates.

These important issues apart, to examine the legacy of Calvin and his colleagues in the educational and academic field is worthwhile, not least because of the enduring impact of the Genevan model on other centers of higher education, especially in France. As those who had studied in Geneva returned to their homeland, they brought with them their newly-acquired knowledge and strong links with the city's leaders, as well as a model of higher education in a Calvinist context, which they could then apply at home.

This paper will start with a rapid overview of the state of education in Geneva prior to the Reformation. Then, by looking both at Calvin's own approach to education in his writings, and the concrete actions taken in Geneva to establish a coherent and useful educational system, we will be able to establish what the Genevan legacy was, and to analyze the ways in which this legacy was taken up elsewhere in early modern Europe.

I

Prior to the Reformation, which was accepted by the Genevan population in May 1536, education in Geneva was a haphazard business, and higher education was largely unavailable in the city itself. Because pre-Reformation Geneva was the seat of a bishopric, the Catholic church was supposed to provide a certain amount of training for its clergy from the area. The third and fourth Lateran Councils, in 1179 and 1215, decreed that each bishop had to create a seminary in his diocese for future priests.[1] Yet this requirement remained an ideal rather than a reality, at least in Geneva, as there is no evidence that a seminary was established while the city was still Catholic.[2] Other schooling options at a lower level included Latin schools, operating at what today would be a high-school level, and vernacular schools, run privately by individuals who taught basic reading, writing and counting.[3] Because no information has survived concerning officially organized schools until 1428, it is difficult to assess what educational opportunities were available to Geneva's young men prior to the early 15th century.

In 1428, however, steps were taken to establish an officially-recognized school. On February 28, 1428, the General Council of Geneva ordered the creation of a public Latin school. This school became known as the Collège de Versonnex, named after the wealthy merchant who put forward the money to have the school buildings constructed. This school primarily taught Latin grammar, and did not offer the option of higher education. The magistrates paid the salaries of those who taught in the Collège de Versonnex. Overall, this represents a first attempt by the Genevan magistrates to organize and control education. Acquiring the right to pay the teachers' salaries, but also to hire these teachers and appoint the rector gave the magistrates a strong voice in educational matters. Indeed, by the time of the Reformation, the magistrates' activity in the Collège de Versonnex provided them with a tradition of involvement in education to call upon when their role in that field was later challenged.[4]

On May 21, 1536, after four years' effort on the part of the Reformers Guillaume Farel, Pierre Viret, Antoine Froment and others, the General

---

[1]Charles Borgeaud, *Histoire de l'université de Genève: L'Académie de Calvin 1559-1798* (Geneva: Georg & Co., 1900), 6.

[2]Louis Binz, *Vie religieuse et réforme écclesiastique dans le diocèse de Genève 1378-1450* (Geneva: Alexandre Jullien, 1973), 352-354.

[3]Louis-J. Thévenaz, "L'Ancien collège de sa fondation à la fin du XVIIIe siècle, précédée d'une introduction sur l'instruction publique à Genève au Moyen-Age," in Thévenaz, Vuilléty et al, *Histoire du Collège de Genève* (Geneva: Département de l'instruction publique, 1896), 1.

[4]Thévenaz, "L'Ancien collège," 5; Jules Vuy, "Notes historiques sur le collège de Versonnex et documents inédits relatifs à l'instruction publique, à Genève avant 1535," in *Mémoires (Institut Genevois)* 12 (1867), 11.

Council of Geneva solemnly agreed "to live under this holy evangelical law and Word of God, as it is declared to us, wanting to leave behind all masses and other papal ceremonies and abuses, images and idols, and to live in unity and obedience to the laws."[5] The previous few years had been very unsettled, not only because of the ongoing confessional debate, but also because of its repercussions on Geneva's political alliances: adopting Protestantism also meant rejecting the rule of the Bishop and princely house of Savoy. The state of affairs in Geneva was such that education suffered as well, since the rector left the Collège de Versonnex in 1534-35, and the pupils began to fall away.[6] Therefore, the renewal of education in Geneva was an urgent priority. The same meeting of the Genevan General council which accepted the Reformation had as a second item of business the reorganization of schooling in the city. The authorities decided that "one should find a learned man [to teach] and that one should pay him a large enough salary so that he can teach and feed the poor [pupils], without asking them for fees, and that all must send their children to school and have them learn…"[7]

By June 13, 1536, the Small Council of the magistrates had found a rector, Antoine Saulnier, from the Dauphiné, and decided to pay him 466 florins a year. Saulnier was to pay part of his salary to each of his two assistants, known as regents. As well, each pupil who could afford to do so was to pay a quarter florin per term. As this modest school fee proved difficult to collect, in essence all pupils attended school for free. The school was now known as the Collège de Rive, taking its name from the area of Geneva in which it lay. From 1544 onwards, the Collège de Rive took over the monastery of the Franciscan friars. While the building, left vacant by the departing monks, was undoubtedly large enough for the school, it was in a poor state of repair. The situation was so desperate that Louis Enoch, rector from 1550-56, complained that several of his pupils had contracted fatal illnesses because of the monastery's ramshackle and unsanitary state.[8]

An anonymous printed pamphlet of 1538, ascribed to Antoine Saulnier, detailed the courses and structure of the Collège de Rive.[9] Admittedly, a comparison with the Collège de Versonnex is difficult, since few sources remain describing the earlier school's teaching. However, it does seem that while the Collège de Rive did address itself to the same age group, it also made certain

---

[5]Amédée Roget, *Histoire du peuple de Genève depuis la Réforme jusqu'à l'Escalade* (7 vols, Geneva: John Jullien, 1870-1888), I: 2.

[6]Thévenaz, "L'Ancien collège," 12.

[7]Roget, *Peuple de Genève*, I: 2.

[8]On the Collège de Rive, see Roget, *Peuple de Genève*, I: 3; Elie-Ami Bétant, *Notice sur le collège de Rive* (Geneva: Fick, 1866), 7, 22.

[9]Bétant, *Notice*, 8.

changes to the curriculum in the light of humanist and Reformation learning. To the French and Latin taught in the Collège de Versonnex, the regents of the Collège de Rive added Greek and Hebrew, taught from the Old and New Testaments. Religious training as a whole began to play a greater role, as the regents led prayers before and after class, and when the school day ended, the children in turn would recite the Ten Commandments, the Lord's Prayer and the Creed in French. In addition, the Rector instructed the entire school daily in the Christian faith. For its boarders, the Collège de Rive offered additional subjects such as basic arithmetic and a more detailed study of Scripture. Otherwise, the school provided classes ranging from reading and writing French and Latin for the beginners, to Latin grammar and written exercises for the more advanced. The preferred Latin authors were Terence, Virgil, and Cicero.[10] There is no sign of higher studies available within the school itself. Outside of the Collège de Rive, however, Saulnier noted that public lectures on the Old and New Testament took place daily. The Hebrew lectures were divided between a grammatical study of each passage, led by an unidentified Hebrew reader, and a study of the scriptural meaning of each passage, led by Guillaume Farel. Calvin provided the Greek lectures on the New Testament.[11]

The aim of Saulnier's pamphlet appears to have been to attract potential pupils to Geneva. The author strongly rejected the charge that Reformed Geneva had cast secular learning aside. In setting out the Reformed attitude towards the liberal arts at this early date, Saulnier provided a useful yardstick against which to measure later attitudes and actions in the same field. He stated that the Reformers considered the liberal arts to be "among the excellent graces of God." He defined clearly the status of the liberal arts. "Even though we give priority to the Word of the Lord, this is not to say that we reject the knowledge of good letters, which certainly can follow and appropriately take second place. And indeed, when these two things are united in this fashion, there is great uniformity and agreement that the Word of God should be the basis of all doctrine, and that the liberal arts act as ways and means (not to be disdained) serving for the true and complete knowledge of that Word."[12] According to Saulnier, study in the arts was held to be a highly useful occupation, but remained a tool of scriptural exegesis.

Some see the Collège de Rive merely as a transitional institution, bridging the gap between Genevan education under Catholicism and Calvin's educational projects brought to fruition in the creation of the Genevan Academy in 1559.[13] This seems unfair, and to do less than justice to the achievements of the

---

[10] *L'ordre et la manière d'enseigner en la ville de Genève au collège* in Bétant, *Notice*, 28-34.

[11] Bétant, *Notice*, 34-5.

[12] Bétant, *Notice*, 37-8.

[13] Henry Fazy, *Le livre du recteur: Etude historique sur l'Académie de Genève* (Lausanne, 1862), 2; and Borgeaud, *Histoire*, 16.

Collège de Rive. Clearly, the education provided by the Collège de Rive was neither as up-to-date nor as complete as possible. There were no standard examinations to regulate progress from one level to another, and no systematic division of pupils into groups of similar ability. As well, apart from the public exegetical lectures given by Calvin and Farel, there was no academic training available in Geneva after one had proceeded through the Collège de Rive. Those who wanted to study further in a university setting had to go elsewhere. Yet the Collège de Rive must not be dismissed completely as an imperfect early version of the Genevan Academy. In spite of the difficulties in recruiting capable personnel, the Collège de Rive saw the application of several Reformed educational principles, such as the emphasis on the ancient languages of Scripture and on comprehensive religious training included in the curriculum. Furthermore, Antoine Saulnier's pamphlet on the Collège de Rive shows how, even in the early years of the Reformation in Geneva, before the Academy's creation, the civil and ecclesiastical authorities were conscious of the need to clarify the relative roles of theological and liberal arts education.

Despite the qualities of the Collège de Rive, the lack of formal training beyond the level of a Latin grammar school in Geneva was a growing problem in the years following Geneva's Reformation, particularly in terms of the education of future pastors. This was especially acute given the high opinion of the ministerial office held by the Reformers, and expressed by Calvin in Geneva's ecclesiastical ordinances.

The ecclesiastical ordinances of 1541 state that candidates for the ministry were to be examined in two areas: on their doctrine and on their morals.[14] Doctrinal knowledge was defined as having "a good and sound knowledge of Scripture," and communicating this to the people in an edifying way. Furthermore, candidates were to agree with the doctrine held in Geneva. Therefore, the required characteristics for ministers in terms of doctrine included knowledge of Scripture, an ability to communicate it clearly to the people, and an understanding and commitment to the Reformed doctrines held in Geneva.

These doctrines had to be learned. Candidates for the ministry could study Scripture and the ways of transmitting its teachings by attending some or all of the twenty weekly services taking place in the Genevan city parishes.[15] Candidates could also attend Calvin and Farel's daily public exegeses on the Old and New Testament, held in the Genevan cathedral of St. Pierre. Finally, candidates may have been able to gain a more in-depth knowledge of Reformed doctrine from the weekly *congrégations*, or gatherings of ministers and interested lay-people, at which theological theses were presented and defended by each of the Genevan ministers in turn. These *congrégations* were

---

[14]"Ordonnances écclesiastiques de 1541," in Henri Heyer, *1555-1909: L'Eglise de Genève: Esquisse historique de son organisation* (Geneva: Alexandre Jullien, 1909), 262.

[15]"Ordonnances écclesiastiques de 1541," in Heyer, *L'Eglise de Genève*, 265-6.

one of the major educational innovations of the Reformation, providing as they did an opportunity for ministers already holding posts to gain further training in Scriptural exegesis and public speaking.[16]

By 1557, as well as the *congrégations*, the ministers organized monthly disputations. The registers of the Company of Pastors recorded,

> On Friday, the first day of the year, a disputation was begun in the ministers' presence by some worthy people of this church, who wish to practice the use of Scripture. It was agreed that the proponent would take his conclusions from one of the Apostles' letters, and the Epistle of the Hebrews was chosen to start with. The first proponent, chosen by lot, was Philibert Grené, and M[aster] Calvin provided the answer to each disputed point, to the edification of all. These disputations, depending on the grace of the Lord, will continue and take place on the first Friday of each month. Of course, no one can attend apart from the ministers and those who wish to debate in turn.[17]

Once again, it is likely that candidates for the ministry were the ones who used this opportunity to further their knowledge of Scripture and to increase their ability at communicating it effectively.

Ministry candidates in Geneva could therefore extend and deepen their understanding of Scripture, its languages, and of the doctrine drawn from it by the Genevan church from sermons, exegetical lectures, the *congrégations*, and latterly from the monthly theological disputations. Yet all these elements were not organized into any system or pattern, making it difficult for the candidates to acquire relevant knowledge in any methodical fashion, and for the ministers to transmit their learning in any formal context.

Increasingly, therefore, the Company of Pastors and magistrates of Geneva were aware of the need for a more structured approach to higher education, particularly as preparation for the clergy. This plan had already been voiced in the ecclesiastical ordinances of 1541. Having established the need for professors of Old and New Testament, the ordinances continue, "but because one cannot benefit from these lectures unless one is taught languages and humanities, and because we need to raise up a harvest for coming years, so as not to leave a barren church to our children, we should establish a college to teach them and prepare them both for ministry and civil government."[18] In 1559, the city of Geneva was finally able to put this aim into practice in the creation of the Genevan Academy.

---

[16] *Registres de la Compagnie des Pasteurs de Genève* (Geneva: Droz, 1969-) (henceforth RCP), I: 167-82

[17] *RCP*, II: 70.

[18] "Ordonnances écclesiastiques de 1541," in Heyer, *L'Eglise de Genève*, 266.

II

Before giving a description of the Genevan Academy and its impact and legacy for Reformed higher education, it is worth examining in more detail what Calvin's own views were regarding education and the form it should take.

Unlike Reformers such as Zwingli, Bullinger, Luther and Melanchthon, Calvin himself did not write any work specifically dealing with education and the form which it should take. Thus, his educational views have to be pieced together from his writings. The most important feature of Calvin's perspective on education was the centrality of education in the faith: in his commentaries and catechisms, he highlighted the necessity for children to learn and understand the grounds of their beliefs. In his commentary on Psalm 78, Calvin states,

> In the first place, the fathers, when they find that ... they are instrumental in maintaining the pure worship of God, and that ... they are the means of providing for the salvation of their children, should ... be the more powerfully stirred up to instruct their children. In the second place, the children on their part, being inflamed with greater zeal, should eagerly press forward in the acquisition of divine knowledge, and not suffer their minds to wander in vain speculations, but should aim at, or keep their eyes directed to the right mark.[19]

Thus parents had a responsibility to teach the doctrines of the faith to their children, while children were expected to be enthusiastic recipients of religious instruction.

Calvin's comment about avoiding "vain speculations" is significant. Indeed, as mentioned before, the issue facing Calvin and other Reformers was that of the integration of religious studies (of the Bible, the doctrines of the church, etc.) with the humanist curriculum and the revival of interest in classical Roman and Greek texts. Once again, Calvin himself did not deal directly with this issue in any writing on education. However, in his commentary on First Corinthians 1, verse 17, Calvin does explain his views on the right relationship between religious education and the liberal arts. When discussing Paul's use of "the wisdom of words," Calvin writes,

> ... it were quite unreasonable to suppose, that Paul would utterly condemn those arts which, it is manifest, are excellent gifts of God, and which serve as instruments, as it were, to assist men in the accomplishment of important purposes. As for those arts, then, that have nothing of superstition, but contain solid learning, and are founded on just principles, as they are useful and suited to the common transactions of human life, so there can be no doubt that they have come forth from the Holy Spirit; and the advantage

---

[19]John Calvin, *Commentary on the Book of Psalms*, trans. James Anderson, (Grand Rapids: Eerdmans, 1949), 233.

which is derived and experienced from them, ought to be ascribed exclusively to God. What Paul says here, therefore, ought not to be taken as throwing any disparagement upon the arts, as if they were unfavorable to piety'.[20]

Clearly, for Calvin the liberal arts had a significant role to play in education, but they also had to be understood as part of the knowledge coming from God, rather than existing as a separate category of knowledge. It is essential to understand that Calvin did not reject humanist learning altogether, even if its models came primarily from among pre-Christian philosophers. Calvin did reject what he called "vain speculations" when wanting to emphasize the importance of a simple approach to faith, but he still saw the liberal arts as more than that.[21] According to Calvin, if all knowledge comes from God, then the liberal arts too can be seen as God's gifts, and, crucially, can be used to reinforce faith. Calvin's view here is linked to that of other reformers such as Heinrich Bullinger of Zurich, for instance. Bullinger also felt that there was value in the study of liberal arts, but made a significant distinction between the categories of knowledge represented by the liberal arts and the study of Scripture. In his *Haussbuch* of 1558, Bullinger writes, "As well, it is well-known that the liberal arts serve to explain and illuminate something, so that they are used for a good reason and a right reverence for God, but one must always leave the mastery to Holy Scripture, and all foreign and separate areas of knowledge must be subject to it."[22]

III

Preserving a balance between theological education and liberal arts training was one of the key features of the Genevan educational system as established in the Academy in 1559. The rest of this study will deal with the ways in which the Genevan church and city leaders approached this problem, and the Genevan impact on other Calvinist colleges and academies in the 16th century. One aspect of the Genevan system that needs to be made clear is that Calvin and his fellow ministers did not intend to create a university in Geneva. Medieval and early modern universities normally had four faculties: an entry-level arts faculty, and three higher faculties, in law, theology and medicine. Hence theology was only one possible course of study open to students in such institutions. The Genevan Academy, however, in its early years at least, had as its main aim the preparation and training of Calvinist ministers for areas outside Geneva, especially France, but later on also other areas of Europe. With this goal in mind, lib-

---

[20]John Calvin, *Commentary on the Epistles of Paul the Apostle to the Corinthians,* trans. John Pringle (Grand Rapids: Eerdmans, 1948), 75.

[21]The best source for this section is François Wendel, *Calvin et l'humanisme* (Paris: Presses universitaires de France, 1976), esp. chapter III.

[22]Hans Ulrich Bächtold, *Heinrich Bullinger vor dem Rat: Zur Gestaltung und Verwaltung des Zürcher Staatswesens in den Jahren 1531 bis 1575* (Berne: Peter Lang, 1982), 230.

eral arts training was integrated into the curriculum, but once again it served as a means to an end, namely the theological training that would result in well-educated and competent ministers. When the Academy was founded, the professors who were first appointed taught in arts (chiefly Latin rhetoric, ethics and eloquence), Greek, Hebrew, and theology. The speech given by Theodore Beza at the inauguration of the Genevan Academy in June 1559 made mention of future plans to perhaps expand the curriculum to add law and medicine, but this was not set in place from the beginning. Most scholars agree that the impetus for study in fields other than theology was more a product of Beza's influence rather than Calvin's.[23] However, Beza, too, in his speech was careful to establish both the parameters and ultimate goal of all learning, namely the service of God. He stated, "you have not come here as most of the Greeks of old went to their gymnasia to watch vain wrestling matches. Instead, prepared by the knowledge of the true religion and all sciences, you can contribute to the glory of God and become the honor of your homeland and the support of your family. Remember always that you will have to account for your service in this holy militia before the supreme commander."[24]

Although Beza, Calvin and their successors in Geneva were careful to establish a system of learning that would emphasize the service of God, rather than the pursuit of learning for its own sake, the curriculum of Geneva did not differ greatly from that of other centers of higher studies at the time. The academies of Strasbourg, Lausanne and Zurich, for instance, all of which predate Geneva, each had as one of their main goals the training of ministers for the surrounding area. Each emphasized, as did Geneva, studies in Latin, Greek and Hebrew as preparatory courses for Scriptural exegesis, which was the culmination of the curriculum.[25] In other words, one cannot claim that Geneva's curriculum was particularly innovative as compared with other contemporary institutions of the same caliber. Instead, the particular legacy of the Genevan educational system was the effective way in which this curriculum was implemented, and specifically, the way it was integrated into the life of the churches and their future pastors.

The strength of the Genevan Academy lay in several factors. First, except in times of financial straits, the magistrates and Company of Pastors of Geneva

---

[23]Borgeaud, *Histoire*, 51-2

[24]*Discours du Recteur Th. De Bèze prononcé à l'inauguration de l'académie dans le temple de Saint Pierre à Genève le 5 juin 1559* (Originally published Geneva, 1559; reprinted Geneva: Slatkine Reprints, 1959), trans. H. Delarue, 19.

[25]On Strasbourg, see Anton Schindling, *Humanistische Hochschule und Freie Reichsstadt: Gymnasium und Akademie in Strassburg 1538-1621* (Wiesbaden: Steiner, 1977); on Lausanne, see Henri Vuilleumier, *Histoire de l'Eglise réformée du Pays de Vaud sous le régime bernois* (4 vols, Lausanne: Editions la Concorde, 1927-1933), in particular vol. 1: *L'Age de la Réforme*; on Zurich see Ulrich Ernst, *Geschichte des Zürcherischen Schulwesens bis gegen das Ende des sechzehnten Jahrhunderts* (Winterthur: Bleuler-Hausheer & Co., 1879).

were in agreement that in order to maintain the Academy's strong reputation, they had to attract the best possible professors. While Calvin was alive and still healthy enough, he and Beza taught theology on alternate weeks. Together, these men established the Academy's reputation in the field of Scriptural exegesis, and indeed, many of Calvin's published commentaries were the result of his lectures in the Academy.[26] Yet significantly, the civic and ecclesiastical leaders of the city did not rely on local talent alone to fill the professorial chairs. For instance, in order to fill the Hebrew professor's post, Calvin contacted Immanuel Tremellius, a converted Jew who had taught at the University of Heidelberg, and who was one of the foremost Hebraists of his day.[27] Although Tremellius did not come in the end, the fact that Calvin and his colleagues were prepared to seek out faculty from well outside their own immediate circle is both striking and significant in terms of the Genevan legacy in education.

This approach differed, for instance, from that of Zurich, where already by 1562, only citizens of Zurich could be appointed as professors in its academy.[28] Restricting these posts to Zurich citizens meant that the city council did save money on professors' salaries, as they did not have to attract and retain expensive foreign scholars. However, this policy also meant that Zurich did not manage to achieve the same level of international recognition and reputation as Geneva, both in terms of its level of enrolments and the geographic provenance of its students. Geneva consistently attracted more students and from a wider variety of locations, especially after the 1560s, than did Zurich.[29] Lausanne too was a smaller operation, handicapped by the mass departure of its faculty in 1559 for Geneva at the culmination of a long-standing dispute with their Bernese overlords.[30] The Lausanne Academy's prime objective remained training pastors for the immediate area of the Pays de Vaud, rather than preparing them for ministry further afield.

The second strong point for the Genevan Academy was the effective collaboration between the city authorities and the Company of Pastors in running the Academy. This is not to say that the two powers always saw eye to eye. Indeed, the magistrates were always more conscious of the financial bottom line than

---

[26]See for instance Calvin's preface in his *Leçons et expositions familieres sur les douze petis Prophetes* (Lyon, 1563).

[27]Borgeaud, *Histoire*, 37, 41.

[28]Hans Nabholz, "Zürichs Höhere Schulen von der Reformation bis zur Gründung der Universität 1525-1833," in E. Gagliardi, H. Nabholz, et al. (eds), *Die Universität Zürich 1833-1933 und Ihre Vorläüfer* (Zurich: Verlag der Erziehungsdirektion, 1938), 28.

[29]Although the matriculation records of Geneva and Zurich are not complete, especially not for Zurich, the available data suggests that Zurich only attracted about a third of the number of those enrolling in Geneva. See Karin Maag, *Seminary or University? The Genevan Academy and Reformed Higher Education, 1560-1620* (Aldershot: Ashgate, 1995), 136.

[30]See Henri Vuilleumier, *Histoire de l'Eglise Réformée du Pays de Vaud*, vol. 1.

many of the pastors liked, and the city fathers, for their part, did not always feel that the ministers understood how difficult their financial situation was. This stress was particularly evident during the years of the Savoy blockade of Geneva in the 1580s. In October 1586, the Small Council of Geneva decided to dismiss the Academy's professors because of the blockade: few students were coming, and the city needed the money from these salaries to cover some of their war costs. Yet the ministers petitioned the Small Council on several occasions during that fall not to dismiss the professors, on the grounds that one of the reasons for Geneva's enduring survival against the plots of its enemies had been the Academy, which contributed significantly to the city's strong international reputation.[31] Apart from these moments of crisis, however, the magistrates and ministers did achieve a strong partnership in maintaining the academy, in large part due to Theodore Beza's constant vigilance in making sure that the Academy received the support it needed from each group. This collaboration was vital, for it meant that ordinary Genevans felt that the Academy was being monitored and overseen by their representatives, while the clergy saw the Academy as the institution which would provide the training for a future generation of pastors in their image.

The third area of strength of the Genevan Academy was the close links built up between the Company of Pastors of Geneva and the churches which sent and received students trained in the Academy. These churches, primarily in France, maintained close contacts with the Genevan authorities in order to keep abreast of their student's progress. The Genevan Company of Pastors had an obligation to write to the French churches, not only to provide progress reports, especially on students receiving scholarships from the churches, but also because as an Academy, the school could not confer degrees. Awarding degrees was the prerogative of universities, which held a charter from the Pope or the Holy Roman Emperor. Not surprisingly, neither of these options was open to Geneva, although it is clear that in Calvin's time at least, there was no perceived need to have the Academy mimic the universities.[32] Instead of degrees, the pastors of Geneva provided a letter of testimony for every student who had completed his studies in Geneva and who intended to serve the churches as a minister. These letters provided information on the moral and academic performance of the students. This approach meant that the Genevan Academy's training was not separate from the world of the pastorate which the majority of students, especially in the early years, was heading for. In fact, this link through correspondence enabled the churches to help shape the education as provided in Geneva.

---

[31]For this episode, see Maag, *Seminary or University?*, 61-4.

[32]Borgeaud, *Histoire*, 51; J.-E Cellerier, *L'Académie de Genève: Esquisse d'une histoire abrègée de l'académie fondée par Calvin en 1559* (Geneva: A. Cherbuliez, 1872), 15; Fazy, *Le livre du recteur*, 4; Thévenaz, "L'Ancien collège," 40.

For instance, the church of Rouen wrote to the Company of Pastors on September 24th, 1613, and made the following request regarding their sponsored student: "If such a thing is allowable among you, we would ask that he could have entry to your consistories, to learn that good order which was first born among you and then spread to the churches of France. We also ask that you use him sometimes, as you do others of the same status, to preach in the villages of your area, so that by speaking in public, he may be able to train his voice and grow in confidence."[33] Clearly, the Rouen church confidently expected that the Genevans would be able to adapt their training to include these requests. The close cooperation between the churches and the Genevan authorities meant that the students could undergo a relatively smooth transition from their home churches to the Academy and then on to their future careers.

Significantly, having the day to day operations of the Academy under the control of the Company of Pastors also meant that the students looked at the Genevan clergy as mentors as well as educators. In several instances, former students of the Academy would write back to the Genevan pastors, requesting advice or assistance, on the strength of the contacts built up during their stay in Geneva. One such student was Nicolas Le More, a young man who went from Geneva to a two-point charge in south-western France, and who had problems with the transition from studies to the life of a minister. On November 1st, 1561, he wrote to the Genevan pastors, stating that his congregation refused to take him seriously, because of his youth. He also complained that some people thought he had preached Anabaptist views. He admitted that part of his difficulties stemmed from a language problem: he tended to speak too fast, and the inhabitants of the region did not understand his French.[34] This was not surprising, since the dialect of that area of France was closer to Basque and Spanish than to French. Faced with this combination of problems, Le More turned to his Genevan mentors, and in fact asked to be allowed to return to Geneva to continue his studies, evidence once again of the strong ties which former students felt for their center of learning.

IV

Thus, as we have seen, the strengths of the Genevan Academy lay primarily in its approach to education, and particularly in the strong links built up with the churches. As the Academy was the main conduit for education in the city, it is to the legacy of the Genevan Academy for international Calvinism that we shall now turn.

---

[33]Bibliothèque publique et universitaire, Geneva, Ms Fr 421, fol. 99.

[34]Nicolas Le More to the church of Geneva, November 1st, 1561, in *Bulletin de la Société de l'histoire du Protestantisme Français* 46 (1897), 466-468.

In the same way as the Genevan Academy had been built on the model of previous institutions, such as the academies of Strasbourg and Lausanne, as well as the Collège de Guyenne in France, so the Genevan Academy too served as a model for other institutions. The Genevan model was particularly influential in areas where the Protestants found themselves unable to take over previously Catholic institutions and were forced to create new ones instead, as in France and the Netherlands.

In France, the Huguenots rapidly saw the advantage of establishing centers of learning for their own young men, rather than sending them outside the country for their studies. Both the expense of foreign studies and the potential lack of direct supervision of students' progress were strong motivators to keep these young men close to home. Already by 1565, the fifth national synod of the French Calvinist churches, meeting in Paris, called on the churches to provide financial support for those studying for the ministry, because of the great need for pastors for the French congregations.[35] In 1578, the National Synod of Sainte Foy asked all the provincial assemblies of the church to work to create schools to teach young people and train young men to serve as ministers.[36] In the end, six Huguenot academies were established in France and its dependent areas: in Orthez in the Béarn in 1565, in Montpellier in 1596, in Montauban in 1600, in Sedan in 1602, in Saumur in 1604, and in Die in southeastern France in that same year. There were also a few colleges, which offered classes closer to a Latin school level, as in Orange. Other cities offered some Protestant educational opportunities for a brief period, as in Nîmes, for instance, where the university was Protestant from 1561 to 1634, and had a chair of Reformed theology, and at Orléans, where there was a Protestant theology faculty from 1561 to 1568.[37]

Among the Academies, the three strongest were Montauban, Saumur and Sedan. Sedan had the advantage of being outside French territory, and thus direct royal control, until 1642, when the area became part of France. All of these academies shared similar aims: to train the future generations of pastors for their churches, but also to offer a wider curriculum calculated to appeal to those wanting to engage in higher studies but not become part of the clergy. In theory at least, the larger academies intended to offer courses in law and medicine as well as the standard arts and theology curriculum, though in most instances, the expansion into these other fields remained a plan rather than a

---

[35] *Actes écclesiastiques et civils de tous les synodes nationaux des églises réformées de France*, ed. Jean Aymon (The Hague: Charles Delo, 1710), I: 70.

[36] *Actes écclesiastiques*, I: 126.

[37] On the Huguenot academies, see Pierre Daniel Bourchenin, *Etude sur les académies protestantes en France au XVIe et au XVII siècle* (Geneva: Slatkine Reprints, 1969; originally printed Paris, 1882).

reality, due to the chronic lack of funds.[38] As the French church had only inter-mittent support from the crown, any money that was available had to go to cover the main activity of the Huguenot congregations, namely the salaries of the ministers. However, the commitment of the Huguenots to their academies was such that when they received a contribution of 43,300 *écus* from Henry IV for their churches, their first disbursement was to the academies.[39] The model for this strong commitment to higher education as a combination of theologi-cal and liberal arts studies in a firmly Reformed context was the Genevan Academy.

As in Geneva, the Huguenot academies offered courses in Latin, Greek and Hebrew as well as theology, and here too, the liberal arts had an important role to play even in the preparation of future pastors.[40] For instance, although the French academies were forced to cut back because of financial difficulties in 1623, eliminating the chairs of Greek, this expedient was only temporary, and by 1626 the teaching of Greek had been restored.[41] The influence of the church on educational affairs was stronger if anything in the French academies than in Geneva, since both the financial support and the oversight of the French academies came primarily from the national and provincial synods. The main difference between Geneva and the French academies was that while Genevan students preparing for the ministry were given practical experience by preaching in rural parishes, the French did not follow this approach. Instead, French theology students were to practice their preaching skills by giv-ing test sermons in the presence of experienced ministers from their area.[42] The two largest academies, Sedan and Saumur, also had professors whose inter-national reputation rivaled those of the professors in Geneva, although enrol-ments remained smaller in the French institutions, largely because they were aimed at a specific clientele, namely young French Protestants.

The Calvinist educational system in the Netherlands was also shaped by the Genevan experience, once again particularly as regards the training of clergy. Here, too, the Calvinists were faced with the difficulty of training their young men to be leaders of their community without having the option of sending them to strongly Catholic universities like Louvain. In response to this need, the Dutch Calvinists followed two routes. The first was to create a university, as

---

[38]Richard Stauffer, "Le Calvinisme et les universités," in *Bulletin de la Société de l'histoire du Protestantisme Français* 126 (1980), 44.

[39]*Actes écclesiastiques,* I: 225.

[40]On the curriculum of the Huguenot academies, see Bourchenin, *Les académies protestantes,* 239-256.

[41]Stauffer, "Le Calvinisme et les universités," 45.

[42]Bourchenin, *Les académies protestantes,* 256-258.

in Leiden in 1575.[43] Although this institution was a university, rather than an academy, and although the role of the church was restricted in its oversight in favor of greater control by the civil authorities, Leiden did take on some elements of the Genevan model. In particular, it left room for the training of ministers by creating two separate residential colleges for future clergy: the Staten Collegie for Dutch speakers, and the Walloon College for those who spoke French.[44] Thus the university authorities still recognized the importance of theological training for the ministry as one of the objectives of study at Leiden. Interestingly, the Remonstrant theologian Jacob Arminius had studied at the Genevan Academy and later taught in the theology faculty at Leiden.[45] Among his opponents, the Counter-remonstrant Sibrandus Lubbertus had also studied in Geneva in the early 1580s, and went on to teach theology at the university of Franeker.[46] In this instance at least, one would want to be careful in weighing the educational legacy of Geneva on one side or other of that particular theological debate.

The other route followed by those wanting to ensure a sufficient number of qualified pastors for the Calvinist church of the Netherlands was once again the creation of small-scale academies, as in Ghent, for instance. There, students followed informal lectures given by professors of varying caliber. One of the most influential, and one who had also had experience of the Genevan model was Lambert Daneau, who had taught in Geneva from 1576 to 1580, and who came to Ghent after a brief stay in Leiden. Although Daneau only remained in Ghent for a year, he did speak very highly of the city and its academy.[47] Indeed, one of the reasons for Daneau's favorable view of Ghent was the close collaboration in the city between magistrates, pastors and professors, a situation which was very similar once again to Geneva's.[48]

---

[43]On Leiden, see M. W. Jurriaanse, *The Founding of Leiden University* (Leiden: Brill, 1965).

[44]On the Staten Collegie see P. A. M. Geurts, "Voorgeschiedenis van het Staten Collegie te Leiden 1575-1593," in *Lias* 10 (1983), 26. On the Walloon college see G. H. M. Posthumus Meyjes, *Geschiedenis van het Waalse Collegie te Leiden 1606-1699* (Leiden: Universitaire Pers Leiden, 1975).

[45]*Livre du Recteur de l'Académie de Genève,* ed. Sven and Suzanne Stelling-Michaud (Geneva: Droz, 1959-1980), II: 64.

[46]H. de Vries, *Genève pépinière du Calvinisme hollandais,* (2 vols, Fribourg: Fragniere Frères, 1918-1924), I: 98-99.

[47]Olivier Fatio, *Nihil Pulchrius Ordine: Contribution à l'étude de la discipline écclesiastique aux Pays-Bas, ou Lambert Daneau aux Pays Bas (1581-1583)* (Leiden: Brill, 1971), 98-102.

[48]Ibid.

V

Thus France and the Netherlands offer examples of the ways in which the Genevan Academy and the Genevan educational system in general provided a legacy which other areas were quick to build on. By highlighting the importance of the liberal arts in higher education, even for future pastors, the Genevans helped ensure that the humanist current of emphasis on ancient learning would continue to play a significant role in the studies and homiletic activity of the Calvinist clergy. Insisting that the liberal arts were necessary for well-rounded students meant that the Genevan Academy and its daughter institutions remained attractive to those seeking higher studies without intending to enter the pastorate. By broadening the base of its student recruitment, Geneva in fact ensured its longer-term survival as an academic institution, particularly as the areas which had sent students to Geneva for training began to establish their own schools closer to home.

The Genevan legacy of close contacts and cooperation in the educational sphere between civic and ecclesiastical authorities is also noteworthy. One of the reasons for the support of civic leaders for the Reformation, whether in Geneva or elsewhere, had been their desire to exercise greater control over city institutions, such as schools and the charitable hospitals. The Genevan approach allowed for magisterial involvement, but also preserved a significant role for the church through the day to day work of the Company of Pastors. This system only worked, however, in cases where the civic and ecclesiastical authorities had enough objectives in common to be willing to work in tandem. Although the French and Dutch political systems did not provide the possibility for the same level of collaboration, the Genevan legacy of a joint approach shows the results which could be achieved when favorable circumstances arose.

Finally, we should consider what John Calvin's academic and educational legacy actually was. As an individual, he did not establish anything particularly innovative in Geneva, nor was he solely responsible for the Genevan system. But his role in getting Geneva to the point where the pastors and magistrates could work together, instead of against each other, and in focusing on the all-important training of the future generations of leaders for the Calvinist church, was indeed a crucial one. Furthermore, in refusing to reject outright the contribution of the humanist liberal arts to the educational process, and in ensuring that higher education was not perceived solely in a narrow sense, even for future pastors, Calvin's impact was significant. In this sense, his academic and educational legacy was and is still fundamental and should not be ignored.

A Response to "Calvin's Academic and Educational Legacy"

W. Fred Graham

Dr. Maag's paper is an important contribution to a subject that has not received the attention it deserves, partly because historians of the epoch simply expect the Reformed churches to major in education because of their stress on the necessity to raise ministers well-trained in scripture, and the parallel emphasis on the obligation of believers to study the Bible. What is common knowledge is thus commonplace and escapes the historian's research. Harro Höpfl can write: "The [Reformed] Church's main task is to teach,"[1] and give no more than a side-long glance at how the church in Geneva carried out that mandate.

William Bouwsma tells us that "As God's school," Calvin's church was more like a humanist academy than a school of theology.[2] Bouwsma goes on to tell us that Calvin's educational views were strongly anti-authoritarian, suggesting that "lash-loving executioners" were not useful in the classroom, for harsh treatment can so intimidate pupils as to make them incapable of a liberal discipline.[3] But Bouwsma's aim is to portray Calvin the person rather than his activities as head pastor of the church in Geneva. The best, easily-accessible study I have found on the effect of his own education on Calvin's "Laws for the Genevan Academy," which includes the influence of Jean Sturm in Strasbourg, is a paper entitled "The Place of the Academy in Calvin's Polity," by Charles Raynal, III, and is found in *John Calvin and the Church*, edited by Timothy George.[4]

We knew before Dr. Maag's study that in Geneva elementary education was universal and free. Even the orphanage at the city's hospital had a schoolmaster appointed to teach the youngsters there, who were also given apprentice-like schooling so they would be employable. That education was also

---

[1]Harro Höpfl, *The Christian Polity of John Calvin* (Cambridge University Press, 1982), 203.

[2]William Bouwsma, *John Calvin: A Sixteenth Century Portrait* (New York: Oxford, 1988), 227.

[3]Ibid., 90.

[4]Timothy George, ed., *John Calvin and the Church: A Prism of Reform* (Louisville: Westminster/John Knox Press, 1990),

compulsory. When the pastor at the small village of Jussy complained that parents were neglecting to send their children to the village school, Geneva's city council appointed Calvin and council member Michel Roset to investigate, and then sent Roset to announce that the teacher's salary would be raised—and the raise would be levied from fines on parents who encouraged truancy.

E. William Monter complains that the city council received a good deal of income from the sale and rent of ecclesiastical properties abandoned by the pre-Reformation church, which were invested in non-church activities. But he also admits that when the college was founded, it immediately soaked up those stray funds and a good deal more.[5] It was the only building constructed during Calvin's life there, tucked near the ancient south wall of the town. Its immediate expense was covered by those ecclesiastical revenues, as well as by gifts, wills and fines. But the major monies used for the building and tree-filled campus were the properties, confiscated and sold, of Calvin's enemies who fled the borough in 1559.[6]

Because Karin Maag has done a fine study of the relationship between Geneva's Academy and higher education among the Protestants of France and the Netherlands, I decided to take a quick look at some of the effects of the Reformation on education in Scotland. A few years ago I was enticed into giving the talk on Robert Burns at a local Burns Night dinner, and I commented in passing that so far as I knew Burns was the only peasant poet of any nation ever to achieve international fame. (James Hogg, the "Ettrick Shepherd," a young contemporary of Burns fits into that mold and had some notice as poet and novelist during his lifetime, but only Burns' poetry has endured.) An Ulsterman present came up afterward and said that surely the reason a tenant farmer's son had the historical and literary background to write poetry beloved by Great Britain's cultural elite was the Reformed insistence on a good elementary education for all youth in society. Chastened by this good word from a food scientist, I did a little reading (not research!) and came up with what follows.

As you probably do not know, most Scottish children go to public schools. These public schools are also *called* public and not private schools, as the English confusion of tongues might lead us to think. It appears that this uniformity goes deep into the Scottish educational tradition, where, after the Reformation of 1560, every local kirk, and its elders, was tasked with the duty of erecting and staffing an elementary school.

No one believes that Knox and other Reformation leaders invented schooling in Scotland. Knox himself was a product of Haddington Grammar School and probably had a degree from the University of St. Andrews, one of three pre-Reformation institution of higher learning in Scotland. So the Scots reformers

---

[5]E. William Monter, *Studies in Genevan Government, 1536-1605* (Geneva, 1964), 20.

[6]W. Fred Graham, *The Constructive Revolutionary* (Richmond, Virginia, 1971), chapter 8.

had no need to create an institution like the academy or college in Geneva. When Knox and others wrote the *First Book of Discipline* (1560), they asked that the revenues from ecclesiastical properties be given to the reformed Kirk for three purposes: to support local churches, for poor relief, and to establish a lower elementary system throughout the land, with high schools (as we would call them) in good enough number for promising scholars to hone their skills before attending one of the three universities: St. Andrews, Aberdeen or Glasgow. (The college at Edinburgh was founded about 1585.) Since revenues from the Auld Kirk probably amounted to half the wealth of the realm, it had long been in secular hands, and there was little prospect of the reformed Kirk getting much of it. Finally, a compromise was reached, whereby the Queen received one-third of those revenues, which she split between her needs at court and the Kirk. Two-thirds for the devil and one for God, Knox sputtered, and certainly both church support and universal education gained only gradual funding as the decades went by.

The *Second Book of Discipline* (1578) continued to ask for the same reforming program from Parliament, as the rejected *First Book*. Ministers and teachers (the *dominie*) were to be appointed with the congregation's consent, not by a system of patronage, and "schools and universities were also to receive sufficient aid to recruit more teachers to instruct the youth, for whom bursaries night be found, and to train aspiring ministers ...."[7] Sometimes the local schoolmaster was a lay person, perhaps an elder, sometimes a minister, especially a younger one. Whether lay or clergy, they were members of presbytery, as set up in the *Second Book*.[8]

One contemporary writer on Scottish education writes that Knox and Company "intended to make more effective and universal the educational work which, in at least some parishes, had been carried on for centuries previously. What they drew up was, in effect, the first truly modern educational system in all Europe." She goes on to recite the initial failure in this attempt, but adds that "it did supply an ideal which lingered on in the Scottish imagination."[9] This "ideal undreamt of ... in any other European nation" envisaged a ladder of education, reaching from the parish school to the university. There was to be a school in every parish, each town kirk was to appoint a schoolmaster who was to teach Latin and grammar, the larger towns to have colleges, and poor children who were "apt for learning" were to be aided all the way through the universities. As Mackintosh says, this equality of opportunity is in the fabric of the Scottish educational system, for "neither in Knox's time nor at the present day does the Scot take kindly to privilege or class."[10] This radical notion

---

[7] *The Second Book of Discipline,* ed. James Kirk (1980), 122.

[8] Ibid., 87.

[9] Mary Mackintosh, *Education in Scotland, Yesterday and Today* (1962), 23.

[10] Ibid., 24.

that the children of the poor might proceed up the educational ladder to the university did not take root south of the border until the end of the nineteenth century.

Of course, our author, Mary Mackintosh, is quick to point out that implementing this universal, compulsory educational system took place only piecemeal, and cannot be said to affect all of Scotland, especially the Highlands, until 1696, and even then progress was slow in the north and west. But the aim of both books of discipline for such a system was never forgotten. Until well into the last century the schoolmaster's house and plot of garden was a feature of each Scottish parish, along with the minister's manse and glebe; and, like the minister, the teacher was a freeholder, the school an adjunct of the parish church. The teacher was examined and approved by the presbytery, and was required to subscribe to the Confession of Faith. All of that until the Education Act (Scotland) of 1872, which transferred the managing of schools to newly elected school boards which function pretty much as local boards of education do in America today.

Perhaps it is time for someone to take on the role of historian for education among churches affected by the reformation coming out of Geneva and Zurich. Karin Maag has made a good beginning here, and further study might show that insistence upon education for everyone is just as important to an understanding of the Reformed churches as recent work by Mentzer, Schilling and Michael Graham and others on church discipline—and lots more congenial to the modern temperament!

Calvin's Exegetical Legacy: His Reception and Transmission of Text and Tradition

John L. Thompson

"Calvin's exegetical legacy" is an ambitious title. Inevitably, one runs the risk of tendentiousness, if not hagiography, and it is fair to ask, "Did (or does) Calvin *have* an exegetical legacy?" To be sure, the adjective ("exegetical") has already pulled the noun ("legacy") away from its literal center and well towards the orbit of metaphor. We know from his last will and testament that Calvin's literal legacy consisted of 225 crowns, a bit of which was left to the college in Geneva and to the *bourse française* while most was parceled out among his relatives. Beza reported that Calvin's net worth, including his library, "scarcely amounted to 300 gold pieces."[1] It matters little which estimate is closer to the truth, of course, because the material and monetary goods from Calvin's erstwhile estate have long since been scattered and forgotten. So what would it mean to say that Calvin left any additional legacy, exegetical or otherwise?

I pose this difficulty not to be captious, but to underscore the danger of begging the question. When taken in its figurative sense, a "legacy" (like beauty) often lies in the eyes of the beholder. An entity such as the Calvin Studies Society is predicated on the belief that Calvin still matters. For this very reason, our claims about Calvin's putative legacy could easily be more wish-fulfillment than matters of fact. Who is to say that Calvin left a legacy? At worst, *we* could say so — just by taking a vote, as if saying were enough to make it so. Indeed, at least some parts of Calvin's "legacy" among us today are current and cogent thanks largely to Karl Barth's insistence that Calvin left a legacy and to Barth's distinctive appropriation of Calvin's theology. So, would Calvin now have the same legacy if Barth had not breathed new life into the study of Calvin? Should we be speaking now of Calvin's legacy or, instead, of some new hybrid of Barth, Calvin, and others?

Such interweaving of influence and appreciation is probably impossible to sort out, at least by a mortal historian. Nonetheless, to deconstruct a legacy is

---

[1] Cf. "Last Will and Testament of Master John Calvin" (CTS-Letters 4:376; CO 20:300–1); and Theodore Beza, "Life of John Calvin" (CTS-Tracts 1:xcix; CO 21:170).

by no means to destroy it. On the contrary, there is much to be gained by trying to unpack this complicated notion. What, exactly, constitutes a "legacy"? At
the very least, the term admits of two dimensions. On the one hand, one's
legacy may be that which one receives from the past, so that a search for Calvin's
exegetical legacy would entail looking for his debt to his exegetical predecessors or, perhaps, his neglect or ignorance of the exegetical past. On the other
hand, a legacy may also reverse the roles, so that a search for Calvin's exegetical legacy would assay his impact as an exegete on those who came after. To
these two dimensions, one might also add a third: a legacy might well be merely
the inventory in one's last will and testament, regardless of how that inventory
is later distributed or dispersed. The bleakness of this deathbed image is actually fruitful, insofar as it reminds us that it is not always helpful to think of a
legacy as only that which is useful to or admired by one's heirs. Legacies may
include stores of treasure, but they may also include lots and lots of garage sale
items, white elephants or household discards.

In the wake of such considerations, I have analyzed Calvin's exegetical legacy
into two parts and four questions. The first two questions pertain to Calvin's
"subjective" legacy, the legacy he received from his predecessors and contemporaries; the second two pertain to Calvin's "objective" legacy, which is the
legacy he left to those who came after him, whether they knew it or not and
whether they liked it or not. These are my four questions: first, what might
Calvin's exegesis have taken or received from the past, explicitly or accidentally? Second, of that potential inheritance, what did Calvin himself actually
use, own, or reject? Third, what did Calvin's exegesis leave or bequeath to his
survivors, explicitly or accidentally? Fourth and finally, of that potential estate,
what did his survivors actually use, own, or reject?

I cannot answer any of these questions comprehensively, but I will use the
distinction between Calvin's subjective and objective legacy to structure my
own analysis, which will combine some observations about Calvin's exegesis
and sources with some tentative generalizations about Calvin's influence and
neglect among later exegetes.

I. The subjective legacy: Calvin's reception of exegetical tradition

In addressing the first aspect of Calvin's exegetical legacy, I wish to draw on
a host of observations and findings that have arisen from my recent research
into the history of exegesis. Most of my observations will therefore be drawn
from various topics and passages in the book of Genesis. What may appear to
be a restriction in the database is actually not so confining. Calvin's work in
Genesis has lately received some exceedingly helpful scrutiny from other scholars, including specialized studies from Max Engammare, Richard Gamble,
A. N. S. Lane, and David Steinmetz. My consideration of Calvin's legacy has

been especially stimulated by Lane's painstaking analysis of Calvin's use of sources.[2] Where Lane's research has been intensive in its analysis of Calvin, however, my own research has leaned more towards an extensive approach, in that I have read selected stories and problems in Calvin's exegesis of Genesis in the widest possible context of his predecessors and contemporaries. My sample of Calvin's "peers" has extended to thirty or forty commentators, often beginning with Philo, then ranging east and west to end with Vermigli and some of the later Lutherans. Stories examined have included the so-called patriarchal immoralities, the question in Genesis 17 of the correlation between circumcision and baptism as covenant signs, and some of the tales of violence done to women in Genesis. As this brief account would suggest, most of my interest has been fixed on Abraham and his descendants rather than the accounts of creation and fall, and I have lately begun to consider the career of Abraham, whom St. Paul styles the father of faith, as marking a convenient boundary for my own inquiries into the book of Genesis. In posing afresh the question of Calvin's exegetical legacy, then, I would like to begin with my recent study of Calvin and Hagar. But, as we will see, to understand Calvin in context, one must go back far before Calvin.

The central problem of John Calvin's "exegetical legacy" — in fact, the crucial problem of all Christian exegesis — is, in simplest terms, the problem of the Old Testament. All other exegetical issues pale by comparison. All other exegetical issues are merely satellites of this one. The problem of the Old Testament is embedded in the earliest Christian preaching and confessions, whether one study the opening chapter of Mark's gospel, Stephen's speech in the book of Acts, or the opening line of the Apostles Creed.

It is also a problem that nowhere comes to such a congested intersection as one finds in St. Paul's depiction of the collision between Sarah and Hagar and between Isaac and Ishmael in Galatians 4 — the only instance in the New Testament where the much-controverted term *allegoria* is used, and a passage that T. H. L. Parker called the *locus classicus* of Calvin's hostility to allegory.[3] When Paul drew forth his allegory from the narrative of Genesis 21, he not only correlated Old Testament with New, he also bequeathed to later interpreters an exciting if cryptic road map for exploring Old Testament narratives. The historical Hagar and Ishmael are thus taken up into an allegory of the contrast between law and gospel, faith and works. Hagar and Ishmael become emblems for the failings of the religion of Paul's kindred and contemporaries.

---

[2]A. N. S. Lane, "The Sources of Calvin's Citations in His Genesis Commentary," in *Interpreting the Bible: Historical and Theological Studies in Honour of David F. Wright*, ed. A.N.S. Lane (Leicester, England: Inter-Varsity Press, Apollos, 1997), 47–97. A substantially revised version of this essay has since appeared as "The Sources of the Citations in Calvin's Genesis Commentary," chapter nine of Lane's book, *John Calvin: Student of the Church Fathers* (Edinburgh: T. & T. Clark, 1999), 205–59. My page citations refer to the revised essay, hereafter cited simply as "Sources."

[3]T. H. L. Parker, *Calvin's New Testament Commentaries* (Grand Rapids: Eerdmans, 1971), 63.

None of this, of course, is news to us or to Calvin, whose engagement with the text and characters of Galatians 4 was regular and prolonged: he commented on the whole of Galatians in 1548; beginning in 1550, delivered lectures on Genesis that were published in 1554; preached on Galatians in 1557–58; then preached through Genesis in 1559–60. The question, then, is whether Calvin will be content with Paul's severe synopsis of Hagar's story. What will the Genevan Reformer take from his exegesis of Paul when he delves into Genesis a few years later? Given the widespread tendency of Christian commentators to read the Old Testament in light of the New, there is ample reason to expect Calvin to follow suit, to bring Paul with him as his authorized interpreter. Yet there are at least two reasons to think otherwise, too. First, Calvin was known in his day as well as our own for his general restraint in interpreting the Old Testament in light of the New.[4] Second, Calvin's more specific (and equally well-known) distaste for allegorical exegesis might lead him to distance himself even from an apostolic allegory in favor of the literal history to be found in Genesis.

The obvious starting point is his commentary on Galatians, not only because of its chronological priority, but also because Calvin explicitly defers to this work when he comments on Genesis 21.[5] Calvin's exposition of Galatians 4:21–31 can be surveyed in three sentences. First, Calvin addresses how previous commentators have misread and misapplied what Paul meant to warrant by his use of the term *allegory* and argues that the apostle's brand of allegory does not violate a literal reading of the story. Second, Calvin goes on to explain how this text exemplifies a much broader typological or figurative relationship between the household of Abraham and the Christian church throughout its history, so that whatever happened to Abraham corresponds to the experience of the church in general. This second point is absolutely crucial to the one that follows, wherein Calvin applies the passage by identifying himself and his own flock with "the lawful children" who are today persecuted by modern-day "Ishmaelites and Hagarites," namely, by the "Papists."

These same three sentences are nearly as adequate to summarize Calvin's later exposition of Genesis 21. To be sure, he has much to say about all of the various turns and twists of the plot line, but when he comes to the ejection of Hagar and Ishmael at 21:12, these are the three points he wishes to make: the

---

[4]David L. Puckett revisited the issue of Calvin's supposed "judaizing" exegesis (in *John Calvin's Exegesis of the Old Testament* [Louisville: Westminster John Knox, 1995], 1–4, 52–81) — that charge which was leveled with such vengeance by the Lutheran Aegidius Hunnius in 1595 — but the same point was addressed a generation ago by Parker in *Calvin's New Testament Commentaries*, 66–68. The episode has been addressed more recently still by David Steinmetz, "The Judaizing Calvin," in *Die Patristik in der Bibelexegese des 16. Jahrhunderts* (Wiesbaden: Harrassowitz, 1999), 135-45.

[5]Calvin, *Comm. Gen.* 21:12 (CO 23:302, CTS 1:546): "I here allude in a few words to those things, which my readers will find copiously expounded by me, in the fourth chapter to the Galatians; yet in this short explanation, it is made perfectly clear what Paul designs to teach."

proper understanding of allegory, the typological status of Abraham's household, and the "Papists" as modern-day equivalents to Ishmael and Hagar. The only assertion that is startlingly amplified by Genesis concerns the more or less final destiny of the historical Hagar and Ishmael. In a word, Calvin treats as sufficiently clear that Hagar and her son were reprobate. He sees no desert in either; he sees no sign of repentance; he excoriates Hagar's obtuse and repeated ingratitude; and he takes the message of 21:20, that "God was with the lad," as denoting not the favor God shows the elect but merely the earthly blessings God sometimes grants to strangers.[6]

With respect to the potential gulf between Paul's allegorical reading of Genesis 21 and Calvin's commitment to a literal reading of the Old Testament, Calvin proves intent on bridging the gap. He vehemently distances himself from *bad* allegories precisely by embracing what he considers good allegory, which he would be happier to term "typology" or "similitude" or even "anagogy." Accordingly, Calvin insists that Paul's allegory represents the literal history, so that the Hagar and Ishmael of Genesis are finally dismissed as actually being the reprobates that they merely represented in Galatians. It is a somber note indeed upon which to end their tale.

So much for Calvin's exposition. Now we can address the interesting question of Calvin's exegetical legacy, namely, *Where did Calvin get all this?* Did he make it up, or is it traditional? Lane's study of the Genesis lectures suggests Calvin drew on a modest working bookshelf:

> Calvin clearly made extensive use of the first two volumes of Luther, for the first twenty-four and a half chapters. He also relied heavily upon Steuchus's *Recognitio* throughout his commentary. ... These two works have pride of place. Also important are three translations with notes that Calvin used throughout: the 1545 Stephanus Bible with the Vulgate and Zurich translations and the Vatable notes, Münster's 1534-35 *Hebraica Biblia Latina* and Fagius's *Thargum*. Calvin most likely read the Servetus marginal notes together perhaps with some or all of the Pagninus translation. ... From chapter four he used Augustine's *Quaestiones in Heptateuchum* and for the whole commentary he consulted Jerome's *Hebraicae quaestiones*. These are the works needed to account for Calvin's citations.[7]

What is striking about this list is not merely its economy, but also that Luther is the only entry resembling anything like a theological commentary. Steuchus's

---

[6]Calvin, *Comm. Gen.* 21:12–20 (CO 23:302–6, CTS 1:545–51). Also see John L. Thompson, "Hagar, Victim or Villain? Three Sixteenth-Century Views," *Catholic Biblical Quarterly* 59 (April 1997): 213–33.

[7]Lane, "Sources," 233.

Recognitio offers, for the most part, selected philological comments,[8] and the other works might be similarly characterized as reference tools and translation aids. Moreover, while Calvin's use of Luther's commentary is complicated and multi-layered, it is clear that he often used Luther less as a conversation partner than as a sourcebook; many of Calvin's references to rabbinic exegesis, for example, seem to be drawn from Luther, who himself obtained these reports from Lyra.[9] In any case, with respect to the Hagar and Ishmael story, my own comparison of Luther and Calvin suggests that Calvin not only knew Luther's exegesis of Hagar but also that he deliberately rejected it.[10] Indeed, one could easily argue that Calvin and Luther were polar opposites with respect to Hagar, for Calvin's coldness towards the Egyptian concubine is more than matched by Luther's extravagant warmth. Calvin's reprobate Hagar and Ishmael stand utterly opposed to Luther's "saintly Hagar" and his picture of Ishmael as an inspired evangelist for Jehovah and for the gospel faith of Father Abraham.

In weighing and esteeming Calvin's exegesis, as well as his exegetical legacy as both received and bequeathed, the contrast between Luther's affection for Hagar and Calvin's hostility is no trifling matter. The issue is not their varying taste in making friendships among the Bible's dead, but rather how Luther and Calvin relate to the exegetical tradition and who can best claim to represent the letter — as each Reformer aspires to do. I can settle this issue: for better or worse, Luther's exegesis (despite its ample embroidery and psychologizing) stands in closer continuity not only with traditional interpretations of Hagar but also with the literal and historical details of Genesis. Indeed, however much Christian interpretation of Hagar and Ishmael in the book of Genesis may have been initially jaundiced by the Pauline allegory, the story of Hagar and Ishmael in Christian exegesis, beginning even with Origen, is a tale of how the amazing details of Hagar's story in Genesis gradually emerged from the shadows cast by Galatians 4.

Needless to say, it is impossible to survey the thirteen centuries of exegesis from Origen to Calvin here. A few highlights must suffice.[11] To begin with, if all

---

[8]Agostino Steuco was the Vatican librarian from 1538 until his death in 1548; his *Veteris testamenti ad Hebraicam veritatem recognitio, sive in Pentateuchum, Annotationes* was published in Venice in 1529 and 1531. I have consulted a microfilm copy of the three-volume *Opera Omnia* (Venice, 1591). In the *Recognitio*, Steuco promised not to discourse on matters "lofty or obscure" but rather "to interpret mere words" (*meras voces*, 1:85ᵛ), namely, to interpret and correct sundry translation errors in the Vulgate on the basis of Hebrew manuscripts, the *Targums*, and rabbinical commentaries. While considerable attention is devoted to the first three chapters of Genesis, later chapters receive about a folio page apiece. See also Ronald K. Delph, *OER* 4:112a, s.v. "Steucho, Agostino."

[9]See Lane, "Sources," 226–27.

[10]For a detailed illustration, see Thompson, "Hagar, Victim or Villain?" 224–25, esp. n. 53.

[11]Full details may be found in chapter one of my book, *Writing the Wrongs: Women of the Old Testament among Biblical Commentators from Philo through the Reformation* (New York: Oxford University Press), forthcoming.

one were to remember about Hagar were filtered through Paul's account in Galatians 4, one might be surprised to learn that in addition to being "the slave woman" who was "cast out" so that her son "might not inherit" with "the son of the free woman," Hagar was also the first person in the Bible to be visited by an angel (16:7), as well as the first to receive an annunciation (16:11–12). She is the only woman in all of scripture ever to receive a promise of innumerable descendants (16:10). She is important enough to God to be rescued, apparently twice, by God or by the angel of the Lord, as well as to be blessed, twice, with an epiphany from God or the angel of the Lord. She is evidently the only woman in the Bible to choose a wife for her son. Perhaps most striking of all, in the wake of her first epiphany, Hagar is depicted in Genesis 16:13 as boldly bestowing a name on God — again, something no other woman seems to have done. Alongside these credits, however, are some less cheery facts, those that concern her forced surrogacy, her mistreatment by Sarah, her own pride, her first flight into the desert, and her later banishment with inadequate supplies. One might wonder, as some recent interpreters have done,[12] if Abraham and Sarah were not just a bit too harsh here.

These are the data that are increasingly reckoned with by Christian commentators, so that when Origen elaborates the Pauline allegory of Hagar as the mother of the flesh, which persecutes the spirit, he does so by adding a *historical* detail from later in Genesis 21. When Hagar was dismissed, Genesis 21:14 reports that Abraham gave her a bottle of water. Origen allegorizes the bottle as the Law, which runs dry. But Hagar and her thirsty son were then divinely shown the way to a well in the desert — and that well (says Origen) is Christ. All of a sudden, Hagar has gone from being a pariah to being an example of repentance and mercy. Origen explicitly compares her to the Samaritan woman, who learned about living water beside yet another well.[13] What must be noticed, however, is that while the Christology of the well is purely Origen's allegory, the mercy Hagar received (and also her repentance, perhaps) are not figurative but part of the historical narrative. Hagar and Ishmael were rescued, and scripture reports that God was with them.

By and large, Origen points the way for much of Latin exegesis ever after: those who want to mine Genesis for more elaborate allegories of Hagar do so by unearthing also the story's literal elements. Consequently, there is more and more attention paid to Hagar's epiphanies, to her perception of God, and to her role as a penitent. Isidore, Bede, Rabanus, and others thus mingle allegorical and literal-historical aspects of their exposition in ways that will call attention to the historical Hagar even when later commentators lose interest in the

---

[12]In particular, Phyllis Trible must be credited for recovering many of the textual observations in this paragraph; see her *Texts of Terror: Literary-Feminist Readings of Biblical Narratives* (Philadelphia: Fortress, 1984), 14–18.

[13]Origen, *Homily 7.3–6 on Genesis*, PG 12:200–3 (FC 71:130–35).

mystical sense of the text. A further development occurs with Lyra, who brings to the fore the ethical dimension of the story, raising with some urgency the question, long since considered among rabbinic interpreters, of whether Abraham and Sarah sinned against Hagar and Ishmael by banishing her.

All of these developments appear to bear a rich harvest in the sixteenth century. Even where allegory is disdained, few will follow St. Paul in ignoring the divine favor Hagar received. Thus Cajetan goes out of his way to defend Hagar and Ishmael from what he sees as rabbinic slanders; he compares Hagar's epiphany to the Magnificat; he worries much over Abraham's severity in expelling his wife and daughter. Zwingli confesses to be deeply moved by Hagar's sufferings and finds in her a model of piety; despite the banishment, both Hagar and Ishmael belong to God. Conrad Pellican also sees Hagar as one of God's own, a model of humility and repentance, and of thanksgiving and prayer. Similar moves are made by Vermigli and by Musculus, and if Luther's exploration of the trials of "St. Hagar" is the longest, it is by no means the first. All of these commentators see God virtually as Hagar's patron, and they derive this insight from the repeated and abundant evidence of God's concern for Hagar that they find plainly indicated in the literal, historical narrative of Genesis 16 and 21.

Why, then, is Calvin so harsh? I should note at the outset that Calvin's singularity here mirrors my findings with respect to other lines of his Old Testament exegesis.[14] But if Calvin refuses to credit the fanciful excuses dreamed up by other commentators on behalf of the immoralities of the patriarchs, here his resentment seems to fly in the face of specific textual evidences. In other words, Calvin seems determined to vilify — indeed, anathematize! — two figures of the Old Testament whom God saw fit to pursue, address, rebuke, instruct, rescue, console, and bless. Let the reader make no mistake on this point: while there are plenty of commentators who harbor sharp and dismissive views of Hagar and Ishmael and who see some measure of divine justice in sending them into the desert, only Calvin sends them to hell. From everyone else, Hagar's divine rescue and Ishmael's divine promises elicit exegetical restraint and a charitable judgment of Hagar and Ishmael, if not upon their descendants — but not from Calvin. Why?

So far as the question of Calvin's harshness bears on his exegetical legacy, I think the answer must point to three factors. First, Calvin the busy pastor is often remarkably innocent (if not ignorant or contemptuous) of the exegetical tradition, even when it might have served him well.[15] Second, there is good rea-

---

[14]I have argued for Calvin's singularity in two essays, "The Immoralities of the Patriarchs in the History of Exegesis: A Reassessment of Calvin's Position," *Calvin Theological Journal* 26 (1991): 9–46; and "Patriarchs, Polygamy, and Private Resistance: John Calvin and Others on Breaking God's Rules," *Sixteenth Century Journal* 25 (1994): 3–27.

[15]There is, to be sure, a partial precedent to be found for Calvin's harshness towards Hagar, but only one. Hagar and Ishmael repeatedly star as villains in Augustine's anti-Donatist writings, but there is little reason to think that Calvin is consciously building on Augustine here.

son to think that while Calvin appreciated Luther's lectures on Genesis as a sourcebook, there is an equally good argument that Calvin was embarrassed by Luther's excesses as a commentator. We can draw this conclusion not only from Calvin's 1555 letter to Francis Burkhard, but also from instances both demonstrable and probable where Calvin ponies Luther for his sources but slights Luther's own exegesis: so when Calvin tells Burkhard that he prefers to "bury errors in silence" and to guard readers against "hallucinations," it is surely Luther whom he castigates here.[16] A third factor, however, and perhaps the one of greatest weight, is Calvin's hostility to Roman Catholicism. The story of Hagar and Ishmael was offered to Calvin in Galatians 4 as a template for gauging fidelity to the gospel. Calvin did not hesitate to use this template in the obvious way, against the Hagarites and Ishmaelites, against the spiritual hypocrites, strangers, and bastards of his own day — against the tyrannical and persecuting church of Rome. That Calvin should feel so pained by the injustices he felt were perpetrated by "papists" against the people of God is nothing surprising. But that his animus should so thoroughly skew his exegesis of the Old Testament, and do so in the face of both scripture's counter-evidence and an articulated and even evangelical tradition, is truly remarkable.

So far as concerns Calvin's exegetical legacy, then, for the moment we may simply observe that Calvin could not have handed on what he himself failed to receive. Surely he can be expected to transmit only what he himself possessed or modeled, whether consciously or not. In the case at hand, Calvin seems to be modeling a passion for application that has led him to ignore some of the sounder traditional insights that weigh with determination upon the letter of the text.

II. The objective legacy: Calvin's reception among his exegetical heirs

Obviously, there are many ramifications of these observations about Calvin and Hagar, as well as Genesis and Galatians, that could be pursued at greater length and in greater detail. But I want to deliver at least a side-dish that pertains to what I have called Calvin's "objective" legacy, the exegetical legacy that he can be imagined to have bequeathed to his survivors and that they may also have embraced and appreciated — or, one must allow, despised or ignored.

Again, the question of method is difficult, the data can easily remain ambiguous, and the task is potentially that of Sisyphus. Arguably, one could search for Calvin's legacy in surefooted fashion only by reading every exegete since Calvin, looking for conscious or unconscious use, for reliance or defiance. Not too long ago, Andrew Pettegree made a preliminary inquiry merely into the ownership of Calvin — that is, of how relatively numerous copies of

---

[16]Calvin to Francis Burkhard, CO 15:454 (CTS-Letters 3:153–55). For a brief discussion, see Parker, *New Testament Commentaries*, 86.

Calvin's works were among estate inventories in England in the late sixteenth and early seventeenth centuries.[17] Ownership, of course, is an uncertain mark of influence or legacy (would that we actually read all of the books we own!), but it is a start, and one that is responsibly quantified so as to avoid the pitfalls of merely casual expressions of preference or admiration. And yet the quantifying impulse still carries within it spores of frustration, for to quantify Calvin's legacy under the guise of ownership or print histories would still leave unanalyzed the meaning or shape of that legacy.

One alternative, of course, would be to troll through the ensuing centuries in search of testimonies to Calvin's exegetical virtues or faults. This too would be a huge labor, but not impossible. In fact, there exists a handy arsenal of depositions gathered in the 1840s and 1850s by one of the Calvin Translation Society's translators. These "Opinions and Testimonies Respecting the Writings of John Calvin" appear immediately after the English translation of Tholuck's essay on "Calvin as an Interpreter of the Holy Scriptures" in the original CTS edition of Calvin's commentary on Joshua.[18] There, William Pringle reproduced sound bites long and short from a hundred and twenty writers over the course of three centuries. From the twenty or so who addressed Calvin's scriptural exposition, we learn mostly what we expect to learn, namely, that Calvin was valued for his clarity, for his reluctance to impose theology upon the text while simultaneously allowing the spiritual or practical significance to emerge, and for his learning, piety, and independence of judgment. Some, to be sure, lamented the continuity he drew between his exegesis (which they liked) and his theology (which they disliked), while others regretted the intrusion of so much polemic into his exposition of scripture.

Most of these points are recombined in the longer studies of Calvin's exegesis, whether it be Tholuck's 1831 essay[19] or the plethora of studies that have blossomed in the waning years of our own century. Parker, for instance, remarked in passing on a few of the older evaluations — Simon, Tholuck, Reuss, and Schaff — even as he crafted his own.[20] Puckett's recent study surveys Calvin's reputation as weighed and analyzed by Childs, Cranfield, Kraeling, Kraus, Ganoczy and Scheld, Parker, Torrance, Dowey, Fullerton, Forstman, and

---

[17]Andrew Pettegree, "The Reception of Calvinism in Britain," in *Calvinus Sincerioris Religionis Vindex: Calvin as Protector of the Purer Religion*, ed. Wilhelm H. Neuser and Brian G. Armstrong (Kirksville, Mo.: Sixteenth Century Journal Publishers, 1997), 267–89.

[18]See John Calvin, *Commentaries on the Book of Joshua*, trans. Henry Beveridge (Edinburgh: Calvin Translation Society, 1854). Tholuck's essay comprises pp. 345–75. The "Opinions and Testimonies" are found on pp. 376–407, to which the CTS edition has added "Additional Testimonies" on pp. 408–64.

[19]See previous note.

[20]Parker, *New Testament Commentaries*, x–xi.

many others as well, including himself.[21] And to these lists one could add still other studies, some older and some recent, including those of Strohl, Clavier, Lane, Steinmetz, Muller, Gamble, Balke, McKee, Engammare, Pitkin, and Schreiner. There are still other names and studies that could be mentioned, of course, but the more of these studies I read, the harder it seemed to say anything new about the general legacy of exegesis that Calvin bequeathed. At the same time, while we have accumulated enough pieces of the puzzle to trace the generally stable outlines of Calvin's exegetical legacy, the picture's details are often missing and occasionally contested.

Accordingly, for my own contribution to this Calvinian labor, I have chosen not to digest my predecessors but to follow a slimmer strand, yet one that is both fascinating and apparently unremarked. From Calvin's Genesis commentary, I initially cast my eye to the seventeenth century, to those two great compendia of exegetical opinion, the 1660 *Critici Sacri* of John Pearson — which Basil Hall termed "that Pantheon of exegetes"[22] — and the 1669 *Synopsis Criticorum* of Matthew Poole. These two works seemed not only to open a window into Calvin's legacy at the appropriate remove of one century, when all direct memory of Calvin had been buried, but also to offer a qualitatively different genre for weighing Calvin's exegetical legacy. Specifically, while it costs a theologian very little to utter a passing opinion of Calvin, however high or low, the editor of a compendium is in a different position. On the one hand, an editor is under no obligation to excerpt everything from his sources. If you could freely edit Calvin, or if you had to condense Calvin, what would you retain? On the other hand, an editor (and his publisher) are of necessity making a financial wager that the material gathered will be compelling and marketable, so the stakes are to that extent raised. What complicated my experiment, however, is the fact that on Genesis, *Critici Sacri* excerpts only seven writers: Münster, Fagius, Vatablus, Castalio, Clarius, Drusius, and Grotius — in other words, nothing from Calvin. And the *Synopsis Criticorum* also ignored Calvin on Genesis, despite its editor's avowed admiration for Calvin, and despite Calvin's presence in later volumes of the *Synopsis*.

The absence of Calvin struck me as more than an omission; it seemed a bit of a snub, and an argument against any triumphalist reading of Calvin's seventeenth-century legacy. I still think that judgment is true, but before I could plot an alternate course, I ran aground on yet one more uncharted shoal. As I perused the text of *Critici Sacri*, I wondered why these old glosses of François Vatable should be more highly esteemed in 1660 than the lucid brevity of John

---

[21]Puckett, *Calvin's Exegesis of the Old Testament*, 7–12. Since I am not attempting a survey of this literature, I have taken the liberty of omitting bibliographical data for these studies and those mentioned in the following sentence. Publication details may be obtained either from Puckett's book or from the annual Calvin bibliography.

[22]Basil Hall, "Biblical Scholarship: Editions and Commentaries," *CHB* 3:80.

Calvin, supposedly one of his former students. Actually, the relationship between Calvin and Vatable is sketchy at best. It has commonly been claimed that Calvin began his Hebrew studies in 1532 or so in Paris under Vatable, yet there are few if any known souvenirs of Calvin's coursework.[23] We have reasons to believe, however, that Calvin did obtain a copy of Stephanus's 1545 Latin Bible, in which two Latin translations are augmented by the annotations of Vatable.[24] If any traces of Vatable survive in Calvin's own exegesis, the student notes that Stephanus purported to publish would have been by far his likeliest source. But while there are indeed some faint echoes of the 1545 Vatable notes in Calvin's 1554 Genesis commentary,[25] the Vatablus excerpts found in *Critici Sacri* differ vastly from those in the 1545 Bible both in length and content. As Dominique Barthélemy noted a decade ago, *Critici Sacri* reprinted not the 1545 Vatable annotations, but the fuller edition of Vatable "and others" found in Stephanus's Bible of 1557, published in Geneva after his flight from the doctors of the Sorbonne.[26] While the *Critici Sacri* edition of the Vatablus annotations has frequently been regarded with distrust,[27] published accounts have just as often

---

[23]Max Engammare has recently undermined claims for Vatable's role as Calvin's teacher, arguing instead that Calvin began his study of Hebrew with Sebastian Munster in Basel in 1535. See "*Johannes Calvinus Trium Linguarum Peritus?* La Question de l'Hébreu," *Bibliothèque d'Humanisme et Renaissance* 58 (1996): 37-42.

[24]The 1545 Latin Bible may have been among various books sent to Calvin from Paris, as Gilmont infers from François Bauduin's letter to Calvin late in that year, though the text of the letter refers rather ambiguously to "reliquas chartas bibliorum Stephani quae istic desiderari poterant" (CO 12:231). See Jean-François Gilmont, *Jean Calvin et le livre imprimé* (Geneva: Droz, 1997), pp. 186–87; Tony Lane kindly alerted me to this reference. Both Stephanus Bibles, 1545 and 1557, are found on the inventory of the Genevan Academy; see Alexandre Ganoczy, *La Bibliotheque de l'Académie de Calvin: Le Catalogue de 1572 et ses Enseignments* (Geneva: Droz, 1969), #44 and #50.

[25]Lane notes some in "Sources," 240–59; I have found one or two others.

[26]Dominique Barthélemy, "Origine et rayonnement de la 'Bible de Vatable'," in *Théorie et pratique de l'exégèse: Actes du troisème colloque international sur l'histoire de l'exégèse biblique au XVIe siècle*, ed. Irena Backus and Francis Higman (Geneva: Droz, 1990), 393. In studying the 1557 annotations, I have not had access to the 1557 Bible but have followed the more accessible text in *Critici Sacri*, which is available on microfilm. I am grateful to Mr. Michael R. Rackett of Duke University for patiently checking the Vatablus material in *Critici Sacri* against the 1557 Bible; his examination revealed only five negligible changes in Genesis 12–22, all of which probably represent typesetting corrections.

[27]Suspicions were voiced by Herm. L. Strack (in *Realencyklopädie für protestantische Theologie und Kirche* [Leipzig: J. C. Hinrichs, 1908], 20:431, s.v. "Vatablus, Franz"), who correctly noted the contrast between the 1545 and 1557 annotations and further attested the presence of Calvin in Stephanus's 1556/57 edition of Vatable's annotations on the Psalms — though he stopped short of finding Calvin in the 1557 Bible. A. Strobel (in *Lexicon für Theologie und Kirche* [Freiburg: Herder, 1965], 10:617, s.v. "Vatablus") makes a laconic but accurate reference to Calvin's presence in the 1557 Vatable annotations.

disregarded the disparity between Stephanus's 1545 and 1557 editions of Vatable and the dubious integrity, therefore, of the *Critici Sacri* reprint.[28]

Although I later discovered others who were aware of the blended nature of these notes, including Richard Simon in 1678,[29] I myself came to discover only by hand, so to speak, that — at least in the book of Genesis — Stephanus's 1557 "Vatablus" notes are heavily interlaced with extracts from Calvin's 1554 Genesis commentary. Indeed, while the short glosses in 1557 occasionally reflect the 1545 Vatable notes, the longer, prose sections of the 1557 annotations are almost always taken from Calvin. In other words, while John Pearson may have thought to ignore Calvin's Genesis commentary in compiling *Critici Sacri*, he failed, for by reprinting Vatable from the first book of Stephanus's 1557 Bible, he incorporated more of the anonymous Calvin than of the authentic Vatable. And because Matthew Poole also drew from *Critici Sacri* in compiling his *Synopsis Criticorum*, Calvin's comments on Genesis are there too, albeit in more concentrated doses.[30] The resulting confusion is predictable and sometimes amusing, as when Calvin's nineteenth-century translator tries to demonstrate the Reformer's traditionalism at Genesis 18:18 by citing Vatable as a precedent, only to end up citing Calvin as a precedent for himself![31]

Stephanus's substantial pirating from Calvin's Genesis commentary thus provided that which I had sought in the seventeenth-century compendia, namely, an instance in which an editor was self-commissioned to pick and choose from among Calvin's exegesis as part of a profit-making venture. And although Stephanus and Calvin enjoyed a close working relationship — from his arrival in Geneva in 1550 until his death in 1559, Stephanus published most of Calvin's Latin writings, including the 1554 Genesis commentary — it is difficult to believe that Calvin had any editorial say. Much as Stephanus prized his long-envisioned 1557 Bible, he denied even Beza the time to revise the translation of the New Testament that Beza had specially prepared for it.[32] Indeed,

---

[28]Thus L. F. Hartman's account (in the *New Catholic Encyclopedia* [New York: McGraw-Hill, 1967], 14:543, s.v. "François Vatable") intimates that while these student notes were "sometimes in garbled form" and therefore "disowned by Vatable himself," there was a substantial continuity between the notes in the 1545 Bible and all subsequent editions. Basil Hall's account leaves a similar impression ("Biblical Scholarship," in *CHB* 3:54, 66–67, 82). The account in Ganoczy (*Bibliothèque*, #44) ascribes the Old Testament notes wholly to Vatable.

[29]Richard Simon, *Histoire Critique du Vieux Testament* (Rotterdam, 1685; facsimile reprint; Frankfurt: Minerva, 1967), 443a. Tony Lane has confirmed for me that the remark is unchanged from Simon's first edition (1678).

[30]An example (from Genesis 15) of this convoluted and successive plagiarism is presented in graphic form in Table A, below. A timeline of the publications and authors involved follows as Table B.

[31]See John King's editorial footnote in the CTS edition of Calvin's Genesis commentary, 1:478 n. 1.

[32]Elizabeth Armstrong, *Robert Estienne, Royal Printer: An Historical Study of the Elder Stephanus* (revised edition; n.p.: Sutton Courtenay Press, 1986), 229, 232–33. Cf. CO 17:234.

why Stephanus felt compelled to abandon his more faithful 1545 edition of Vatable[33] in favor of a much-diluted fabrication still mostly in the name of the now-deceased Vatable is not all that clear; for if the 1545 Paris Bible had precipitated the Sorbonne's mistrust or envy of Stephanus into a vague but potent censure, any Bible hailing from Stephanus's Geneva press could be expected to carry only a darker cloud.

Perhaps some clue to Stephanus's motive — and Calvin's legacy — might emerge from the way he insinuates Calvin anonymously into the 1557 annotations. Barthélemy's study compared the 1545 annotations with the extant student *reportationes* of Vatable's lectures and concluded very much in favor of Stephanus's basic fidelity to Vatable. In the 1545 annotations, Barthélemy observes, Stephanus's tendency was not to "protestantize" Vatable but more to "decatholicize" his lectures simply by omitting various references to the church that are found in the student notes, so that Stephanus appears more to omit than fabricate material.[34] Stephanus's use in 1557 of Calvin's 1554 commentary, however, would necessarily be complicated by the need to extract relatively brief annotations from a comparatively huge commentary. What will Stephanus choose?

My examination has focused on the Abraham narratives, Genesis 12–22, expanding both forward and backward from the stories of Hagar and Ishmael. Calvin's pattern in this commentary involves a varying combination of two or three ingredients. He often leads off by explaining some detail of the text, but he cares far more to explain narrative twists and turns than to luxuriate in the niceties of what one might term "technical" exegesis or "criticism." Philology and grammar are of interest to Calvin only as they elucidate the plot. Calvin's comments then examine, almost always, the significance of the plot for the Christian readers of his own day. Such "application" may entail gnomic statements or aphorisms, as in the generalization he drew from the rescue of Hagar: "Note, then, that there are two ways whereby people are regarded and helped by God: either when they implore his help and protection as suppliants, or when even unasked he helps in their misfortunes."[35] But Calvin can also frame his application more parenetically. When Abraham capitulated to Sarah's scheme to use Hagar as a surrogate, Calvin drew forth this exhortation: "Although we may have stood long and firmly in the faith, we must daily pray that God would not lead us into temptation.[36] Just as often, however, Calvin's

---

[33]A point well argued by Barthélemy's article.

[34]Barthélemy, "La 'Bible de Vatable'," 396: "Le constant le plus intéressant que l'on puisse faire est que, là où Estienne cite Vatable, il ne l'a pas tant 'protestantisé' que 'decatholicisé'." Even some of the texts on justification by faith, which the Spanish Inquisition would later censure, are actually rooted in Vatable's own words (p. 399).

[35]Calvin, *Comm. Gen.* 16:11 (CTS 1:433, CO 23:229).

[36]Calvin, *Comm. Gen.* 16:2 (CTS 1:426, CO 23:224).

application of a text will lead him to broader theological issues and, if needed, to polemical excursions. Thus it was not enough to clarify how and why Paul saw his Jewish sisters and brothers as imaging Hagar and Ishmael; Calvin had also to identify and expose the Hagarites and Ishmaelites of his own day. Here one sees the significance of his frequent assertion not only that Abraham was an image or type of the church, but also that Abraham *was* the church in his own day. What happened to and around Abraham parallels perfectly what happens later on and nowadays to and around the church — to us, and around us. For Calvin, the plot is everything, yet the plot is also always the same: the ways of a just and gracious God among sinners.

Not all of these ingredients are of equal interest to Calvin's later editors. In the case of the 1557 Vatable notes — the ones we should call "pseudo-Vatablus" — it seems that the editor, Robert Stephanus, is interested mostly in only one aspect of Calvin. As reprinted in *Critici Sacri*, the 1557 notes require just over 1200 lines of text to cover Genesis 12–22, of which about thirty percent (~380 lines) are culled from Calvin. More to the point, Calvin is quoted to address about fifty-seven different verses and questions.[37] Most of the time — and there are several exceptions — the material that Stephanus presses into service consists of what I have termed Calvin's "semi-technical" exegesis: not precisionist analysis of grammar or etymology, but explanations of phrases or concepts or events that elucidate the plot. Some are quite short, such as his account of what Lot meant when he said his guests had come "under the shadow of my roof."[38] Most excerpts are a sentence or two, or three: thus, Calvin anonymously testifies for Stephanus as to how a covenant works, why Abraham built altars, why it was said that the kings of Sodom fled "into pits," what the twofold office of Melchizedek was, and why Abraham saluted only one of the three angels who visited him.[39]

The longest excerpt, in fact, pertains to the difficult question of Hagar's vision in Genesis 16: What did she say about God, what did she name the well, and why? Hagar's experience of divine providence is explored in this extract, but Calvin's longer discourse in Genesis 21 on the theological significance of Hagar and Ishmael and on their ultimate destiny will be of no interest at all to Stephanus, who draws nothing from Calvin on Hagar's final exile.[40] Stephanus's peculiar interests are perhaps clearest in passages such as the

---

[37]So far as I can tell, Calvin is never the source of the abundant short glosses on the meaning of Hebrew words or phrases, and if the original notes of Vatable survive anywhere, it is here. At the same time, it is obvious that Stephanus has not retained much of the Vatable annotations as they were published in 1545, even though these were the notes that Barthélemy found reasonably faithful to the surviving student transcriptions. One can only assume that he has acquired additional sources for his short glosses.

[38]Pseudo-Vatablus, annotation to Genesis 19:8 (*Critici Sacri* 1:215); hereafter cited as *Ann. Gen.*

[39]Pseudo-Vatablus, *Ann. Gen.* 12:3, 12:7–8, 14:10, 14:18, 18:3 (*Critici Sacri* 1:177, 178, 184, 185, 215).

[40]Pseudo-Vatablus, *Ann. Gen.* 16:13 (*Critici Sacri* 1:199–200).

incest of Lot and his daughters: there, he ignores all of Calvin's moralizing to focus instead on a few matters of philology.[41] Likewise, when Abraham lies to Abimelech about his "sister" Sarah, Stephanus is far more interested in the genealogical considerations that might undergird Abraham's claim than in Calvin's excoriation of Abraham for his feeble excuses.[42]

A mere list of textual dependencies, however, may conceal the more remarkable elements of what Stephanus includes and omits. Sometimes Stephanus clearly but quietly disagrees with Calvin, as when he maintains that in the war against the five kings, Abraham had trained his servants in the art of war — an assertion Calvin had explicitly repudiated.[43] And while Stephanus is generally not interested in Calvin's polemics or paranesis or aphorisms,[44] there are exceptions. At Genesis 15:10, Stephanus is happy to embrace one of Calvin's unadvertised allegories, wherein the halves of the animals severed as part of the covenantal rite signify the hard servitude and the eventual restoration of the sons of Abraham.[45] Stephanus also likes the ensuing allegory — to be sure, Calvin calls it an *analogy* — drawn from the account in Genesis 15:17 of the smoking furnace and the lamp passing between the severed animals: the smoke and the light, Calvin wrote, signify the promise of a future deliverance to Abram's seed, and of how the church retains its hope even in the darkness of afflictions.[46]

Clearly, not all of Stephanus's borrowings from Calvin can be consistently categorized. What can be said with respect to Calvin's exegetical legacy, however, is that at least one editor had no qualms about picking and choosing from among Calvin's potpourri of exegetical offerings. What Stephanus liked in

---

[41]Pseudo-Vatablus, *Ann. Gen.* 19:31–37 (*Critici Sacri* 1:216); cf. Calvin, *Comm. Gen.* (CO 23:281–85).

[42]Pseudo-Vatablus, *Ann. Gen.* 20:12 (*Critici Sacri* 1:221); cf. Calvin, *Comm. Gen.* (CO 23:292–93, CTS 1:530).

[43]Pseudo-Vatablus, *Ann. Gen.* 14:13 (*Critici Sacri* 1:184); cf. Calvin, *Comm. Gen.* (CO 23:199, CTS 1:384).

[44]Thus at Gen. 18:19 (*Critici Sacri* 1:208–9), the aphorism Calvin draws from Abraham's example about the behavior proper to the head of the household is recast so as to apply not to "us" but only to Abraham. Similarly, at Genesis 18:22 (*Critici Sacri* 1:209), Stephanus breaks off from quoting Calvin just where Calvin turns gnomic.

[45]Pseudo-Vatablus, *Ann. Gen.* 15:10 (*Critici Sacri* 1:192); cf. Calvin, *Comm. Gen.* (CO 23:216-17, CTS 1:413–14), and Table A, below.

[46]Pseudo-Vatablus, *Ann. Gen.* 15:17 (*Critici Sacri* 1:193); cf. Calvin, *Comm. Gen.* (CO 23:221, CTS 1:420). These two excerpts from Genesis 15 are pertinent for a consideration of Barthélemy's suggestion that Stephanus "decatholicized" Vatable in 1545. In the 1557 annotations on Genesis 15:10 (previous note, cf. Table A), Stephanus seems similarly to "de-ecclesiologize" Calvin by omitting key phrases in which Calvin makes clear that the ultimate restoration is that of the *church*. Yet at Genesis 15:17, Stephanus does not hesitate to include Calvin's reference to the church as the ultimate subject signified by the furnace and the lamp.

Calvin, at least for this project, the Bible whose composition he had schemed over for more than a decade and in some ways his *magnum opus*, was not Calvin's philology, not his varying modes of application, not so much his theological reflection, certainly not his polemics, but — instead, mostly — his micro-mastery of the Bible's immediate storyline.

It would be unwise, of course, to lose sight of the extent to which Stephanus's genre determined his editorial predilections. He was about the business of producing an annotated Bible, a study-bible for his own day, and that was rather different than commissioning a commentary. Nonetheless, these editorial choices still represent his distillation of Calvin, a selection of exegetical insights gauged to appeal and endure independently of Calvin's commentary — and without either the cachet or the liabilities attached to Calvin's name. And so it happened: the "Vatablus" annotations of 1557, with their many excerpts from a fairly de-theologized Calvin, were taken up and immortalized in "that Pantheon of exegetes," the *Critici Sacri*.

There is, moreover, an uncanny corroboration for the editorial choices made by Stephanus, a deposition of sorts from Matthew Poole, a full century later. I have already noted how Poole's *Synopsis* declined to draw on Calvin for the full stretch from Genesis to Job. What I have not mentioned, however, is that the omission of Calvin is neither accidental nor tacit. In the introduction to the first of his five volumes, after two folio pages that inventory the many commentators and sources upon which he has drawn, Poole offers a strange encomium-cum-apology for why he has bypassed Calvin, even though he says he thinks the world of Calvin as a commentator. Thus he begins:

> Some perhaps may wonder that in the catalog of authors John Calvin does not appear: an interpreter who is acute, learnéd, and solid, even in the judgment of his foes. There are those who construe this as my personal failing, and (if I may say so) they write to me of the injury inflicted on such a great man; while others give thanks that I should omit him whom they hate worse than a dog or snake.[47]

Poole, however, insists he has selected his sources without pandering to Calvin's admirers or detractors, and he defends his right to borrow from Calvin's writings in later volumes wherever he may find it necessary or useful. Later in his long paragraph, Poole goes on to assert that most of Calvin's successors, even his adversaries, have drawn from Calvin to improve their own writings: "Almost everyone," Poole claims, "has Calvin in their hands and libraries." But so far as concerns Calvin's absence from the first volumes of the *Synopsis*, Poole's rationale is clear:

---

[47]Matthew Poole, *Synopsis Criticorum*, vol. 1 (Utrecht, 1684), p. III: "Mirentur forsan nonnulli, in Auctorum catalogo non comparere Joannem Calvinum, Interpretem, vel adversariorum judicio, acutum, doctum, & solidum. Sunt qui hoc mihi vitio vertent, & dicam mihi scribent injuriae tanto nomini illatae: alii gratulabuntur, quod illum praeterierim, quem cane pejus & angue oderint." Poole's *Synopsis* originally appeared in five volumes, 1669–74.

> The commentaries of Calvin are not so much critical (a quality the present undertaking looks to first of all) as practical; nor do they so much explain words and phrases (matters of primary concern to the *Synopsis*) as they solidly treat theological matters and focus on praxis.[48]

Poole writes an odd love letter: Calvin is esteemed, even lionized, but he will not appear in the opening volumes of the *Synopsis Criticorum*, because he is evidently too theological and practical at the expense of the technical, philological, and critical exegesis that Poole is after. How odd to praise and defend Calvin so fiercely, only to dismiss him wholesale, without even a cameo here and there! Does Poole think that, on the Pentateuch and the Writings, and on critical issues at least, Calvin is a lightweight? It is hard not to wonder if Calvin's reputation as a "theological" commentator, or perhaps as a polemicist, has served to relegate much of his Old Testament exegesis to the storeroom.

In the case of Matthew Poole, part of the problem surely is Calvin's reputation, more so than his actual exegesis. We know this, because Calvin *is* in Poole's *Synopsis* — once again, disguised as François Vatable. By examining Poole's use of the pseudo-Vatablus material he drew from *Critici Sacri*, we can see what Poole selected to publish of Calvin without having had the burden of knowing it was Calvin: a blindfolded test, so to speak. As it turns out, Poole actually does like the anonymous Calvin, for he excerpts quite a number of sufficiently critical observations that are derived verbatim from the Genevan Reformer[49] — observations that Poole evidently did not think Calvin had to offer, assuming that Poole ever read the Calvin whom he claimed to have in his own hands and library.

In any event, in Genesis 12–22, Poole happily reports many of the observations and glosses that Stephanus had seen fit to include in the 1557 Geneva Bible. Of course, since Stephanus had declined to incorporate much at all from Calvin's non-technical and theological exegesis, Poole had little to choose from but these short and semi-technical sentences from Calvin. Still, one would expect Poole to favor the anonymous Calvin only where his remarks appear sufficiently "critical" or philological. All the more remarkable, then, is Poole's inclusion of both of Calvin's tropological interpretations of Genesis 15 — the figurative interpretation of the severed animals, and his moral "analogy" of the lamp in the smoking furnace. Presumably, Poole would never have gone look-

---

[48]Poole, *Synopsis Criticorum* 1:III: "Calvini Commentaria non tam Critica sunt, (qualia inprimis respicit praesens institutum,) quam Practica; nec tam verba & phrases enucleant, (in quibus praecipue versatur Synopsis,) quam materias Theologicas solide tractant, & ad praxin accommodant."

[49]Let me offer Genesis 15 as an example. The "Vatablus" material in *Critici Sacri* numbers 812 words, of which 43% (350 words) are verbatim excerpts from Calvin. Poole in turn draws on 174 words of "Vatablus," of which 107 words, or better than 60%, derive from the Calvin excerpts. Note that *Critici Sacri* also retained (via the 1557 Bible) 90 words from the shorter and more reliable Vatable notes in the 1545 Bible, only 30 of which were copied by Poole.

ing for such a "practical" bit of exegesis from Calvin, but he received it gladly in the name of Vatable.[50]

Let us take one more look at Hagar and Ishmael, then conclude. As noted earlier, Calvin's disquisition on Hagar's vision in Genesis 16, along with her naming of both God and a well in the desert, constitute one of Stephanus's largest excerpts from Calvin in the Abrahamic narratives of Genesis. To be sure, the length probably owes more to Calvin's digest of other opinions than to the profundity of his own, but Poole's use of this material appears to give a slight nod in Calvin's favor: for of the eleven exegetical options Poole reports, three are drawn verbatim from Calvin, with first place given to Calvin's own view.[51] Poole, of course, did not know this was Calvin's view, nor did the friends who helped complete Poole's vernacular *Annotations on the Holy Bible* in 1683, whose preface spoke so highly of Vatable, "papist" though he was.[52] On the other hand, when Poole's *Synopsis* turned to Genesis 21, Calvin fared somewhat worse — and Hagar, somewhat better. Because Stephanus had bypassed all but one line from Calvin's commentary for most of this entire episode, from Ishmael's "playing" with Isaac through the subsequent rescue and resettlement of Ishmael and his mother, it is no surprise that Poole himself has nothing more from Calvin here either.[53] Yet Poole drew on many sources besides pseudo-Vatablus in *Critici Sacri*, and if Calvin's angry disposal of Hagar and Ishmael had possessed much currency in Poole's day, one still might hope to find it reported, especially since Poole himself explicitly raised the question of Abraham's harshness toward his concubine and son. Indeed, Poole's *Synopsis*

---

[50]Further confirmation of Poole's appreciation for Calvin's tropology may be gleaned from his last work, the vernacular *Annotations on the Holy Bible* that he began upon completing the *Synopsis Criticorum*. At the time of his death in 1679 (the year after Simon's *Histoire Critique* first appeared), Poole had completed these *Annotations* through Isaiah. Although his friends who went on to complete the work and write its preface claimed that the *Annotations* were not, in fact, a translation of the *Synopsis*, Poole's annotations on Genesis clearly condense and translate selections from the earlier work. And since the English *Annotations* were intended to be less technical than the Latin *Synopsis*, it is no surprise to find that many Calvinian glosses and interpretations from the *Synopsis Criticorum* were welcomed also in the *Annotations* — including, again, the figurative interpretations of Abraham's covenant sacrifice and vision in Genesis 15. The two-volume *Annotations on the Holy Bible* of 1683–84 have been reprinted as *A Commentary on the Holy Bible*, 3 vols. (London: Banner of Truth Trust, 1962).

[51]It is less clear in the *Annotations* which view Poole favors at Genesis 16:13 (p. 39a), where Calvin's view is the first of but three that are listed. However, Poole's opening remark there continues to recall Calvin's enunciation of how Hagar came to recognize divine providence in her rescue.

[52]Preface to Poole, *Annotations*, I:v.

[53]Specifically, in Genesis 21:9–21, Stephanus borrowed only this sentence from Calvin: "Fuit igitur maligna subsannatio qua protervus adolescens fratrem adhuc infantum prae se contempsit" (*Critici Sacri* 1:227, cf. CO 23:300). Poole's *Synopsis* (1:184) condensed this to "Fuit maligna subsannatio qua fratrem prae se contempsit."

offered five possible explanations of Abraham's conduct (including arguments attributed to Cajetan, Rivet, and Mercier), even as Poole's *Annotations* on Genesis 21:12 would synthesize half a dozen traditional considerations.[54] Nonetheless, in neither work is there any echo of Calvin.[55]

III. Conclusion

Only suggestive conclusions can be drawn from such a limited sampling of Calvin's legacy. I have looked at what I think is an important representation, but there are many other texts and themes in Calvin's exegesis. There were also many other users and opinions of Calvin in the seventeenth century. Indeed, Poole himself had another opinion in reserve, for the mixture of enthusiasm and reticence with which he greeted Calvin in the first volumes of the *Synopsis Criticorum* turned, by volume three, to an explicit endorsement of Calvin's technical proficiency in elucidating Hebrew words and phrases along with other obscurities.[56] While these words of praise do not fully square with his earlier reservations, Poole's allegiance was never in doubt: he stood as a successor to those numerous Elizabethans for whom Pettegree found Calvin's theological influence to be simply "dominant."[57] Yet Poole's gritty defense of Calvin reminds us that the Reformer's detractors were also numerous. To some, the Genevan exegete was "a great man"; to others, "worse than a dog or snake."

If the present study has made anything clear, I hope it is that Calvin's exegetical legacy is itself not all that clear. Calvin's reception of exegetical tradition is complicated and subtle. So also is his reception by later interpreters and commentators. My appreciation for this twofold complexity rests on five (concluding) observations:

First, with respect to the legacy he received and possessed, my analysis of Calvin's treatment of Hagar and Ishmael suggests that, at some points at least, he embraced little from the exegetical context or resources of the sixteenth century and earlier. Calvin has often been admired for his independence of mind, but the obverse of his independence may, on occasion, be simply an ignorance of exegetical tradition — an ignorance born not of a considered critique but of heat or haste.

---

[54]Poole, *Synopsis*, I:185; idem, *Annotations*, I:49b.

[55]Poole's utter neglect of Calvin at Genesis 21 is made only more enigmatic by one contemporary's probable embrasure of Calvin, including clear echoes of the rhetoric of Hagar's and Ishmael's reprobation. See George Hughes, *An Analytical Exposition of the Whole first Book of Moses, called Genesis ...* (n.p.: O. Hughes [?], 1672), 268b, 270a. The colophon of this work is dated August 24, 1662.

[56]See Poole, *Synopsis Criticorum*, Praeloquium to volume 3, where he protests that he had planned all along to include Calvin — a claim corroborated by the broad hint in his preface to volume 1 (see p. 47, above).

[57]Pettegree, "Reception of Calvinism in Britain," 280–81.

Second, the commitment to literal exegesis that Calvin espoused and that often is taken as a hallmark of Reformation exegesis is often not what we might mean today by "literal" exegesis. Calvin's use of the allegory of Hagar and Ishmael in his exegesis of Genesis 21 illustrates his discomfort less with the notion of allegory than with its abuse. Consequently, his exegesis here also displays his ability and desire to shelter the fruits of figurative exegesis under a more literal umbrella. It is ironic that Calvin should choose this occasion to vilify Origen's allegoresis for twisting scripture.[58] Ironic, because Calvin himself saw Paul's allegory as not an instance of doctrine per se but merely as a "lovely illustration" (*pulchram exornationem*) unable to bear a proper burden of proof.[59] Ironic, further, because in proclaiming that the "true sense of scripture" lies in "the natural and simple" reading[60] — against the capriciousness of Origen and his ilk — Calvin moves quickly to confess that there is, in fact, an allegory to be found not only here, but throughout the Old Testament: "in circumcision, in sacrifices, in the whole Levitical priesthood" and in all of "the principal and most memorable events that happened in [the house of Abraham]."[61] Ironic, finally, because Calvin's insistence that such allegories "do not involve a departure from the literal meaning"[62] leads him to historicize St. Paul's allegory at the expense of the more sympathetic reading of Hagar that was not only traditional but, arguably, also more literal.

Third, Calvin's commitment to what Matthew Poole called "practical" or "theological" commentary further stretched his fidelity to literal exegesis. Calvin takes pains in all of his expositions of Sarah and Hagar to underscore the typological status of Abraham and his household. As an interpretative strategy, deriving the church from Old Testament roots is by no means original to Calvin — Luther comes at once to mind,[63] though the argument is surely Pauline, if

---

[58]Calvin, *Comm. Gal.* 4:22 (CO 50:236, OODR 2/16:106.10–12; CNTC 11:84).

[59]Calvin, *Comm. Gal.* 4:21 (CO 50:236, OODR 2/16:105.13–15; cf. CNTC 11:84): "Non esset quidem satis valida per se probatio. Sed postquam argumentis satis pugnavit, confirmatio haec non est spernenda."

[60]Calvin, *Comm. Gal.* 4:22 (CO 50:237; OODR 2/16:107.2–3): "Sciamus ergo eum esse verum Scripturae sensum, qui germanus est ac simplex."

[61]Calvin, *Comm. Gal.* 4:22 (CO 50:237; OODR 2/16:107.2–3; cf. CNTC 11:85): "Sicut ergo in circuncisione, in sacrificiis, in toto sacerdotio Levitico allegoria fuit, sicuti hodie est in nostris sacramentis, ita etiam in domo Abrahae fuisse dico."

[62]Calvin, *Comm. Gal.* 4:22 (CO 50:237; OODR 2/16:107.2–3; cf. CNTC 11:85): "Sed id non facit, ut a literali sensu recedatur."

[63]Jaroslav Pelikan argued the case in *Luther the Expositor* (St. Louis: Concordia, 1959), as does Ulrich Asendorf in *Lectura in Biblia: Luthers Genesisvorlesung (1535–1545)* (Göttingen: Vandenhoeck & Ruprecht, 1998); see esp. chapter III.2, "Die neue Kirche Abrahams," 257–65. Luther, however, seems less concerned to enforce a "literal" exegesis of Galatians 4 and can quite comfortably allow Hagar and Ishmael to fulfill contrasting roles, as literal heroes in Genesis and as symbolic villains in Paul. Calvin, on the other hand, seems driven to homogenize the figuration of Paul's self-stated *allegoria* with the history in Genesis, collapsing or dissolving the symbolic into the literal.

not dominical — but Calvin is probably more self-conscious than most in embracing and extolling this strategy precisely because it preserves the *letter* of the Old Testament. Again, because he is not merely a type or figure of the church but also *the* church in his own day, Abraham becomes the agent through whom Calvin procures an abundance of theological insights, polemics, and pastoral applications in his commentaries and sermons on this passage, all of them marketed to Calvin's audience as *literal* exegesis. The crucial question, however, is whether Calvin has really broken free from traditional exegesis, with its various pitfalls and promises, or has he merely repackaged it? There can be little doubt but that Calvin's typology looks for all the world like last year's tropology.[64]

Fourth, for all of Calvin's distinctive and engaging theology and practicality, it was that very attribute that some editors could find mostly expendable. Both Robert Stephanus and Matthew Poole attest that it was possible to value Calvin in piecemeal fashion, even as both men — one wittingly, the other not — enabled Calvin to leave a piecemeal legacy. From Stephanus we learn that the "pastoral" or "practical" or "theological" exegesis for which Calvin would later be so lauded (by Poole, among many others) could be detached and discarded without scruple. From Poole we learn that Calvin's theological exegesis could be expendable in another way, for it was his very reputation for practicality that seems to have caused Poole to shun his exegesis altogether, at least so far as concerned the Pentateuch and the Writings, as having little to offer by way of critical exegesis.

Finally, the eclectic reception and redaction of Calvin further suggests that his exegetical legacy may be rooted less in his actual exegesis than in what his successors thought about his exegesis. As Poole's *Synopsis* demonstrates, Calvin's reputation for practical commentary was so great a century after his death that a loyal Protestant and Presbyterian was unwilling to consider or even examine it for its "critical" virtues — and yet the same writer would happily take Calvin's insights, both those that were semi-technical as well as those that were more inclined toward allegory or tropology, when offered in the name of a respectably critical or technical commentator.

Poole's unwitting ambivalence could be dismissed as a fluke, if it did not so closely mirror our own. Like Poole, we who value the Bible today want to understand it literally and precisely, tutored by the cutting edge of scholarship and criticism. Often enough, as Poole could tell us, Calvin says little or nothing to the technical and critical considerations though which interpreters today must labor in hopes of finding embedded in the text some scrap of the word of God, some echo of God's voice. Yet if we consult Calvin less for information than for inspiration, it does not diminish his legacy among us. As an exegete, Calvin was driven by a passion to find and present the pure word of God, and to this end

---

[64]Once again, the "analogies" Calvin finds in Genesis 15 illustrate the point. See above, notes 45, 46.

he charged unswervingly towards the original text, jettisoning anything that might distract or impede, whether allegory, fable, or popular opinion. We still aspire to this. But Calvin was no mere tourist of biblical antiquities: his journey *ad fontes* was always booked on a round-trip fare and with an eye to the return. And if the present study has suggested that Calvin's journey *ab fontibus* was sometimes imperfect, burdened at times with extraneous concerns or hindered by ignorance, it does not diminish our admiration for the clarity with which he framed the *ideal* — an ideal for exegesis in which criticism and faith, text and practice, letter and spirit are one.[65]

---

[65]I thus conclude in unpremeditated agreement with the observations of Elsie Anne McKee about Calvin's "vision of theology and exegesis as two parts of one whole," but I am especially sympathetic to her characterization of how Calvin's "theological vision of the unity and authority and practical applicability of Scripture" combines with his "unusual architectonic gifts" to give his theology "an *impression* of novelty" (emphasis mine). See "Some Reflections on Relating Calvin's Exegesis and Theology," in *Biblical Hermeneutics in Historical Perspective*, ed. Mark S. Burrows and Paul Rorem (Grand Rapids: Eerdmans, 1991), 224–25.

Annotations on Genesis 15:10 from the 1545 Stephanus Bible, fol. 9ᵛ, sig. b.iᵛ

¶16 Heb. & **quamlibet partem diuis**ionis suae **e regione** sociae suae posuit. Modus loquendi Hebraicus, pro, & **posuit partes illas** sibi respondentes altrinsecus.

> **boldface**
> *represents text of 1545 "Vatablus" preserved in the 1557 Bible*

Excerpts from John Calvin, Commentary on Genesis 15:10 (1554) • CO 23:216f, CTS 1:413f

. . . this, in my opinion, is the sum of the whole: That God, in commanding the animals to be killed, shows what will be **the future condition of the Church.** Abram certainly wished to be assured of the promised inheritance of the land. Now he is taught that it would take its commencement from death; that is that he and his children must die before they should enjoy the dominion over the land. In commanding the slaughtered animals to be cut in parts, it is probable that he followed the ancient rite in forming covenants whether they were entering into any alliance, or were mustering an army, a practice which also passed over to the Gentiles. Now, the allies or the soldiers passed between the severed parts, that, being enclosed together within the sacrifice, they might be the more sacredly united in one body. That this method was practiced by the Jews, Jeremiah bears witness (34:18), where he introduces God as saying, 'They have violated my covenant, when they cut the calf in two parts, and passed between the divisions of it, as well the princes of Judas, and the nobles of Jerusalem, and the whole people of the land.' Nevertheless, there appears to me to have been this special reason for the act referred to; that the Lord would indeed admonish the race of Abram, not only that it should be like a dead carcass, but even like one torn and dissected. For the servitude with which they were oppressed for a time, was more intolerable than simple death; yet because the sacrifice is offered to God, death itself is immediately turned into new life. And this is the reason why | Abram, placing the parts of the sacrifice opposite to each other, fits them one to the other, because they were again to be gathered together from their dispersion. But how difficult is **the restoration of the Church** and what troubles are involved in it, is shown by the horror with which Abram was seized. We see, therefore, that two things were illustrated; namely, the hard servitude, with which the sons of Abram were to be pressed almost to laceration and destruction; and then their redemption, which was to be the signal pledge of divine adoption; and in the same mirror **the general condition of the Church** is represented to us, as it is the peculiar province of God to create it out of nothing, and to raise it from death.

> **underlining**
> *represents text borrowed from Calvin (1554) by Stephanus (1557)*

Annotations on Genesis 15:10 as reprinted in *Critici Sacri* (1660) from the 1557 Stephanus Bible

10. *Per medium.* בְתוֹךְ] i. In partes æquales: *Unamquamque*, &c. 'וּנו אִישׁ] Ad verbum, *virum partes suam eregione sociæ suæ*. i. **Quamlibet partem** animalium ab ipso **divis**orum **eregione** partis correspondentis. q.d. **Partes illas** divisas **sibi respondentes altrinsicus posuit**. Quòd mactata animalia in partes secari jubet, videntur fuisse vetustus ritus in fœderibus pangendis, qui deinde ad Gentes quoque transiit, sive ineunda esset aliqua societas sive exercitus lustrandi. Transibant autem per medias partes vel socii vel milites, ut sanctiùs in unum corpus coalescerent, sacrificio simul inclusi. Judæis quidem usitatum fuisse hunc morem testatur Jeremias, c. 34. 18. Ubi Deum ita loquentem inducit, *Violarunt fœdus meum quum vitulum conciderint in duas partes, & transierint inter divisiones ejus, tam principes Juda quàm proceres Jerusalem, & totus populus terræ.* Hîc res duas ostendit Dominus ipsi Abrahæ, duram servitutem quâ ferè usque ad interitum & lacerationem premendi erant Abræ filii; quod per occisa animalia & in duas partes secta significatur: Deinde redemptionem, quæ insigne pignus foret Divinæ adoptionis, quam indicant partes eregione inter se coaptatæ, quia ex dissipatione rursus colligendæ erant. ¶ *Sed aves* הַצִּפֹּר אֶת] Ad verbum, *& avem*.

• {Critici Sacri 1:192.45–67}

shading *represents text borrowed by Matthew Poole from "Vatablus" material in Critici Sacri*

Matthew Poole, *Synopsis Criticorum* (1669) on Genesis 15:10, p. 159f

Table A: An example of Calvin's transmission as Pseudo-Vatablus.

1530	François Vatable begins teaching Hebrew at the College Royale
1532	Robert Stephanus publishes *Biblia Breves in eadem annotationes, ex doctiss. interpretationibus, & Hebraeorum commentariis* (Paris)
1545	Stephanus publishes *Biblia* with Vatablus notes (Paris)
1547	Death of Vatable
1548	John Calvin's *Commentary on Galatians*
1549	Stephanus's 1545 *Biblia* listed on Paris *Index* (& others later on)
1550	Stephanus flees Paris for Geneva
1550	Calvin begins lectures on Genesis
1552	Stephanus's *Ad censures theologorum parisiensium responsio*
1554	Calvin's *Commentary on Genesis* published by Stephanus (Geneva)
1557–58	Calvin preaches on Galatians
1557	Stephanus publishes *Biblia* with expanded Vatablus notes (Geneva)
1559	Death of Stephanus
1559–60	Calvin preaches on Genesis
1564	Death of Calvin
1584–86	Salamanca Bibles reprint "corrected" annotations of "Vatablus" [?]
1660	*Critici Sacri* reprints annotations from 1557 Bible as "Vatablus"
1669–74	Matthew Poole's *Synopsis Criticorum,* based partly on *Critici Sacri*
1678	Richard Simon's *Histoire Critique du Vieux Testament,* first edition
1679	Death of Poole
1683–84	Poole's (posthumous) *Annotations on the Holy Bible*
1685	Simon's *Histoire Critique du Vieux Testament,* revised edition

Table B: A timeline of persons and publications mentioned

A Response to "Calvin's Exegetical Legacy: His Reception and Transmission of Text and Tradition"

Barbara Pitkin

If the present study has made anything clear, I hope it is that Calvin's exegetical legacy is itself not all that clear. Calvin's reception of exegetical tradition is complicated and subtle. So also is his reception by later interpreters and commentators.—John Thompson

John Thompson begins this meticulously researched study of Calvin's exegetical legacy by heightening our appreciation for the complexity of the topic itself. I am especially appreciative that these reflections come at the beginning of the conference, because the points raised are relevant to our consideration of Calvin's legacy in other areas; I am equally grateful that they are expressed in the context of a paper that is clearly and cogently argued. Regarding Calvin's exegesis, "legacy" is a metaphor that admits of several dimensions. Calvin's exegetical legacy may refer to the fund of traditional and contemporary exegetical insights bequeathed to Calvin by the Christian past, or to the inventory of exegetical writings he left to posterity, or, finally, to the impact his exegesis or Calvin himself as an exegete might have had on those who came after him. Determining the substance of any of these is complicated by the fact that inheritors of legacies make whatever use of them that they will, such that what constitutes the legacy, is, as Thompson reminds us, often in the eye of the beholder.

Having cautioned us about the difficulty of the terrain, Thompson goes on to provide a helpful orientation by exploiting the full range of meanings implied by the title and yet limiting his discussion to two discrete cases: Calvin's commentary on Genesis and the reception of Calvin in two seventeenth-century compendia. These limitations do not mean that the findings are confined to these areas. Rather, as is evident in the concluding reflections, the insights drawn from these two cases are richly suggestive of methodological and substantive insights fundamental to consideration of Calvin's place in the history of biblical interpretation.

I. The "subjective" legacy

Obviously, in order to assess what Calvin could possibly have left to posterity, we need a sense of what Calvin received from the past, how he used what he inherited, and especially how he may have transformed traditional insights in his transmission of them. For this reason, the attention to the "subjective legacy" that Calvin received is especially welcome.[1] It is important to note that in adopting an "extensive" approach, as opposed to the intensive approach take by Tony Lane,[2] this investigation focuses not so much on identifying exactly what Calvin himself received and used of the exegetical tradition but rather on the richer exegetical inventory of the Christian past. This broader discussion raises several more general considerations of importance for anyone interested in the actual exegetical inventory that Calvin left to posterity. These are raised in Thompson's concluding comments, and I would like to underscore and expand on several of them.

A. The question of Calvin's relationship to exegetical tradition.

Many of us who have been plowing Calvin's corner in the field of the history of biblical interpretation have been arguing in various ways for Calvin's relative independence in making exegetical decisions. Few, however, have been willing to face the difficult questions of the actual sources Calvin used in his exegesis of biblical texts and the substantive relationship of his work to these resources. We have literally volumes of sometimes conflicting information about Calvin's hermeneutics, but only a handful of materials, mostly articles, that attempt to *demonstrate* substantively, through either the intensive approach favored by Tony Lane or the extensive approach taken by John Thompson and David Steinmetz, the exact nature of Calvin's alleged independence from his predecessors and contemporaries and, where possible, to name those predecessors and contemporaries whom he might actually have used. And while some, myself included, offer up largely theological explanations for Calvin's peculiar emphases, John invites us to consider a far more mundane reason for Calvin's ignorance of exegetical tradition: he was simply too busy.[3] This is not to say that theological reasons cannot be given, but only to point out that we tend to overlook the most obvious reason for Calvin's alleged independence of mind.

---

[1]For more detailed treatment, see John L. Thompson, *Writing the Wrongs: Women of the Old Testament among Biblical Commentators from Philo through the Reformation* (Oxford University Press, forthcoming).

[2]See especially A. N. S., "The Sources of Calvin's Citations in His Genesis Commentary," in *Interpreting the Bible: Historical and Theological Studies in Honour of David F. Wright*, ed. A. N. S. Lane (Leicester: Apollos, 1997), 47-98; "Did Calvin Use Lippoman's *Catena in Genesim?*" *Calvin Theological Journal* 31 (1996): 404-19; "Calvin's Use of the Fathers and Medievals," *Calvin Theological Journal* 16/2 (November 1981): 149-205.

[3]Tony Lane also stresses this in "The Sources of Calvin's Citations in His Genesis Commentary," 50, 83.

B. Calvin's interpretation of the literal sense of scripture

Everyone who has written on Calvin's interpretation of the Bible has ventured an analysis of Calvin's commitment to the plain, natural sense of scripture that includes the recognition that what passes for the literal sense for Calvin is not what moderns usually mean by the literal sense. However, I do not recall ever seeing the point pressed so far as to claim that Luther stands in closer continuity than Calvin "not only with traditional interpretations of Hagar but also with the literal and historical details of Genesis." Here I would ask John to draw on his research of other passages in Genesis to clarify whether this claim relates only to the passages about Hagar or whether he finds that it holds throughout Genesis. True, the resentment Calvin expresses toward Hagar may fly in the face of some specific textual evidences (primarily Gen. 16: 7, 10-12), but even these are not unambiguously positive; Balaam, too, was "blessed" with epiphanies of the divine, and Hagar's first "rescue" entailed a divine endorsement of her slavery and mistreatment. Moreover, while Calvin may overlook the potentially positive dimensions of these literal details in the case of Hagar, and in the cases of Sarah and Abraham as well, he clearly had enough literal evidence in Genesis for the all-too-human-failings of each of these characters. I agree that Calvin's passion for application stretches the letter of the text, but I find it hard to see that he stretches it any farther than Luther. Thompson says later that Calvin likely embraces typology precisely because it preserves the *letter* of the Old Testament. All this is to state the obvious: Calvin's understanding of the letter is complicated, and further work needs to be done to settle these questions.

C. Why is Calvin so harsh?

I think that the third question John raises is an excellent one and deserves further attention: has Calvin "really broken free from traditional exegesis, with its various pitfalls and promises, or has he merely repackaged it? There can be little doubt but that Calvin's typology looks for all the world like last year's tropology." The issue merits our attention all the more in light of our continuing to emphasize the busy pastor's independence from tradition. I will return to this issue a little later; for now, I would like to offer a comment on Calvin's harshness toward biblical characters, which holds true not only for the patriarchs of the Old Testament but even for the New Testament "faithful."[4] John offers three plausible reasons for Calvin's harsh attitude toward everyone involved in the story, so far as the question bears on the exegetical legacy he

---

[4]On the OT, see John L. Thompson, "Patriarchs, Polygamy, and Private Resistance: John Calvin and Others on Breaking God's Rules," *Sixteenth Century Journal* 25, no.1 (Spring 1994): 3-28; on the NT, see Craig S. Farmer, "Changing Images of the Samaritan Woman in Early Reformed Commentaries on John," *Church History* 65/3 (September 1996): 365-75; Barbara Pitkin, "Seeing and Believing in the John Commentaries of Martin Bucer and John Calvin," *Church History* 68, no.4 (December 1999): 865-885.

inherited. First, Calvin is ignorant of the positive treatment of Hagar, especially, because he does not have time to read others' commentaries. Second, in the case of Hagar, Calvin may be trying to balance out the positive excesses of the one commentary he is consulting (namely Luther's). Finally, his animus toward Roman Catholicism skews his reading of Genesis, which he filters through Paul's allegory in Galatians 4 to focus on Roman Catholics as the Hagarites of his own day. Since John's third suggestion incorporates a polemical-theological justification along with the exegetical one, I venture to suggest an additional theological reason for Calvin's harshness: zeal to illustrate the glory of God by underscoring God's ability to achieve the divine purpose and bestow grace in spite of the obstacles cast up by human sin. Calvin aims in his interpretation to show the basic plot: the ways of a just and gracious God among sinners. Craig Farmer has noted this "deep theological purpose" underlies Reformed commentators' new negative images of the Samaritan woman in John 4.[5] But Calvin's harshness clearly goes beyond that of his Reformed contemporaries. My observations only serve to make the point that attention to the exegetical inheritance Calvin received and his relationship to it cannot fully account for all the interpretive moves Calvin makes. They also demonstrate the need to adopt a kind of "canonical" approach when reading Calvin's exegesis and remember that the *Institutes* too was conceived as a guide for reading scripture.

II. The "objective" legacy

The discussion of Calvin's objective legacy demonstrates that the legacy Calvin bequeathed is also complicated and no less fraught with cases of mistaken and hidden identities than the past he inherited. Thompson nicely lays out several methodological approaches to the question before deciding on one that appeared, at first glance, to be a dead end. We are then astounded (and amused) to discover that this first impression is wrong. Due to Robert Stephanus's "pirating" from Calvin's 1554 Genesis Commentary for the notes to his 1557 Bible, Calvin's legacy lived on under the guise of François Vatable. John shows what Stephanus drew from Calvin for the purposes of his genre of Calvin's semi-technical explanations, or "Calvin's micro-mastery of the Bible's immediate storyline." This picture of Calvin as an exegete does not reflect the "passion for application" that characterizes his interpretation of Genesis 12-22 and for which he was renowned by later generations, including that of Pearson and Poole.

Thompson's concluding suggestion that Calvin's exegetical legacy, as it was taken up by later generations, was rooted less in his exegesis than in his reputation, confirms what every serious student of Calvin's thought has discovered for him or herself: that perceptions of Calvin, both popular and scholarly, often prove to be misperceptions with little or no basis in what he actually wrote or

---

[5]Farmer, "Changing Images of the Samaritan Woman," 375.

did. But before we all congratulate ourselves for our sober and objective readings of Calvin, I would underscore that in John's findings is also a warning to all to be very clear about what is being claimed in our analyses of Calvin as an interpreter of scripture. The careful attention to historical and intellectual contexts in particular serves as a model for investigations into the particular substance and character of Calvin's "legacy."

If we take the least metaphorical understanding of "Calvin's exegetical legacy," we can ask: What "exegetical property" did Calvin actually bequeath "by will"? That is, what exegetical results did he deem worthy enough to publish for posterity? The answer is easy here: a number of commentaries, sermons (some not published; many of which were sold at garage sale and therefore "lost"), and a massive hermeneutical guide for the study of scripture. Some polemical writings also figure in here, to the extent that they reflect arguments over exegetical results or even principles. His exegetical contributions can easily be considered the largest portion of his testament to his contemporaries and to later generations. Our presentations of this enormous bequest in our scholarship need to be guided by the kind of careful consideration modeled by Thompson's paper.

III. Concluding Comments

Thompson shows how intensive and extensive approaches, when done well, can complement each other. Tony Lane is surely correct when he argues that when the question is one of influence—where, exactly, did Calvin get certain exegetical insights—then the intensive approach, the painstaking identification of the exact sources and resources Calvin most conceivably could have used in preparing a particular commentary, is the necessary first step to answering such a question. The intensive approach also sheds important light on Calvin's place in the stream of Christian exegesis and alone can answer definitively how Calvin transformed the tradition he received in shaping his own exegetical legacy. For all its strengths, however, the intensive approach cannot fully answer the question of Calvin's relationship to traditional exegesis. As Thompson's work admirably shows, the extensive approach need not seek to answer questions of influence, nor result in pointing out mere parallels of thought regardless of any historical connection. What the extensive approach offers is an account of the general inventory of Christian exegesis, and—recognizing that Calvin received and availed himself of only part of that material— it can seek to delineate his exegetical positions and determine whether they are distinctive to him or characteristic of other aspects of the historical tradition.

Finally, the paper raises as well the possibility for another cooperative endeavor, between historians of exegesis and historical theologians who recognize that the history of Christian thought is in large part the history of biblical interpretation. For such, engagement with this past is essential to shaping a contemporary theology of scripture. The paper strongly suggests, especially in the last paragraph, that part of Calvin's exegetical legacy was a particular mode of interpretation, probably not unique to him but certainly characteristic enough of his work to become one of the dominant images for describing his approach. What Matthew Poole designates as Calvin's "passion for application" does not, as Thompson shows, figure substantively into the slice of Calvin's "legacy" mediated by Stephanus, the *Critici Sacri*, or Poole himself. Stephanus apparently considered it expendable, but only further study will show whether others judged otherwise. Thompson also notes how Calvin's interest in typology "stretches [his] fidelity to literal exegesis" (at least as some moderns understand it).

We are left with the recognition that Calvin's attitude toward the past in general, including the biblical past, was not simple reiteration but reformation and revision. As he argued against his Roman Catholic opponent, Albert Pighius, "Our constant endeavor, day and night, is to put those things we are faithfully handing on into the form we think will prove best."[6] Hence, I would venture to press the intent of Thompson's final sentences even farther—or at least to lift up a point in his final footnote. Calvin's exegetical legacy rests not only among those who aspire to present the pure word of God by charging, like Calvin, "unswervingly towards the original [biblical] text." It is also to be sought among those theological types who, "with an eye to the return," still journey *ab fontibus* in revisioning the past in the form they think will prove best.

---

[6]CO, 6:250.

Calvin's Ethical Legacy

Merwyn S. Johnson

Like the other topics in this volume, "Calvin's Ethical Legacy" moves in two directions at the same time. On the one hand is Calvin's ethics. What did he actually say about ethical issues and problems? What did he actually do about ethical situations he faced? On the other hand is the legacy of Calvin's ethics. What impact did he have at the time of the Reformation, particularly in Geneva? What influence has he had over the years since then, beyond Geneva and his own life time? And what is the continuing viability and usefulness of Calvin's ethical teachings for Christians at the beginning of the Twenty-first Century?

In his recent study of Calvin's approach to ethics, James B. Sauer raises the question, "Was Calvin an ethicist?"[1] He points to the relatively few, dedicated treatments of Calvin's ethics available.[2] Indeed, the Latin word for ethics *(ethice)* does not appear at all in Calvin's main work, the *Institutes of the Christian Religion.* The Latin word for morality or moral *(moralia)* appears only 17 times, most often in relation to the law of morality and sometimes with negative overtones (e.g. *Institutes,* 3.11.19). Calvin's preferred term is obedience *(obedientia),* which occurs 215 times in the *Institutes.* No one who reads Calvin's writings will doubt that they are full of ethical considerations. The Christian life touches on every aspect of Calvin's life, work, piety, and theology.[3] Further, no one who has read

---

[1]James B. Sauer, *Faithful Ethics According to John Calvin: The Teachability of the Heart* (Lewiston, N.Y.: Edwin Mellen Press, 1997), 55. Gilbert Vincent, *Éxigence éthique et interpretation dans l'oevre de Calvin* (Genève: Labor et Fides, 1984), also raises the question whether Calvin was an ethicist; contrasting Calvin with Thomas Aquinas, he says Calvin aims for an ethos while Aquinas aims for an ethic, 18ff.

[2]Ibid., 56. He mentions only three: Eric Fuchs, *La Morale selon Calvin* (Édition du Cerf, 1986); Georgia Harkness, *John Calvin: The Man and His Ethics* (Nashville: Abingdon Press, 1931, 1958); and Gilbert Vincent, *Éxigence éthique et interpretation dans l'oevre de Calvin* (Genève: Labor et Fides, 1984).

[3]Broader studies of Calvin on ethics and/or the Christian life include (in alphabetical order): W. Fred Graham, *The Constructive Revolutionary: John Calvin and his Socio-Economic Impact* (Richmond: John Knox Press, 1971); Peter De Klerk, editor, *Calvin and Christian Ethics* (Grand Rapids: Calvin Studies Society, 1987); John H. Leith, *John Calvin's Doctrine of the Christian Life* (Louisville: Westminster/ John Knox Press, 1989); Ernst Troeltsch, *The Social Teaching of the Christian Church,* 2 volumes (New York: Harper Torchbooks, 1960), 1: 576-630; Ronald S. Wallace,

Western history of the last 500 years will doubt that Calvin has had a profound influence and impact upon the entire modern world, ambiguities and all. But to appropriate and value his ethical legacy, we still have to grasp his distinctive approach to ethics with modern eyes.[4]

The thesis of this essay is that *Calvin's approach to the Christian life is an ethic of participation.* The aim is not to prove the thesis, but to establish the terminology of participation in Calvin's writings and then develop it in terms of several topics that bear directly upon ethics, or the Christian life, for Calvin. Participation is rooted in Calvin's concern for the believer's union with Christ (Section I). What qualifies that participation are: the use of the law after Christ (Section II), the Ten Commandments (Section III), "handles" by which we take hold of Christian living within the realities of a sinful world and God's activity therein (Section IV), and the equity part of the law of nature (Section V). Section VI pulls things together. Several of these topics suggest different ways we moderns receive Calvin's theology and his ethical legacy. A sub-theme running through the essay highlights the significance of Calvin's legal training for his theology and vision of the Christian life.

I. Participation by Union with Christ

Participation for Calvin refers above all to communion with God or, what is the same thing, to union with Christ, which lies at the heart of Calvin's concern for the Christian religion.[5] Beginning his discussion of the Christian life in the

---

Calvin, Geneva and the Reformation: A Study of Calvin as Social Worker, Churchman, Pastor and Theologian (Grand Rapids: Baker Book House, 1988 and 1990); Ronald S. Wallace, *Calvin's Doctrine of the Christian Life* (Edinburgh: Oliver and Boyd, 1959). Useful treatments of Calvin on the Christian life are also contained in studies of Calvin's theology such as François Wendel, *Calvin: Origins and Development of His Religious Thought* (New York: Harper & Row, 1963), and Wilhelm Niesel, *The Theology of Calvin* (London: Lutterworth Press, 1956).

[4]Sauer, 55-84. Sauer's concern is constructive, not historical. He uses Calvin as a prism to reflect upon the roots of how faith (*fiducia* as trust or confidence, *fides* as knowledge or the concern for knowing) plays a fundamental role in ethical behavior, 47ff. Most scholars subordinate Calvin's ethical views to his theology, says Sauer, a practice which he disputes. The context of Renaissance humanism, he says, focused Calvin's life and thought on wisdom, not doctrine. Calvin's efforts were devoted to approaching the concrete situations of life out of faith, in a time of dramatic change when the indications of what a Christian should do were unclear.

[5]See Willem van 't Spijker, "*Extra nos*' and *'in nobis*' by Calvin in Pneumatological Perspective," *Calvin and the Holy Spirit* (Grand Rapids: Calvin Studies Society, 1989), 39-62. Van 't Spijker traces the theme of union with Christ to the Reformation context of Martin Luther and Martin Bucer, with both of whom Calvin stood closely on this issue. Union with Christ has figured prominently in the recent search for a central dogma in Calvin's theology: see Charles Partee, "Calvin's Central Dogma Again," in *Calvin Studies III*, edited by John H. Leith (Richmond, VA: 1986); and Brian G. Armstrong, "The Nature and Structure of Calvin's Thought According to the *Institutes: Another Look*," in *John Calvin's Magnum Opus* (Potchefstroom, South Africa: Institute for Reformational Studies, 1986), 55-82, especially p. 72. See also Guenther Haas, *The Concept of Equity in Calvin's Ethics* (Waterloo, Ontario: Wilfred

Institutes, Calvin speaks quite openly of God's gathering us together "to join us to himself" *(ut sibi aggregaret, Institutes,* 3.6.2), "union with God *(cum Deo coniunctionis, Institutes,* 3.6.2), "communion with him" *(communione, Institutes,* 3.6.2, 3.8.1), and "fellowship with Christ" *(suorum consortio, Institutes,* 3.8.1).[6] Union with Christ is the only way union with God is possible in any positive sense at all.[7] So Calvin emphasizes union with Christ and what it entails. At the beginning of Book III of the *Institutes*, Calvin underscores the importance of union with Christ.

To share with us what he has received from the Father, he [Christ] had to become ours and to dwell within us. For this reason, he is called "our Head" [Eph. 4:15], and "the first-born among many brethren" [Rom. 8:29]. We also, in turn are said to be "engrafted into him" [Rom. 11:17], and to "put on Christ" [Gal. 3:27]; for, as I have said, all that he possesses is nothing to us until we grow into one body[8] with him *(cum ipso in unum coalescimus),* [or until we] embrace that communion with Christ *(Christi communicationem)* which is offered through the gospel . . . (*Institutes*, 3.1.1.).

Faith is what unites us with Christ and all his benefits (3.1.1): by faith "he makes us, ingrafted into his body, participants *(participes)* not only in all his benefits but also in himself" (3.2.24). And, of course, "faith is the principal work of the Holy Spirit" (3.1.4).

When Calvin turns to repentance, under which topic he places his treatment of the Christian life, he likewise uses the language of *participation*. Both mortification (dying to self) and vivification (coming to life again) happen to us by participation in Christ *(ex Christi participatione)*. For if we truly partake of *(communicamus)* his death, "'our old man is crucified by his power, and the body

---

Laurier University Press, 1997), 1; Leith, 98ff; Niesel, 120ff; Wallace, *Christian Life,* 17-17; and Wendel, 234ff. A number of recent studies of the topic are valuable: William B. Evans, *Imputation and Impartation: The Problem of Union With Christ in Nineteenth Century American Reformed Theology* (Ann Arbor: UMI Dissertation Services, 1996), probes Calvin's treatment in Chapter One on the way to tracing the theme through the history of Reformed theology to the present; Brian Gerrish, *Grace and Gratitude: The Eucharistic Theology of John Calvin* (Minneapolis: Augsburg Fortress, 1993), shows how Calvin's concern for union with Christ is not only personal but also ecclesiastical and sacramental (see especially 71-76, 82-86, 110, and 133); and Dennis E. Tamburello, *Union with Christ: John Calvin and the Mysticism of St. Bernard* (Louisville: Westminster/John Knox, 1994), catalogs Calvin's references to union with Christ and related terms in 111-113.

[6]And negatively 3.6.2: "no fellowship with wickedness and uncleanness."

[7]Because of who Christ is—the second member of the Trinity (1. 13) —and because of what he has done for our salvation—his incarnation, death, and resurrection (2. 12-17)—to be united with Christ is to be united with God and *vice versa*. In his commentary on I John 4:15 Calvin says: "we are united to God by Christ and . . . we can only be joined to Christ if God abides in us"; and further, "men are so engrafted into Christ by faith that Christ joins them to God." Quoted from *The Gospel According to St. John, Part Two, 11-21 and The First Epistle of John,* translated by T.H.L. Parker (Grand Rapids: Wm. B. Eerdmans, 1961), 293ff.

[8]The word "body" is not in the Latin text.

of sin perishes' [Rom. 6:6 p.], that the corruption of original nature may no longer thrive. If we share *(sumus participes)* in his resurrection, through it we are raised up into newness of life to correspond with the righteousness of God." (*Instututes*, 3.3.9). Referring to both repentance and justification Calvin says:

> By partaking of him *(cuius participatione)*, we principally receive a double grace: namely, that being reconciled to God through Christ's blamelessness, we may have in heaven instead of a Judge a gracious Father; and secondly, that sanctified by Christ's spirit we may cultivate blamelessness and purity of life. (*Institutes*, 3.11.1).[9]

Furthermore, for Calvin both repentance (which includes the Christian life) and justification (which includes the forgiveness of sins) are *effects (effectuum, Institutes,* 3.3.1) of faith. That is, they are not steps to be taken in a certain order or even separable actions of their own. They are ways to explain and elaborate the activity and the dynamics of faith, the faith that unites us with Christ. For Calvin both repentance and justification are simply ways of talking about our *faith participation in Christ.* The thesis lies ready-to-hand: *the Christian life for Calvin is a participation in the life, death, righteousness, and on-going life of Jesus Christ.*

As an ethic of participation in Christ and in the on-going, active life of the living God, Calvin's approach to the Christian life stands on its own. But the ethic of participation contrasts with alternative approaches which are widespread today, such as:

- an ethic of command-and-do (God commands general rules, we do them),
- an ethic of the ideal (God/the Bible shows us norms for which we are to strive),
- an ethic of example ("What would Jesus do?"),
- an ethic of action-and-response (God acts, we respond in thanks and praise),
- an ethic of utility (cost-benefit analysis),
- and an ethic of character-and-virtue (this is the way we are and are to be; now act accordingly).

This study of Calvin came across elements of many such approaches in his writings. He resists some of them explicitly; for example, the ethics of character-and-virtue (3.6.1), the ethics of action-and-response (3.14.10), and perhaps the ethics of utility (3.10.2). He uses Christ as an example but does not make the Christian life an imitation of Christ.[10] Mostly he absorbs these alternative

---

[9]Calvin's lengthy and strenuous treatment of Osiander in *Institutes,* 3.11.5, 10, 23, is directly related to the issue of union with Christ. For the full rejoinder to Osiander in the *Institutes,* see 1.15. 3-5, 2. 12. 5-7, and 3. 11. 5-12. Osiander affirmed a union with Christ that moves beyond participation in Christ to an over-emphasis on "Christ in us," which substantially identities Christ with humankind. "Christ in us" transfers to "us" an "essential righteousness" by which we can possess and exercise the same divine righteousness he did, and Christ becomes merely an example of what we can become, i.e., filled with divine righteousness of our own. Calvin's balance between "we in Christ, therefore Christ in us" becomes for Osiander "Christ in us, therefore we *like* Christ." Osiander anticipates in the sixteenth century the direction that seventeenth to twentieth century Pietism will take, including many ambiguities modern Christianity still faces.

approaches into his own, over-arching ethic of participation in Christ. Most impressive is the complex way Calvin's writings draw on, sift, and synthesize so many different impulses. Yet he remains clear and steadfast about his own direction, the ethic of participation in Christ.

II. The Use of the Law after Christ.[11]

When Calvin stepped onto the Reformation scene in the 1530s, the options faced by the Protestant movement were essentially three: the Lutheran, the Papal, and the Antinomian. Following Paul closely, the *Lutherans* said we are justified by faith alone apart from the works of the law (Romans 3:21). The law is fulfilled by Christ and abolished—in its moral as well as its ceremonial and political forms ("Christ is the end of the law," Romans 10:4). Christians do good works, Luther said, but they are justified first and do good works spontaneously from the heart, the way a healthy tree bears fruit. To re-erect the law after Christ would put us back into the same situation we were in before Christ. Over against Luther, the *Papal position*, codified in the Council of Trent, said that our faith does not justify us alone but requires obedience to God's law as well. Christ fulfills the law but does not abolish it (Matthew 5:17). The law remains in force and is binding on Christians after Christ as much or more than before Christ. "Faith working through love" (Galatians 5:6) is the way they put it, also quoting from Paul. The *Antinomian* option was represented by the early Anabaptist movement as it was associated with the Peasants Revolt of 1525 and the radicals who took over the city of Münster in 1534/35. For these people Christ fulfilled the law and abolished it. We are justified by faith alone apart from the works of the law. We no longer need the law, or if we do, God places the law in our hearts at conversion (Jeremiah 31:33, Revelation 21:22-27). Either we are already justified by Christ, or we are capable of doing what the law requires out of ourselves. Either way we can do no wrong. After the Peasants Revolt of 1525, the Papal side accused all Protestants of Antinomianism: by eliminating the law, they said, the Protestants lost their capacity to foster a responsible Christian life.

That was the situation Calvin and the Reformers faced in the 1530s. Calvin quickly added a fourth option, already apparent in the 1535/36 edition of the *Institutes*. Starting with Luther's accent on Law and Gospel, Calvin agrees that

---

[10]Gilbert Vincent makes a convincing argument for this point in *Éxigence Éthique et Interprétation dans l'Oeuvre de Calvin*, 141ff. Calvin is certainly aware of the limitations and ambiguities of example: see Calvin's comment on John 4:20, in *The Gospel According to St. John, Part One, 1-10*, translated by T.H.L. Parker (Grand Rapids: Wm B. Eerdmans,1959), 95ff.

[11]See I. John Hesselink, *Calvin's Concept of the Law* (Allison Park, PA: Pickwick Publications, 1992). In a most excellent way, this book sifts Calvin's writings and the secondary literature concerning the "third use of the law." The treatment here differs from Hesselink in certain emphases, but not on any essential point.

Christ fulfilled the law and abrogated it in all its forms as something that is required for salvation.[12] The law does not thereby lose its validity: as Paul argues throughout the early chapters of Romans, the law is holy, spiritual, and righteous altogether. But for Calvin the law itself is transformed by Christ, who fulfills it and makes himself—God's own self (Emmanuel, God with us, which the law is not and never will be)—the sole avenue of our life with God. How does Christ transform the law? *Christ removes from the law its demand character.* The law remains valid, but no longer threatens the person in Christ with a curse. The law remains in the imperative form, hence the role of exhortation; but its force is descriptive rather than prescriptive. The law points back to the Lawgiver: it gives us clues to the character, the will, the purposes, even the activity of God in the present moment. Meditating upon the law gives us, who by grace love and want to serve the Lord, clues to doing what lives with and works for, not against, God.[13]

---

[12]In his otherwise very helpful treatment of Calvin's concept of equity, Haas, while discussing the third use of the law in Calvin, asserts that "Calvin clearly rejects the view that the moral law has been abrogated as a guide for believers" (*The Concept of Equity in Calvin's Ethics,* 66). This supports the position, taken by many, that Calvin thought Christ abrogated the law in its political and ceremonial forms, but not in morality. For his position Haas cites a sentence from the *Institutes* (2.8.57) but leaves out the crucial phrase (here in italics) which distinguishes the law before (first use) and after (third use) Christ: "To be Christians under the law of grace does not mean to wander unbridled outside the law, but to be engrafted in Christ, *by whose grace we are free of the curse of the law,* and by whose Spirit we have the law engrafted upon our hearts." Calvin deals with the abrogation of the law most clearly in *Institutes* 2.7.14-16. There he concurs with Paul's (and Luther's) treatment of the matter (cf. Romans 7:6 and Galatians 3:10-14) and says plainly: "we must be released from the bonds of the law, unless we wish to perish miserably under them, . . . [t]he bonds of harsh and dangerous requirements" (2.7.15; see also 3.19.2-3). For Calvin all kinds of law are rooted in the law of nature (God's will), whether moral, ceremonial, or judicial (see 4.20.14-16). Hence also for Calvin "Christ is the end of the law" (Romans 10:4), including all its forms, in the sense of Christ being its purpose, its complete fulfillment, the substitution of his own life for the curse and/or demand requirements of the law upon humanity, and the redirection of its focus or teaching *(torah)* back upon God (cf. Calvin's argument in 2.6, 2.7, 2.8, and 2.9-11). Following the accents in his quotation, Haas brings the matter back to where it belongs when he says: "This ongoing place of the law in the Christian life must be seen as based upon and determined by union with Jesus Christ" (Haas, 66). In fact, Calvin qualifies himself in a similar manner whenever he talks about abrogating the law, in any sense of it. For example, "The ceremonies . . . have been abrogated not in effect, but only in use. Christ by his coming has terminated them, but has not deprived them or anything of their sanctity; rather, he has approved and honored it." (2.7.16; see also 4.20.15.).

[13]The key to the understanding of Calvin's third use of the law is his image of the faithful servant in *Institutes* 2.7.12, which was put forth in 1536 and modified only slightly in 1539: "It is as if some servant, already prepared with all earnestness of heart to commend himself to his master, must search out and observe his master's ways more carefully in order to conform and accommodate himself to them." In this image the faithful servant does not wait to be told what to do, but *studies* previous commands (i.e., the law) in order to *anticipate* the master's purpose and will, hence *to do with the master* (either in harmony with the master's will or in fellowship with what the master is doing at the same time) what the master is going to do.

Calvin specifically rejects the notion that Christ and salvation enable followers to do after Christ what they could not do before Christ, namely, keep the law. Calvin is emphatic that salvation takes place by faith alone, without any assistance from works of the law (3.11.19). He states plainly in a line from the 1559 edition of the *Institutes* that goes back to the 1536 edition:

God does not, as many stupidly believe, once for all reckon to us as righteousness that forgiveness of sins concerning which we have spoken in order that, having obtained pardon for our past life, we may afterward seek righteousness in the law; this would be only to lead us into false hope, to laugh at us, and mock us. (3.14.10)

For Calvin at least, the Christian life (after Christ) is as much a function of God's grace as salvation itself. Here Calvin surely rules out an ethic of response, i.e., that the Christian life is a human response to Christ, to the Gospel, or to saving grace. The Christian life for Calvin becomes a constant, energetic search for the will and present activity of God in the present moment.[14] The search takes place in union with Christ, energized by the Holy Spirit. The law engages our attention as a clue to the will of God in the present moment, as does the cross of Jesus Christ and the example of his life. So, the law as a guide to the Christian life—the third use of the law—cannot become after Christ what it was before Christ. The law after Christ—the third use of the law—does not tell us what to do under the threat of condemnation. The law after Christ —the third use of the law—does not focus our attention upon itself instead of the Lawgiver. And the law after Christ—the third use of the law—does not put us back on the treadmill of works righteousness which turns the law into the power of idolatry and sin (I Cor. 15:56). For Calvin *God* remains the Supreme Guide for the Christian life, and the law remains a descriptor of God's will and present activity.

The law thus transformed by Christ takes on its intended role in the Old Testament, that of teaching (*torah*) us about the will and present activity of God. Notice that the descriptive force of the law as a reflection upon the Lawgiver (third use) parallels directly the descriptive force of the law in revealing our sin (first use). In fact for Calvin the law describes the image of God in the positive sense of delineating the humanity God made in the first place. "The law of God contains in itself that newness by which his image can be restored in us," he says (3.6.1). From Calvin's earliest writings the law thus provides the characteristic jumping-off point for his running dialectic between humanity in the light of God and God in the light of humanity. The third use of the law gives Calvin the leeway to explore all the possibilities of the law for both God and humanity. He does not have to ground everything in the order of creation or a self-sufficient law of nature. In fact, he would be reversing himself and his best insights to do so.

---

[14]This is the thrust of James Sauer's book, *Faithful Ethics According to John Calvin: The Teachability of the Heart.*

Perhaps the best analogy for Calvin's treatment of the law is a game which involves a number of people playing together. The rules of the game define the game, what the players can do and what they cannot do. While the rules are in the imperative form, the force of the rules is descriptive. The players play the game together within the sphere of activity outlined by the rules. The purpose of the game is to enjoy the interaction between teammates, opponents, and even the creator of the game. Hence, playing the game is the focus, not keeping the rules—though the players will constantly study the rules to see what they can and cannot do, and they will push the rules to the limit in order to get the most out of the game, for example, the tactical use of fouling in the game of basketball. However, when keeping the rules of the game becomes the focus instead of playing the game, the game becomes a perversion of its original form, an exercise in control and "no fun."

In the analogy of the game, the Christian life sounds like this: the rules of life, commanded by God, set the sphere of interaction with God, with fellow human beings, and with the world all around. The rules of life are rules of goodness, because God is good. Living within the sphere of interaction outlined by God's rules, humans honor and commune with the living God, which is the aim of the Christian life. Humans do not, however, live just to keep the rules or to make themselves "good" according to the rules. God alone is good, and goodness comes from God alone. Keeping the rules for their own sake leads humans to seek a goodness that does not require God or God's goodness—perverting the rules, distorting humanity, and breaking off communion with God. By God's gracious action the rules circumscribe the place where humans abide—live vigorously—with God (John 15:1-10) together with other humans and nature.[15]

III. The Ten Commandments

The first topic, the law after Christ, reflects Calvin's distinctive treatment of the third use of the law, which corresponds very closely with Calvin's concern for union with Christ, communion with God. *The second topic picks up on the content of the law, the Ten Commandments.* Calvin's handling of the law, exemplified by his treatment of the Ten Commandments, is fluid, dynamic[16] and, one could add, modest. Calvin was, after all, a trained lawyer, as were many of the Protestant Reformers. Following Paul and large parts of the Old Testament, the Protestant understanding of the Gospel generally follows a juridical model. Calvin's handling of the Ten Commandments offers a glimpse of Calvin's legal mind at work.

---

[15]This is the thrust of the famous first question of the *Westminster Shorter Catechism* (1646), which says: "Man's chief end is to glorify God and enjoy Him forever." See John 15:7-11. Significantly, the *Catechism* does not say that "man's chief end" is to be saved or to be good.

[16]Hesselink, *Calvin's Concept of the Law,* 34ff. and 277ff., is concerned to say that Calvin's treatment of the law is dynamic. He rightly emphasizes the role of the Holy Spirit. For his treatment of the Ten Commandments, see Chapter III, 87ff.

Calvin deals with the Decalog in general and in summary. He also goes through the Ten Commandments one-by-one.[17] Calvin is not content merely to state what the commandments order or prohibit. He handles them dynamically, developing a broad range of meaning, as if from within, far beyond any mere definition of terms or appeal to authority. He announces his formula plainly, up front, in four items. First, he asks how the commandment reflects the character of the Lawgiver (*Institutes,* 2.8.6-7), whose righteous activity the law projects. What does the law say about the Lawgiver? What kind of God wants us to act this way? For example, in the case of the Sixth Commandment ("thou shalt not kill"),[18] God is the one who made humans in God's own image, which is sacred (2.8.39). God is the one in whose eyes human life is precious, so that the way we act toward one another is the way we act toward God.

Second, Calvin declares the commandments to be *synechdoches*. A *synechdoche* is one instance that stands for a whole class of things (2.8.8). Each commandment (or at least most of them) is a worst-case scenario for a whole pattern of human behavior (2.8.10). In the case of the Sixth Commandment, murder is not the only way to act badly toward another human, but it is the most heinous way of all (2.8.40). Indeed, says Calvin, killing is not limited to murder: killing entails planning anything against the safety of a neighbor and goes even to the anger which burns within to seek the harm of another person (2.8.39).

Third, to get at the larger class of actions, Calvin asks of each commandment what is God's intention for it. Why—for what purpose—did God give it to us? In the case of the Sixth Commandment the intent is to act with reverence toward God's image imprinted in our humanity and to cherish our own flesh therein (2.8.40). In his love for us and for others Christ acts to show us the way. Fourth, still within the realm of God's intent, Calvin asks of each commandment not only what it forbids negatively but also the opposite: what does the commandment positively encourage us to do? The Sixth Commandment, accordingly, stipulates that

---

[17]Calvin deals with the Decalog in three places: *The Institutes,* Book 2, Chapter 8, written for the 1536 and 1539 editions, with only minor revisions thereafter; sermons on the Ten Commandments, delivered in the summer of 1555; and a harmony of the four books of Moses (Exodus-Deuteronomy) written between September 1559 and November 1562. Calvin's general and summary treatments are in the *Institutes,* 8.1-12 and 8.51-59; the detailed handling of each commandment is in the *Institutes,* 8:13-50. For the sermons on the Ten Commandments see Ben Farley, editor and translator, *John Calvin's Sermons on the Ten Commandments* (Grand Rapids: Baker Book House, 1980). For an overview of Calvin's *Harmony* see T.H.L. Parker, *Calvin's Old Testament Commentaries* (Louisville: Westminster/John Knox Press, 1993). The *Harmony* is contained in the published *Commentary on the Five Books of Moses,* 1564, which is in fact a separate commentary on Genesis, originally published in 1554, combined with his *Harmony of the Last Five Books of Moses,* originally published in 1563. The discussion here leans most heavily on the *Institutes* and the sermons, and builds on the author's prior study of Calvin on the Ten Commandments, presented as a paper to the Sixteenth Century Studies Conference in 1993.

[18]See also Daniel Augsburger, "Calvin and the Sixth Commandment," in *Calvin and Christian Ethics,* edited by Peter De Klerk (Grand Rapids: Calvin Studies Society, 1987), 101-118.

If we find anything of use to us in saving our neighbors' lives, faithfully to employ it; if there is anything that makes for their peace, to see to it; if anything harmful, to ward it off; if they are in any danger, to lend a helping hand. (2.8.39; 2.8.10, 40).

With his fluid and dynamic treatment of the law, John Calvin is a prime example of "Act"[19] as a mode of theological language.[20] For Calvin, we cannot know God's essence or inner being, "not as he is in himself, but as he is toward us" (1.10.2). We know God, that is, by God's works (1.5.9-10),[21] what God *does*, pre-eminently the acts of creation, providence, salvation, and glorification. And what God wants from us is not ceremony or understanding, but obedience—to

---

[19]Gilbert Vincent, *Éxigence éthique et interprétation dans l'oevre de Calvin*, sees this plainly, 71ff., where he discusses "La Grammaire de l'Action." In succeeding chapters he traces Calvin's language mode notably through the commentaries.

[20]Theological language typically expresses itself in one of three familiar modes:

Being is the preferred mode of ontological discourse; it dominates Patristic theology and the major streams of Scholasticism. Prominent examples are the Nicene Creed, 325/381 (the Son is of the same substance or being *[homoousias]* as the Father. The being of God as Trinity establishes the being of everything else.); Thomas Aquinas, 1225-1274 (God is the first being, whose essence is being itself and whose being is pure actuality); and Paul Tillich, 1886-1965 (God is being itself.).

Act is the mode of Calvin's theological language, which comes through above all in his treatment of law. Besides Calvin, 1509-1564 (we know God by God's works), prominent examples are the Synod of Dort, 1619 (the decree of God is God's supreme act of mercy in Jesus Christ for the salvation of sinful humans.); and Karl Barth, 1886-1968 (we know God only from God's trinitarian act of self-revelation, as the One who loves in freedom and whose love embraces the acts of creation, reconciliation, and redemption).

Relation is the truly modern one—including the terms relationship and relativity, and the accents on the personal relationship with Jesus Christ and historical-contextual relations. Prominent examples are Friedrich Schleiermacher, 1768-1834 (The feeling of absolute dependence entails the relation between God and the World, but also—overlaid by the antitheses of sin and grace—the relations between the self and Jesus Christ/God, the self and others, the self and the world); Ernst Troeltsch, 1866-1923 (The truth of any perspective becomes clear in how it is related to other perspectives in its own time and through history); Hendrikus Berkhof, 1914- (The truth of the Christian faith lies with its place in historical context/relationships and in God's economy of things, from creation to the renewal of the world); Jürgen Moltmann, 1926- (The inter-relations of the social Trinity tell us who God is and how God relates to us, the world, and all humanity.).

The mode of theological language affects the content of theology indirectly, in nuances of expectation or requirement. Act favors practical over speculative habits of thought, and the logic of divine and human activities over propositional logic. As Calvin's mode of theological language, Act overlays—it does not replace—Calvin's rhetorical patterns of discourse. Associations with Aristotelian logic and the orders of Being may have enticed the heirs of Calvin back to the Being mode of theological language, but the Reformed Tradition is capable of all three modes.

[21]Calvin focuses upon the activity of God in his handling of the Trinity: "To the Father is attributed the beginning of activity, and the fountain and wellspring of all things; to the Son, wisdom, counsel, and the ordered disposition of all things; but to the Spirit is assigned the power and efficacy of that activity" (1.13.18).

do God's will from the heart (2.8.1, 5). Furthermore, law is a natural vehicle for "Act" as a mode of theological language. Law functions primarily as a regulator of what people *do*—toward God, toward other persons, toward the world around them, and even toward themselves. As a medium of discourse (or theology), law is incisive—it pertains to what happens mainly *between* people, how they *interact*—it does not try to comprehend the whole of reality in a single embrace, explanation, or string of relations. Like the law, God's decree(s) (God's activity of predestination by another name) and God's covenant with humanity (whether of works or of grace, etc.) typically belong to the language mode of "Act," exactly as they emerged in Reformed Protestantism. Compared with Scholasticism (Being) and modern Pietism (Relation), Calvin's theology (Act: divine and human actions and interactions) is highly fluid, dynamic, and characteristically modest.

IV. Handles for Taking Hold of the Christian Life

Calvin's ethic of participation is qualified by the role of the law after Christ, his distinctive treatment of the "third" use of the law which coincides closely with the aim of union with Christ, communion with God. His ethic of participation is also affected by the fluid, dynamic, even modest way the law, notably the Ten Commandments, comes into play. The law, rightly considered, leads to the Lawgiver, who is the real focus of Christian living. But the Christian has to face the realities of life in a sinful world, which includes sub-human activity, suffering, and the misuse of the things of this world. How can we penetrate such a fog and commune with God in living daily on this earth? *The third topic deals with "handles" by which we take hold of Christian living within the realities of a sinful world and God's activity therein.* Calvin draws "handles" for taking hold of the Christian life from the three spheres of God's primary activity, namely, creation, redemption, and glorification.[22] He presents these "handles" succinctly in the

---

[22]The approach to Christian ethics is strikingly different when considered primarily from the vantage point of:

Creation: Emphasizes the order and goodness of creation as God made it before the Fall. Sin takes away from that goodness, but sin also confuses us terribly: are we to consider foremost the goodness of the world we live in or the sin-and-tragedy of it? Redemption in Christ restores us to the way things were before the Fall, and the future (glorification) will consolidate that outcome. Creation and the orders of creation established before the Fall remain the absolute standard against which everything else is measured.

Redemption: Emphasizes Jesus' teachings, especially about the kingdom of God, and the new reality God establishes with the life, death, and resurrection of Jesus Christ. From the vantage point of Jesus Christ and redemption, Christians look back upon the marvelous goodness of creation in its original state, and they gauge the horrors of sin, evil, and death at the Fall. Likewise from the vantage point of redemption, Christians look forward to what God has in store for humanity—already begun in Jesus Christ—which is greater than before the Fall (the City of God in Revelation is greater than the Garden of Eden in Genesis).

Glorification: Emphasizes the future reality of the kingdom of God. Our redemption introduces us to that future by the life, death, and resurrection of Jesus Christ, who will come again to draw us to himself. This future is not a dream for which we merely hope, nor an ideal toward

Institutes, 3. 6-10, dating essentially from the 1539 edition. The "handles" are the image of God in humanity, cross-bearing, and meditation on the future life.

The image of God in humanity obviously derives from creation.[23] We are made in the image of God, a mark of God's special favor on humanity. At the Fall the image of God was seriously defaced and distorted, but not utterly destroyed or obliterated. By his life, death, and resurrection as a human, Jesus Christ restores the image of God, so that those who are redeemed in Christ may recover that image and live before God once again. The image of God in Christ becomes both the likeness to which God conforms us in our redemption and an example for us to follow in our lives (3.6.3). The image of God in humanity makes all humans our neighbors (3.7.6), a point that echoes frequently in Calvin's commentaries and sermons. No human is so depraved, corrupt, or needy that the image of God in each one is not precious and worthy of honor. And Calvin makes plain that to despise another human who carries the image of God is to despise ourselves, which is unnatural and self-defeating. The way we deal with the image of God in others is the way we deal with the God in whose image they are made. Our love for other humans, accordingly, must come from the heart, and the only limit to our helping others in their need or distress is the limit of our resources (3.7.7).

Cross-bearing (3.8) obviously derives from Jesus Christ and the redemption he brings, in and with his crucifixion. On the one hand we cannot expect to be treated any better than our Lord, who was crucified: Christ is for us, accordingly, an example (3.8.1). On the other hand, being conformed to Christ means sharing in his sufferings. Christians are to worship God in thick or in thin and obey God's will without swerving (3.8.3). Calvin recognizes fully the pain of suffering; he never tells us simply to "grin and bear it" in Stoic fashion (3.8.9ff.). Pain and difficulty make suffering what it is. Suffering effectively focuses our attention upon God, God's will, God's righteousness, and God's active presence precisely at the points where we assume God is absent, at the points where we need God the most (3.8.10ff.). Suffering quickly exposes

---

which we strive, but a reality already accomplished toward which we are moving. Set up by both creation and salvation, our present lives anticipate the future reality God has in store for us, and we experience that future even now.

Every Christian theologian has to cover all three spheres of God's activity. But ethics and the Christian life look very different when the emphasis is placed on one of them. With his particular accent on union with Jesus Christ, Calvin emphasizes redemption (and its corresponding ethic) more than creation or glorification (and their corresponding ethics). The range of possibilities, however, sharply divides Calvinists, who all try to justify their positions in terms of Calvin.

[23]Calvin develops his understanding of the image of God from three vantage points, while dealing with "the knowledge of ourselves" (1.15.1): "what we were like when we were first created" (ibid.); "what our condition became after the fall of Adam" (ibid.), i.e., humanity corrupted in every part by sin; and what Christ does to "restore us to God's image" (1.15.4). The third vantage point becomes primary for Calvin (see 2.3.6-14 and further references in the text).

hypocrisy or half-hearted commitment; it presses us to complete honesty with ourselves and others. Suffering tests our patience (3.8.3,10ff.), instructs us in an often costly obedience to God (3.8.4), and even corrects us along the way (3.8.6ff.). God, however, promises to sustain us through our sufferings (3.8.8). God even transforms suffering associated with persecution for righteousness' sake into a singular comfort and blessing for Christians (3.8.7).

Meditation on the future life obviously derives from glorification at the end time, eschatology by another name. In this matter, too, we are to be conformed to Christ our head (3.9.6), receive instruction in the school of Christ (3.9.5), and share in his happiness (3.9.6). For in contrast to our own, dim circumstances, which Calvin describes typically as the "unstable, defective, corruptible, fleeting, wasting, rotting tabernacle of our body" (3.9.5), Christ has attained for us "a firm, perfect, incorruptible, and finally heavenly glory." This future inheritance manifests once again the goodness of God and helps us make sense out of it (3.9.3). Our present lives, especially the various ways God has benefited us, allow us to "taste the sweetness of the divine generosity" and "whet our hope and desire to seek after the full revelation of this" (3.9.3). Fear of death no longer grips us (3.9.5), for in Christ we "joyfully await the day of death and final resurrection." We experience the things of this life with joy for what they are and what they do for us (3.10.2).[24] We experience the things of this life with gratitude to God who out of kindness gives them to us (3.10.5). But we do not cling to them. We live in this world fully, for our duty is to obey God's will; our vocation is to follow God's calling (3.10.6); and we are accountable to God in all things (3.10.5). But we live in the world "as if not," because the world does not in the end draw or bind us to itself as God does (3.10.4, following Paul in I Cor. 7:29ff). We learn "to bear poverty peaceably and patiently, as well as to bear abundance moderately" (3.10.4, 5)—to which Calvin adds the masterful comment: "He who, not content with a slender meal, is troubled by the desire for a more elegant one, will also intemperately abuse those elegances if they fall to his lot."

---

[24]The passage is worth quoting: "Now if we ponder to what end God created food, we shall find that he meant not only to provide for necessity but also for delight and good cheer. Thus the purpose of clothing, apart from necessity, was comeliness and decency. In grasses, trees, and fruits, apart from their various uses, there is beauty of appearance and pleasantness of odor [cf. Gen. 2:9]. For if this were not true, the prophet would not have reckoned them among the benefits of God, "that wine gladdens the heart of man, that oil makes his face shine" [Ps. 104:15 p.]. Scripture would not have reminded us repeatedly, in commending his kindness, that he gave all such things to men. And the natural qualities themselves of things demonstrate sufficiently to what end and extent we may enjoy them. Has the Lord clothed the flowers with the great beauty that greets our eyes, the sweetness of smell that is wafted upon our nostrils, and yet will it be unlawful for our eyes to be affected by that beauty, or our sense of smell by the sweetness of that odor? What? Did he not so distinguish colors as to make some more lovely than others? What? Did he not endow gold and silver, ivory and marble, with a loveliness that renders them more precious than other metals or stones? Did he not, in short, render many things attractive to us, apart from their necessary use?" (3.10.2)

Notice that in discussing these "handles" of the Christian life, neither the Ten Commandments nor any normative sense of law comes into play. When Calvin does introduce the language of God's command (3.8.10), he does not talk about keeping set laws or norms. He talks about doing God's will at the moment and how God commands us to follow the will of God wherever it takes us.[25]

Notice, too, that all three of these "handles" of the Christian life entail some form of self-denial. The image of God in humanity requires us to acknowledge, honor, and serve that image in other humans—no matter how lowly, corrupted, or perverse they may be. The effect is to humble us before other humans and God when we do so. Similarly, cross-bearing—suffering by another name—requires us to ask, "What are God's good purposes when close at hand we see only pain, injustice, malice, and the utter senselessness of it all?" Suffering requires us finally to seek and to serve the will of God at precisely such moments. The effect is to humble us before the experiences of life and God when we do so. Yet again, meditation on the future life requires us to cast off any binding affection for the present life except as it anticipates the future glory God has in store for us. The effect here, too, is to humble us before the things of this world and God when we meditate upon the future life.

These "handles" of the Christian life set us on task with a focus upon God and keep us on task with a humility that keeps us from the presumption of our own good intentions.[26] The "handles" establish mechanisms or levers of humility that keep things in perspective while cutting through the corruption of a corrupted world. With penetrating simplicity and brutal honesty they focus upon actively living with God as the sole purpose of our existence, in the world as it is. God, of course, remains the central Actor in this drama of life, and the Christian life is a constant engagement with other humans, the world at large, and the things of this world.

V. The Law of Nature: Equity and the Golden Rule

We need to ask *whether Calvin treats the law of nature in the same fluid and dynamic manner he treats the Ten Commandments.* Twentieth century literature about Calvin has spent a great deal of energy on Calvin's treatment of natural

---

[25]Eric Fuchs, in his book *La Morale selon Calvin* (Paris: Les Éditions du Cerf, 1986), regards providence—the providential moment—as the structural foundation of Calvin's approach to ethics (Chapter II, 26ff.). The law of God is then the external norm for ethics (Chapter III), and sanctification/regeneration—notably the accents in 3.6-10—is the corresponding internal requirement for practical Christian living (Chapter IV, see notably 78ff.).

[26]See Calvin's brief discourse on humility in 2.2.11. He begins by quoting approvingly Chrysostom, who said, "the foundation of our philosophy is humility," and then Augustine, who said, "If you would ask me concerning the precepts of the Christian religion, first, second, third, and always I would answer, 'Humility.'"

law.[27] Calvin's references to natural law are undeniable. Does "natural" here refer mainly to the inbred order and character of creation, or does it pertain more clearly to the will, wisdom, and character of God—the rule or kingdom of God by another name? In Calvin's treatment of the Ten Commandments, law mediates the interaction between God and humans, and the interaction of humans among themselves. The mediating function of the law becomes distorted or misunderstood if it gets locked in too closely with an independent reality such as nature or creation. The law of nature over-identified with creation can quickly become a competitor with Jesus Christ for focus and attention. Calvin does not allow that.

Calvin shares with others of his time a strong conviction that the world we live in, the world God created, is a structured one which reflects God's wisdom and God's command. In fact, however, Calvin spends remarkably little time and attention on God's original act of creation. Book One of the *Institutes* is entitled "The Knowledge of God the Creator." Yet in the early chapters of the *Institutes* he mainly talks about the wisdom of God in the world around us and how sin makes that wisdom inaccessible to the natural human. For sinners the knowledge of God the Creator requires a prior knowledge of God the Redeemer (1.2.1), albeit by right of creation humans made in God's image owe God everything (1.2.2). Calvin really gets to the basic concerns about creation only at the end of Chapter 14 (paragraphs 20-22), almost as an afterthought. Chapter 15 deals with humanity as a special case of creation—humanity created in God's image and Christ the restorer of that image in his work of redemption. From there to the end of Book One Calvin deals with God's providential activity in each new moment of history—three full chapters devoted to the subject of providence. The same accents come through in his commentary on Genesis, chapters 1-3. Calvin refers to various orders of creation, including humanity created in the image of God. But his principal concern remains: God actively governs all the things God has made. The resulting view of creation could be described as a *creatio continua*.

The missing link here is most likely the concept of equity, to which Gene Haas calls attention in his recent book, *The Concept of Equity in Calvin's Ethics.* Following the conventions of his legal studies, Calvin identifies equity with the Golden Rule, and the Golden Rule with the law of nature.[28] Why the Golden

---

[27]See the excellent overview article by William Klempa, "Calvin and Natural Law," in *Calvin Studies IV,* edited by John H. Leith and W. Stacy Johnson (Richmond, VA: 1988), 1-24. On the dynamic character of the law, see the earlier references to Hesselink, *Calvin's Concept of the Law,* in footnote 16. Hesselink also has a fine review of the literature and his own treatment of the law of nature in Chapter II, 51ff.

[28]Haas, 49-63, shows how Calvin explicitly identifies equity with the Golden Rule in his commentary on Matthew 7:12 (and elsewhere), and, 65-77, how Calvin further identifies the Golden Rule with the second table of the Ten Commandments and the Ten Commandments with the law of nature. John T. McNeill makes essentially the same connections in *Institutes,* 2.8.1, footnote 5.

Rule? Because it portrays the regulative interaction among humans and ulti-mately between God and humanity. Equity means "to give someone their due," most often what they deserve. Equity can also be used in the sense of giving someone mercy if the grounds for it are clear.[29]

The Golden Rule in Scripture takes three forms: "Do unto others as you would have them do unto you" (Matt. 7:12, Luke 6:31), "love your neighbor as yourself" (Matt. 22:39, Lev. 19:18), and "love one another as I have loved you" (John 15:13). The Rule had a "golden run" up to about 1800, and since then it has been reduced to the first form and become little more than a platitude.[30] Through the Middle Ages the Golden Rule was accepted as part of the law of nature. For John Locke in the seventeenth century it became a tool of socio-political analysis, the theological basis for a society based on law.[31] For Immanuel Kant the Golden Rule became the root form of the categorical imperative, the way any person of reason would act. But after 1800 commenta-tors and theologians have little to say about it. They note the discovery of the Golden Rule in its negative form, "do not do to others what you do not want them to do to you," but little more. Ethicists today prefer to talk about "the love command."

The Golden Rule, of course, is part of the Lord's summary of the Ten Commandments (Matt. 22:37-40). The Golden Rule also gets us quickly into the legal concept of equity, and into a dynamic concept of God's righteousness (see 3.8.11 in the *Institutes*). Calvin's oft-repeated, heavy accent on self-denial is obviously working on the *self* part of "love your neighbor as your*self*." He is keenly aware that unless and until we reduce the level of our own self-concern, self-interest, and the constant calculations of our self-advantage, we will never love either our neighbor or God. We have to have "handles" to keep us humble and to remind us how crucially important God and other people are for us. Only with such humility and constant reminders will we seek what is really good for God and the people around us.

---

[29]See Haas' treatment of equity in its historical development from Aristotle and Cicero to Aquinas, 17-31, and further among Calvin's contemporaries such as Erasmus, Budé, and Melanchthon, 33-46. Klempa, "John Calvin and Natural Law," 14, borrowing from David Little, may go too far in defining equity as "the perpetual rule of love." Equity requires the elements of fairness and reciprocity which are necessary for justice in human interactions whether love is active or not. Mercy is a special case of equity which gives regardless of deserving, instead of demanding on the basis of deserving (rewards or punishments). The narrative discussion explains further.

[30]See the recent, full-length treatment of Jeffrey Wattles, *The Golden Rule* (New York: Oxford University Press, 1996). Wattles' study does not explicitly expand the Golden Rule beyond the for-mula, "do unto others as you would have them do unto you," nor does he recognize the connec-tion with Christ that makes the Golden Rule more than a platitude in Biblical or Reformation thought. As a wide-ranging survey of its use, however, the book is most interesting and helpful.

[31]See John Locke, *Second Treatise on Government*, paras. 5 and 6, any edition. See also Merwyn S. Johnson, *Locke On Freedom: An Incisive Study of the Thought of John Locke* (Austin: 1978), 53-74.

The equity side of the Golden Rule binds us to our fellow humans in a shared, interactive doing.[32] The "as" in the Golden Rule, e.g., "love your neighbor *as* yourself," by definition sets up an interaction—an equity of doing—between us and our neighbors. The "as" functions like an equals sign, which covers the whole range of our interactions with others on a sliding scale. Now, the quality of that interaction is not automatically guaranteed. For if we hate ourselves, how will we treat our neighbors? Or if we are merely neutral toward ourselves, how will we act toward our neighbors? If we are fearful or expect others to act badly toward us, how will we act toward our neighbors? When will we ever get to *loving our neighbors*—much less our enemies—if caring for ourselves is ambiguous or worse? The Golden Rule thus calls our attention to different levels of interaction. In the Seventeenth Century John Locke would name three of them the State of War, the State of Nature, and Civil Society.[33] Equity, giving people what they are due, is involved at every level. And society, by its appointed means, obviously has to regulate equity at every level.

At the level of greatest humility, however, equity means giving someone what they are due as a human made in the image of God and loved by God, regardless—nay, in spite of—what they otherwise deserve. Equity then leads us to give without calculating the cost of our giving and without calculating what we will get in return. If everyone acted with such equity, what a remarkable community we would have! Scripture, however, and Calvin are fully aware that the Golden Rule cannot be accomplished so easily by sinful humans. It was accomplished ultimately only by Jesus Christ, who establishes thereby its on-going operation at the level of greatest promise. John's version, "love one another as I have loved you," pegs the Golden Rule to the cross of Jesus Christ, who guarantees its operation with his life's blood. Indeed, "while we were yet sinners" (Romans 5:8) Jesus loved us utterly and gave himself for us without counting the cost. At the most, sinners that we are, we can only participate in Christ's love for God and our neighbors, even when we allow the Golden Rule to inform our activities.

V. Pulling It All Together

We now need to *pull together and summarize Calvin's approach to the Christian life as an ethic of participation in Christ*. Participation starts at the believer's union with Christ, which is already a sharing in God's own, on-going, active life. The law after Christ qualifies that participation: by Christ's transformation of the law (Calvin's distinctive accent on the "third use of the law"), the law points to who God is, what God wants, what God is actively doing, and the sphere within which living with God can take place. The Ten Commandments add further

---

[32]For the following analysis, based on an earlier study of Luke 6:27-38, see Johnson, *Locke on Freedom*, 55-58.

[33]See ibid., 62-66. A devout, trinitarian Christian, Locke's own piety and life experiences led him to see the Golden Rule at the level of freedom in God (see ibid., 145-169).

specificity to the sphere of action and interaction, a specificity which Calvin identifies in fluid, flexible, yet dynamic terms. But Calvin does not stop there. With characteristic realism he provides "handles" for taking hold of life in Christ, albeit in the real world of sinners and suffering. The "handles" keep us humble so we can focus upon God and the best interests of others as we commune with God. The equity part of the law of nature—the several forms of the Golden Rule, which also leads us back to Christ—reinforces and extends the "handles" a step further, but remains fluid and dynamic for Calvin in his vision of union with Christ and communion with God. What follows are five observations drawn from the previous discussion of topics.

First, participation in Christ immediately puts Calvin into the characteristic dialectic of the knowledge of God and the knowledge of ourselves (1.1.1). The knowledge of God triggers the language about God's majesty, God's glory, and the active presence of God which bathes everything everywhere in every moment with brilliant light and breath-taking color. We cannot fail to recognize immediately how puny and unworthy we are (the knowledge of ourselves), how we depend upon God for every good thing, and what an awesome thing it is to live day-by-day in the presence of such a One (the knowledge of God). Indeed, the majesty and glory of God (the knowledge of God) provoke in us two strong reactions simultaneously (the knowledge of ourselves). On the one hand we marvel and love, worship and adore, praise and celebrate God in all God's splendor and grace towards us. On the other hand, we dread that same presence to the point of hiding from it. For in God's penetrating light we see the shadowy landscape of our own lives illuminated with excruciating clarity, and we fear doing anything that might work against—or put us at odds with— God's present purposes and actions.

Calvin brings out these sentiments regularly in his sermons, for example, his sermon on the Second Commandment not to take the Lord's name in vain.[34] Typically Calvin points out the positive as well as the negative side of the command: "By these words [of the second commandment] we must carefully recognize the proper and lawful usage of his name."[35] "God in this text," says Calvin, "has decided to show us [the nature] of that majesty which is contained in his name in order that we might use it in our speech with complete reverence and honor."[36] Calvin speaks then of different occasions when people use God's name: in oaths, sometimes appropriately, but often casually, ignorantly, mockingly, maliciously. Calvin relates each instance to how it looks in the light of God's majesty, and he counsels simplicity and reverence.[37] "When we think of

---

[34]This is the fourth sermon in Ben Farley's translation of *John Calvin's Sermons on the Ten Commandments*, 81-96, on Deuteronomy 5:11.

[35]Ibid., 82.

[36]Ibid.

[37]Ibid., 87.

God," says Calvin, "we are in the presence of his inestimable glory, before which the angels tremble."[38] The recognition of God's majesty and glory leads us constantly to be careful how we use God's name and to be fearful of misusing it.[39]

Second, participation in Christ is a shared doing. When we do what God is doing at the same moment, we commune with the living God in the doing. We have a "fellowship of righteousness with him" *(iustitiae societatem . . . cum eo,* 3.11.10). The actions of humans are simultaneous with the action of God. The interaction between God and humanity is not thus a sequence of God's act and our response, nor our act and God's response. Whatever we do, we do it toward God in the context of God's activity toward us. Whatever God does entails a human action that is bound up with God's activity at the moment. Participation in God's activity is a communion with God in a shared doing.

Such is Calvin's meaning when, borrowing from Romans 12:1, he identifies our worship as the obedience of the whole self to God and God's Word, Christ living and reigning within by the power of the Holy Spirit (3.7.1). "Now the great thing is this," he says: "we are consecrated and dedicated to God in order that we may thereafter think, speak, meditate, and do nothing except to his glory." And with that he breaks out into the stirring litany: we are not our own, we are God's:

> We are not our own: let not our reason nor our will, therefore, sway our plans and deeds. We are not our own: let us therefore not set it as our goal to seek what is expedient for us according to the flesh. We are not our own: in so far as we can, let us therefore forget ourselves and all that is ours. Conversely, we are God's: let us therefore live for him and die for him. We are God's: let his wisdom and will therefore rule all our actions. We are God's: let all the parts of our life accordingly strive toward him as our only lawful goal. (3.7.1)

Third, participation in Christ leads us to seek God's will in the present moment. In order to do what God is doing at the same moment, we have to discern what God is doing. Romans 12:1ff. provides Calvin's focus on the will of God here, too; we are not to be conformed to the fashion of this world, but be transformed by the renewal of our minds, so that we may "prove what is the will of God" (3.7.1). A critical step is the extremely difficult task of denying ourselves. But here, too, the law or command of God plays a pivotal role.[40] The law

---

[38]Ibid., 92.

[39]Ibid., 92-96.

[40]In the *Institutes*, 2.8.5ff., before taking up the Ten Commandments one-by-one, Calvin explicitly refers the law pre-eminently to the will of God: "The Lord, in giving the rule of perfect righteousness, has referred all its parts to his will, thereby showing that nothing is more acceptable to him than obedience" (2.8.5). The law yields its greatest benefit by pointing beyond itself to the Lawgiver—not to itself, its own absolute claims or demands upon humankind, even its own inherent righteousness. The law, after all, is not God. After Christ (and in Christ) we are to "look to the Lawgiver, by whose character the nature of the law also is to be appreciated" (2.8.6).

of God, presented by the Word of God (Scripture) and accompanied by the example of Christ, all function to give us *descriptive clues* as to what the will of God is, what God wants, what God is like, and what God may be doing in the present moment. By meditating upon these, we will learn *not what we should do,* which simply reintroduces the demand character of the law. We learn *what God is doing* and the purposes for what God does.

The command of God, with specific reference to the law of God, has the effect of defining the moment. It defines the moment in terms of God's presence, God's activities, God's intentions, and the glorious prospect of participating in what God is doing at the moment, no matter how desperate or costly.[41] The decisions we make, the actions we take, may not be easy to do, but they will—by the grace of God—put us in communion with God in God's own active life, which is the participation of our doing in God's doing. When Calvin speaks of God's command to us, as under the topic of cross-bearing, he becomes much more situational.[42] He cites the example of Peter going to a martyr's death:

> Even though he obeyed the divine command with the utmost fervor of heart, yet, because he had not put off his human nature, he was pulled apart by a double will. For while he contemplated that bloody death which he was to die, stricken with dread of it, he would gladly have escaped. On the other hand, when it came to his mind that he was called to it by God's command, having overcome and trampled his fear, he willingly and even cheerfully undertook it. (3.8.10)

Fourth, participation in Christ involves a vigorous social interaction. The Golden Rule and the concept of equity make the interaction plain at every level, both positively and negatively. Calvin brings out these dimensions in every commandment of the Decalog. The Christian life entails interacting with God and with other people, never the one without the other. The Christian life entails interacting with fellow Christians but also with all humans, for all are alike made in the image of God. The Christian life entails protecting people from those who would overwhelm them. The Christian life entails lifting up those who are overwhelmed. The Christian life entails showing mercy when equity suggests it, sometimes to those who do not deserve it. Calvin keeps the individual clearly in view, but his own theology will not let him see the individual alone. Before God we cannot be Christian alone: we cannot be saved apart from the Church! Before God we cannot be human alone: we cannot retire from the human community! Calvin never called these considerations social justice: they are for the Christian faith simply the weave of the fabric.

---

[41]See the last 13 lines of *Institutes,* 3.8.10, dealing with *synecdoche.* See also 3.8.11, which is explicit about using the Scriptures and God's law to discern God's will with respect to righteousness and equity.

[42]Sauer's analysis of Calvin is instructive on this point as well.

Fifth and finally, participation in Christ has a gift character. The gift character seals the ethic of participation and keeps it from becoming merely an ethic of cooperation or response. All that Calvin says about the Christian life points to the gift of sharing in God's own, on-going, active life. We cannot miss the vigorous, active sense of Christian living for Calvin. Humans can share no greater adventure.

The gift is more than an opportunity we have to seize, more than a capacity we have to use, more than a change of heart or head we have to exercise, more than some essence or pill that enables us to do out of ourselves what we need to do, more than a restoration upon which we have to build. *Beyond the offer and the opportunity, God gives us the added gift of the doing itself.* Has Calvin not already said that faith—the activity of believing in Christ—is the work of the Holy Spirit? We believe. God does not believe instead of us. We believe because God gives us the believing with which to believe and commune with God in the believing. Similarly, we do good works. God does not do them for us. We do good works because God gives us the doing with which to do them and commune with God in the doing. God actually gives us the believing and the good works with which to participate in Christ and commune with God.

To put it another way: by the gift of believing in Christ come the effects of such believing—repentance (and Christian living in communion with God), justification (and the cleansing that puts us in the constant presence of God), and every moment of them both. With repentance and justification we participate in that "perfect gentleness" which is God's most complete accommodation to our humanity. Calvin says it well in the words of the hymn he wrote:

I greet Thee, who my sure Redeemer art,
My only Trust and Saviour of my heart,
Who pain didst undergo for my poor sake;
I pray Thee from our hearts all cares to take.

Thou art the King of mercy and of grace,
Reigning omnipotent in every place:
So come, O King, and our whole being sway;
Shine on us with the light of Thy pure day.

Thou art the life, by which alone we live,
And all our substance and our strength receive;
Sustain us by Thy faith and by Thy power,
And give us strength in every trying hour.[43]

---

[43]Quoted from *The Hymnbook* (Richmond: Presbyterian Church in the United States, 1995), number 144.

Preaching and Presence:
Constructing Calvin's Homiletical Legacy

Thomas J. Davis

I. Introduction: The Need for a Legacy

How is God to be known, especially if one is a Calvinist? The problems, on the face of it, are insurmountable. Or, at least, *the* problem. For, if one takes a view— mistakenly but still commonly held—that at the heart of Calvin's theology sits an absolutely transcendent God, one is left in a quandary about how the human and divine can be bridged at all.[1]

Perhaps this is said as a Calvin scholar who knows better, a little tongue-in-cheek. The truth of the matter is, however, that Calvin's God remains unknown to many. Calvin's teaching about God's presence has been presented in such an unbalanced manner that it affects not only popular attitudes toward Calvin but even those who do research on the theology of John Calvin. A few examples should suffice.

Back some years ago, Leroy S. Rouner, a professor at Boston University and sometime general editor of the Boston University Studies in Philosophy and Religion series, wrote a piece called "Transcendence and the Will to Believe." Though the piece was somewhat wide ranging—a comparative look at eastern and western philosphical and religious ways of belief with William James serving as the bridge between the two—the Calvinist tradition was repeatedly seen as one of the West's problematic ways of thinking. The problem? Calvin's theology of God's transcendence, which leads to the bugaboo of predestination. As Rouner put it, "Calvin, obsessed with the need for clarity and logical consistency, carefully crafted an increasingly monstrous doctrine which even he found hard to believe." In all this, Rouner used Calvin as a straw man to argue

---

[1]This line of thinking has led David Wright to remark on the "fearful caricature of the Calvinist Deity: an arbitrary, heartless despot, disposing of the destinies of human beings in this life and the next with capricious cruelty—the kind of God tailor-made by and for the tyrant of Geneva, John Calvin himself, for whom dispatching awkward dissidents to the funeral pyre was all in a day's work." David F. Wright, "Calvin's Accommodating God," in *Calvinus Sincerioris Religionis Vindex. Calvin as the Protector of the Purer Religion*, ed. Wilhelm H. Neuser and Brian G. Armstrong (Kirksville, Missouri: Sixteenth Century Journal Publishers, 1997), 3.

for the need of the experiential in religion. Of course, Calvin held to a notion of the transcendence of God, but he also balanced that with a notion of God's presence. One does not find reference to that balance in Rouner.[2]

A second, more anecdotal story. I once worked with a woman whose husband's father was a Unitarian minister. She told me of an article he had written—I have never tracked it down—in which he places the blame for modern day atheism at the feet of Calvin; in particular, Calvin's notion of the transcendence of God is the culprit behind rampant secularity. Calvin removed God so far from humanity, the argument goes, that it is like having no God at all.

Third example, which details how a one-sided focus on God's transcendence works its way even into Calvin scholarship. A 1995 dissertation by Christopher Elwood, in a chapter on Calvin's eucharistic theology, speaks of the separation of sign from reality in Calvin's rendering of eucharistic meaning. The author explains that such separation is due, in fact, to the transcendent God one finds in Calvin.[3]

I bring up these examples for a reason: to show how one aspect of Calvin's thought—the notion of God's transcendence—is perceived to overwhelm any notion of God's presence with humanity, thus rendering God unknowable. This widely held misreading of Calvin makes the job of a Calvin scholar difficult because it throws up barriers to a more honest rendering of Calvin's theology if one is trying to convey the range and depth and beauty of Calvin's theology to the non-specialist. Everyone thinks they already know Calvin.

Frankly, one could speak here of Calvin scholars as well. For the very subject that Calvin most insistently called upon to show how God is to be known, cognitively and affectively, is the very subject which scholarship, traditionally and

---

[2]Leroy S. Rouner, "Transcendence and the Will to Believe," in *Transcendence and the Sacred*, eds. Alan M. Olson and Leroy S. Rouner (Notre Dame: University of Notre Dame Press, 1981), 161-175; see quote on p. 171.

[3]Christopher Lee Elwood, "The Body Broken: The Calvinist Doctrine of the Eucharist and the Symbolisation of Power in France, 1530-1570" (Ph. D. dissertation, Harvard University, 1995). Elwood's chapter on Calvin is chapter three, "The Doctrine of Sacramental Signification in Calvin's French Writings on the Eucharist, 1541-1550," 101-140. Elwood argues that the Eucharist must be viewed within the context of God's absolute power (134). If this is *the* context from within which the Eucharist must be viewed, then it is not surprising that Elwood thinks, finally, that sign and signified are separated in Calvin's eucharistic thought. The sacramental signs have no inherent power (127), they are "inferior instruments" (130), and they are "in effect degraded" and "reduced to the status of mere instruments" (136). Therefore, we read that Calvin's sacramental view is representational (133). What is lacking, of course, is any sense of balance; certainly the Eucharist is only an instrument, but it is an ordained instrument of God's power. The cross itself is instrumental. If one starts from God's self-revelation, rather than some absolutist stance, then, of course, the role of the Eucharist takes on a different character than that outlined above—a character that has to do with God making Godself known rather than an absolute (and therefore unknowable) God. There is, as Calvin fully knows and teaches, an absolutely transcendent aspect of God; but that is God in Godself, not God for us.

as a whole, has not been very good at dealing with—the real presence of Christ and union with him as the crux of Christian existence. The reason Calvin is perceived to present a transcendent God *absolutum* is because the thing he balances transcendence with, Christ's presence, is perhaps the least appreciated aspect of his theology—perhaps because it is the thorniest.[4]

Brian Gerrish is correct in his assessment of this situation as he addresses Calvin's views on the Eucharist: real presence is at the heart of Calvin's eucharistic piety, and that is expressly what has not found a home in the mainstream of Reformed thought. Gerrish is also correct, in my opinion, that such a presence as Calvin experienced in the Eucharist is, in fact, the same presence given by the proclaimed Word.[5] Thus, in a roundabout way, I finally come to the thesis of this essay: by and large, Calvin left no homiletical legacy, because that which he left has not been received; or, if we want to speak in terms of the ancient church doctrine of *paradosis*, what Calvin handed down has been dropped. Thus, to speak of Calvin's homiletical legacy is to point to the need to construct that legacy and to see what impact it can have for us as we teach Calvin's theology. In fact, serious attention to Calvin's homiletic goes a long way toward balancing off overblown emphasis on transcendence. Whatever else homiletical theory and homiletical practice shows us in Calvin, it is a God with us.

II. Calvin and Preaching, or, What Is It We're Looking For?

When one speaks of Calvin's preaching, one speaks of one of the two final frontiers in studies of Calvin; the other is exegesis. Calvin the theologian, at least in the sense of quantity, has been the subject of a great tradition of scholarship. Within the last generation, however, many within that tradition find it no longer acceptable to study Calvin as theologian in the traditional manner: by reading solely the great *Institutes of the Christian Religion*. With great vigor, a number of scholars have begun the task of taking on the commentaries and are beginning to relate Calvin's theology and exegesis in fruitful ways.[6]

---

[4] The best that much of the Reformed tradition has done is to make of Christ's presence a spiritual (non-bodily) presence. When pushed to see the evidence in Calvin for some experience of bodily presence, the tendency is and has been to reject such a presence as alien to Calvin's *real* concerns, such as predestination. The clearest example here is Charles Hodge, who will be noted below.

[5] It is a "settled principle that the sacraments have the same office as the Word of God: to offer and set forth Christ to us, and in him the treasures of heavenly grace." *Institutes*, 4.14.17 (CO, 2:953). Thus Calvin asserts that in both Word and Sacrament one first receives Christ, then his benefits. See also Brian Gerrish, "Calvin's Eucharistic Piety," in *Calvin Society Papers, 1995-1997: Calvin and Spirituality; Calvin and His Contemporaries*, ed. David Foxgrover (Grand Rapids, 1998), 63-65.

[6] Much headway has been made in working on Calvin's commentaries since T. H. L. Parker's observation that "apart from some well-trodden paths," the study of exegesis in the sixteenth century "has been neglected." T. H. L. Parker, *Calvin's New Testament Commentaries* (Grand Rapids: Eerdmans, 1971), vii. A brief review of some of this literature, mostly books, can be found in

Calvin's preaching, however, is just now beginning to come into its own as an area of study. A handful of books and articles have begun to form a locus of inquiry from which to examine Calvin and preaching.[7] I want to point briefly to three ways we can look at Calvin's homiletic and suggest that one of these areas, however interesting historically, is really accidental in some ways to the concern for a legacy; the second is helpful but not foundational; while the third holds promise as a key to unlocking something new and exciting for how Calvin is studied and understood.

A. The Logistics of Preaching

Pioneer work on Calvin's preaching starts in many ways with T. H. L. Parker's *Oracles of God*; this was later revised as *Calvin's Preaching*. This book represents the kind of historical spade work necessary to establish the actual work of Calvin's preaching. Here we find detailed information on when Calvin preached on what, how many times a week Calvin ascended the pulpit, the number of sermons to be reckoned with, and some analysis of the form of Calvin's preaching. The book reveals something to us especially of the day-to-day work of Calvin's preaching.[8]

I will not rehearse here what is said in this book; it is easily enough obtained. What I would say is that, while it serves as a foundation for the study of Calvin's preaching, such studies as this one are not capable, by their very nature, of serving as an entry point for a discussion of Calvin's homiletical legacy. Such works are intrinsically biographical. They tell us something of Calvin, his situation, the routines of sixteenth-century Genevan church life, and the like. As such, biography, while shedding light on the circumstances of Calvin, is a writing of a life, not a legacy. Invoking Calvin's principle of distinction without separation, we can say that the legacy flows from the life in a sense—but they are not the same

---

Richard A. Muller, "Directions in Current Calvin Research," in *Calvin Studies IX: Papers Presented to the Ninth Colloquium on Calvin Studies*, ed. John H. Leith and Robert A. Johnson (Davidson, N. C., 1998), 83-84. A collection of important articles, many of which touch on Calvin's exegesis, can be found in Richard Gamble, ed., *Calvin and Hermeneutics* (New York: Garland, 1992). David Steinmetz made a statement similar to Parker's in "John Calvin and Isaiah 6: A Problem in the History of Exegesis," *Interpretation* 36 (1982): 156-170. Steinmetz then set out to address the problem. His efforts have been celebrated with a volume of essays, complete with a bibliography of Steinmetz's work. See Richard A. Muller and John L. Thompson, eds., *Biblical Interpretation in the Era of the Reformation* (Grand Rapids: Eerdmans, 1997).

[7]These will be listed in what follows as they come up, rather than being listed here all at once.

[8]T.H.L. Parker, *The Preaching of John Calvin* (Louisville: Westminster/John Knox Press, 1992); T. H. L. Parker, *The Oracles of God: An Introduction to the Preaching of John Calvin* (London: Lutterworth, 1947). Serious work on Calvin's sermons began with Erwin Mülhaupt, *Die Predigt Calvins: Ihre Geschichte, ihre Form, und ihre Religiosen Grundgedanken* (Berlin: De Gruyter, 1931). This led, in part, to work on Calvin's manuscript sermons and their publication (little by little, ongoing) in the *Supplementa Calviniana*.

thing. No one would say, for example, that Calvin's pattern of preaching should be duplicated in some form, or the length of his sermons are normative, or any such thing. One must look elsewhere for something that constitutes a legacy in preaching.

B. The Method of Preaching: Pedagogy and Persuasion

Calvin preached through books of the Bible. Parker and others can be consulted on how many sermons were preached on which books.[9] But the point is that, as far as pedagogy was concerned, Calvin believed that the Bible's message was contained in its books, which had authors. For Calvin, in preaching as well as in exegesis, the point in studying books of the Bible was to "unfold the mind of the writer."[10] Since he believed in a contextual reading of Scripture—that verses fit within larger fragments that were held together by an authorial mind in an overall view of the subject[11]—Calvin thought it best to go through each book of the Bible a few verses at a time, *lectio continua*, explicating with clarity and brevity the meaning of the author. Once explicated, the meaning was universalized in the sense that fit with Calvin's belief that the message of the Bible had as much to do with the present as the past. This process is called, perhaps somewhat mistakenly, application.[12]

By briefly running through this procedure for preaching, it should be clear that what we speak of here is the craft of homiletics, which has two distinct parts: determining the message of Scripture, a matter of pedagogy (if one takes

---

[9] See Parker, *Calvin's Preaching*, appendix 1, 153-162.

[10] Since preaching is an oral interpretation of Scripture, I assume Calvin's statement applies as much to preaching as to the written commentary. The quote comes from Calvin's dedicatory letter to Simon Grynaeus in his first biblical commentary, an exposition of Romans. See John Calvin, *The Epistles of Paul to the Romans and Thessalonians*, tr. Ross McKenzie (Edinburgh: Oliver and Boyd, 1960; repr. Grand Rapids: Eerdmans, 1973), 1; CO, 10:403. Most articles written during the last twenty years on Calvin's exegesis start with this statement.

[11] See Calvin's remarks in his commentary on Isaiah 14:12: "But when passages of Scripture are seized upon thoughtlessly and the context is ignored, it should not surprise us that mistakes arise everywhere" (sed quum temere arripiunture scripturae loci, nec attenditur contextus, nos errores passim oboriri mirum non est). CO, 36: 277. See also Parker, *Calvin's Preaching*, 81-82, 90, 93, 132-133, 137-138.

[12] Parker, *Calvin's Preaching*, part four: "From Exegesis to Application." Application seems to me too "external" a word; it implies the past being taken and put into contact with the present. Although Scripture speaks of the past activity of God, it is not about the past. As Richard Muller says about Calvin's understanding, "Scripture, as God's Word, is a present revelation." Richard A. Muller, "The Foundation of Calvin's Theology: Scripture as Revealing God's Word," in *Duke Divinity School Review* 44 (1979): 15. Maybe the word "transformation" would better convey Calvin's notion of how the message of God's Word works than application. Dawn DeVries states it nicely when she says of Gospel story, "The hearer does not so much intellectually appropriate the story as *participate* in it." Dawn DeVries, *Jesus Christ in the Preaching of Calvin and Schleiermacher* (Louisville: Westminster/John Knox Press, 1996), 32.

pedagogy to mean how one is taught and how one best learns), and then an appropriate presentation of the meaning of that message, or persuasion. Let us look briefly at each of the two parts.

By all accounts, Calvin used all the available critical tools at his disposal to wrestle with the meaning of Scripture. One can find in his sermons and his commentaries references to ancient history, geography, philology; one also finds that Calvin used the tradition of interpretation available to him. Though the hand of the scholar is displayed more lightly in sermons than commentaries, it is there nonetheless, and Calvin certainly saw it as the preacher's task to equip himself for the task of interpretation as fully as possible with all the tools available, disdaining not to use even pagan authors if therein one could find help in shedding light on a problem of scriptural interpretation.[13] Once one has so educated oneself, in a sense, then it became a matter of teaching the congregation what is necessary in order to realize the meaning of a passage of Scripture in its fullness. Preaching has, thus, a didactic function: the congregation leaves worship knowing more about God's word than when they entered.

This knowledge, however, is more than cognitive; it is affective. And this is where the notion of persuasion comes in. To simply convey bare Gospel history, for example, is not sufficient for preaching. To be sure, one should know the Gospel history, but such knowledge by itself is not sufficient; the message, after penetrating the mind, must make its way to the heart.[14] And the approach appropriate to such affective appeals is that of persuasion.

There have been a number of works that deal with the notion of persuasion in Calvin. Bouwsma, for example, speaks of Calvin's desire to persuade in his theology within the context of the general Renaissance environment, one that placed a kind of pragmatic value on thought, a pragmatism of action. For Bouwsma, this means an anti-systematic Calvin, because the rhetorical by nature militates against a strict systematic approach.[15] Also jumping off from

---

[13]As Calvin says in the *Institutes*, "If we regard the Spirit of God as the sole fountain of truth, we shall neither reject the truth itself, nor despise it wherever it shall be found." *Institutes*, 2.2.15; CO, 2:198.

[14]"Faith rests not on ignorance, but on knowledge" (*Institutes*, 3.2.2; CO, 2:399); "Indeed, most people when they hear this term [faith], understand nothing deeper than a common assent to the gospel history" (*Institutes*, 3.2.1; CO, 2: 397-398); "And it will not be enough for the mind to be illuminated by the Spirit of God unless the heart is also strengthened and supported by his power" (*Institutes*, 3.2.33; CO, 2: 425); knowledge of God, to be true, must take "root in the heart" (*Institutes*, 1.5.9; CO, 2:47).

[15]On the general place of rhetoric in Calvin's theology, see William J. Bowsma, "Calvinism as Theologia Rhetorica," in *Calvinism as Theologia Rhetorica*, ed. Wilhelm Wuellner (Berkeley: Center for Hermeneutical Studies in Hellenistic and Modern Culture, 1986), 1-21; esp. 1, where Bowsma states, "The rhetorical tradition, given new life by Renaissance humanism, supplied *the* dynamic element in Calvin's thought" (emphasis mine). On Calvin as "anti-system," see William J. Bowsma, "Calvin and the Renaissance Crisis of Knowing," *Calvin Theological Journal* 17 (November, 1982): 190-211, esp. 194, 199, 208-209. For a more appreciative view of "system" in Calvin—understood as a coherent whole held together by governing principles—see Gerrish, "Calvin's Eucharistic Piety," 54-56.

the Renaissance interest in rhetoric, Millet has written as well on the drive within Calvin's theology to work persuasively, that is, rhetorically.[16]

What interests me most, however, is to examine what in language Calvin finds to constitute persuasive speech, and on this matter he is quite clear. It is the language of metaphor that moves hearts, and Calvin states how he is willing to sacrifice some exactness of definition, inherent in the use of metaphor, in order to find that persuasive metaphor that impresses upon the heart the meaning of Scripture.[17] This seems to me to be an extremely important principle in Calvin's preaching; though he does, in fact, for pedagogical reasons, want to make the things of Scripture clear, he also wants to make those things clearly present to the heart of believers. The fact that he thinks metaphor works best to accomplish this end is something we will return to—for now it is just to be noted.

Still, are pedagogy and persuasion, considered in and of themselves and as Calvin expressed them, something that we want to consider as constituting Calvin's homiletical legacy? While I think they lend themselves a bit more toward the making of a legacy than logistics, in and of themselves I do not think they make up the heart of a legacy, though certain aspects of them can be helpful as we reflect upon preaching.[18]

---

[16]"La rhétorique ... est en effet la doctrine à visée pratique don relève entièrement cet exercice de la parole dans *la mésure où* il se veut efficace, c'est-à-dire persuasif." Olivier Millet, *"Docere/Movere.* Les catégories rhétoriques et leurs sources humanistes dans las doctrine Calvinienne de la foi," in *Calvinius Sincerioris Religionis Vindex,* 35. Speaking of faith as persuasion, Millet powerfully explains the implications for preaching: "La foi définie comme persuasion restaure la prédication chrétienne, parole prononcée comme instrument du salut, elle invite aussi implicitement les prédicateurs chrétiens à assumer dans toutes ses dimensions les ressources du language humain" (51). David F. Wright, "Was John Calvin a 'Rhetorical Theologian'?" in *Calvin Studies IX,* calls into question some of the trends in using rhetoric as a way of talking about Calvin the theologian. While critically appreciative of Millet's work, Wright is less impressed by others who have recently worked on Calvin as "rhetorical theologian." Wright argues that Calvin is more concerned with biblical truth than with rhetoric (see p. 69).

[17]"Although a figurative expression is not so distinct, it gives a more elegant and significant expression than if the thing were said simply, and without figure. Hence figures are called the eyes of speech, not that they explain the matter more easily than simple ordinary language, but because they attract attention by their elegance and arouse the mind by their lustre, and by their lively similitude better penetrate the soul." John Calvin, "True Partaking of the Flesh and Blood of Christ," in *Selected Works of John Calvin: Tracts and Letters,* vol. 2, *Tracts,* part 2, ed. and tr. Henry Beveridge (Edinburgh: Calvin Translation Society, 1849; repr. Grand Rapids: Baker, 1983), 567; CO, 9: 514. The last part of the translation has been slightly altered to better represent what Calvin actually wrote. See also Jane Dempsey Douglass, "Calvin's Use of Metaphorical Language: God as Enemy and God as Mother," *Princeton Seminary Bulletin* 8 (1987): 19-32; esp. 19-20.

[18]"Indeed, it will be an unattractive way of teaching, if the masters do not work out carefully what are the needs of the times, what suits the people concerned, for in this regard nothing is more unbalanced than absolute balance [perpetua aequalitas]." Calvin commenting on Matthew 3:7 in John Calvin, *A Harmony of the Gospels: Matthew, Mark, Luke,* vol. 1, tr. A. W. Morrison (Edinburgh: St. Andrews Press, 1972; repr., Grand Rapids: Eerdmans, 1980), 120; CO, 45:116. Here Calvin is

C. The Purpose of Preaching

There is a sentence from one of Calvin's sermons that should give every preacher pause as he or she ascends the pulpit. It is his strongest statement on the purpose of preaching, or, if you like, its role in the great drama of salvation. "If the gospel be not preached," Calvin proclaimed, "Jesus Christ is, as it were, buried."[19] Is this exaggeration on Calvin's part? I think not. He is putting to his congregation what he considers to be the usual means of God's redemptive activity. [20] Preaching is the instrument God uses to span time and space and to bring Christian, Christ, and cross together. Preaching is the bridge between

---

commenting on John the Baptist's preaching repentance to the Pharisees; but the point has general application. It speaks to whether or not one should speak or preach, rhetorically or otherwise, in the same manner as Calvin. Obviously not. But it is not only audience and rhetorical methods (persuasive speech) that change. What I have called pedagogy changes as well. Pedagogy, broadly understood, is about the means of teaching—oneself as well as others. Calvin approached the text pedagogically with the resources of humanistic learning, especially a concern for language and context. Some see this approach as the start down the path of modern historical criticism. Luke Timothy Johnson, for example, lays the "sins" of modern historical criticism at the feet of the early Protestant Reformers (primarily Luther, who represents "the reformation"), especially in their insistence on the literal meaning of Scripture, and in what he considers to be their flawed approach to the text: historical. See Luke Timothy Johnson, *The Real Jesus: The Misguided Quest for the Historical Jesus and the Truth of the Traditional Gospels* (San Francisco: Harper, 1996), 67-69. Johnson talks about how the *real* Jesus is the Jesus that lives in the community of the faithful. Yet this is exactly Calvin's point—but he ties that real presence in community to the instrument of Scripture by the power of the Holy Spirit. Still, Johnson's point is well taken if one understands him to mean that the *method* of interpretation (modern historical criticism) cannot by its nature be what reveals the living Jesus. This is why, as helpful as Calvin is—precritical or precursor to modern, depending on one's interpretation—as one example of how to approach Scripture pedagogically, one can certainly distinguish that approach from what I take to be the purpose of preaching. Simply put, prevailing paradigms of interpretation change over time.

[19]John Calvin, *The Mystery of Godliness and Other Selected Sermons* (Grand Rapids: Eerdmans, 1950), 25 (on 2 Timothy 1:8-9, CO 54:41; there is a bit more punch to the French: "Or si l'Evangele ne se presche, voilà Iesus Christ qui est comme enseveli"). See also sermon on 1 Timothy 2: 5-6: "We may therefore perceive that the death and passion of our Lord Jesus Christ would be unprofitable to us, unless it were witnessed by the gospel" (Ibid., 208; CO 53:176); and the sermon on 2 Timothy 1:9-10: "If the Gospel were taken away, of what advantage would it be to us that the Son of God had suffered death, and risen again on the third day for our justification? ... Jesus Christ shows himself openly to those who have the eyes of faith to look upon Him, when the gospel is preached" (Ibid., 48; CO 54:61; the original text does not contain the words "for our justification").

[20]See Calvin's comments on Romans 10:14: "The Word, accordingly, is required for a true knowledge of God. But it is the preached Word alone which Paul has described, for this is the normal mode which the Lord has appointed for imparting His Word." See also comment on Romans 10:17: "This is a noteworthy passage on the efficacy of preaching, for Paul declares [testatur] that faith is produced by preaching. He has just stated that by itself preaching is profitless, but when the Lord is pleased to work, it is the instrument of his power." Calvin, *Epistles of Paul to the Romans and Thessalonians*, 231, 233 (CO, 49:205,206). Later, at Romans 10:21, Calvin says, "In procuring our salvation by the ministers of His Word, God stretches forth His hands to us exactly as a father stretches forth his arms" (Ibid., 236; CO, 49:210).

the work of the cross and the grace of God experienced in the present. This is one of the many attributes that preaching and sacraments share with one another: grace is offered in the here and the now through the instruments God has chosen to present and to make present the new life in Christ.[21]

We shall consider at greater length below what it means to Calvin to have new life in Christ. Let it be sufficient here to say that new life is had only in Christ, with an emphasis on the "in." The Christian experience is defined by the fact that it is an experience of Christ, and Calvin is quite clear that such an experience has to do with the present rather than with the past. It is the living Christ with whom the Christian has to do, and it is the living Christ to whom the Christian must be joined to gain the benefits of Christ.

But to speak of communion with Christ, one must ask in what way one has access to Christ. The answer is that one has access to Christ through the means appointed by God, and the primary means is through preaching. "We receive [Christ]," Calvin says, "clothed with his Gospel."[22] What is more, what Calvin means here by Christ being clothed in the Gospel is that Christ comes in the Gospel as proclaimed. This is not to place the written Word in an inferior position—it is God's revelation and testimony to the incarnate Word, and all preaching must be measured against it. But it is the spoken Word, proclaimed to the community, that embodies Christ. This may well be because, for Calvin, the written Word that testifies to Christ must come alive in contemporary circumstances.[23] Preaching spans the gap that separates the "then" nature of the

---

[21]As Brian Gerrish has said, "The idea of Christ's living presence, effected through the Word of God, is the heart of Calvin's gospel." B. A. Gerrish, "John Calvin and the Reformed Doctrine of the Lord's Supper," *McCormick Quarterly* 22 (1969): 92. Though Calvin makes this point in numerous places, it is said particularly well in his sermons: "So, then, may we esteem the spiritual grace which is given us in our Lord Jesus Christ, and which is offered us every day by the preaching of the gospel." John Calvin, *Sermons on the Saving Work of Christ*, selected and tr. Leroy Nixon (Grand Rapids: Eerdmans, 1950; repr. Hertfordshire, England: Evangelical Press, 1980), 148 (on Matthew 27:27-44; CO, 46: 913-914); and preaching on Matthew 28:1-10: "He is willing to have a common life with us, and that what He has may be ours, even that He wishes to dwell in us, not in imagination, but in fact" (Ibid., 195; CO, 46:953).

[22]*Institutes*, 3.2.6; CO, 2:401.

[23]It is, of course, by the power of the Holy Spirit that the Word comes alive. On the relation of Spirit, Word and preaching, Richard Muller says, "God's Spirit is so conjoined to the Word that preaching becomes at once a communication of God's will and an instrument of the Holy Spirit in working salvation. Calvin establishes the closest possible relation between the words of the preacher, the Word of God and the work of the Spirit without exalting the human instrument beyond his station. Preaching makes the Word of God present to faith because God has so willed." Richard A. Muller, "The Foundation of Calvin's Theology: Scripture as Revealing God's Word," *Duke Divinity School Review* 44 (1979): 125. I would expand this train of thought, however, to make explicit that the Word presents Christ, and him bodily. More will be made of this in what follows. Because the role of the Spirit is to unite believers with Christ, Willem van 't Spijker is correct when he states, "Unity with Christ keeps the scriptural principle from degenerating into a legalistic scheme used in a formulatistic way. Scripture comes alive in fellowship with Christ." Willem van't Spijker, "Calvin's Friendship with Martin Bucer," in *Calvin Studies Society Papers, 1995-1997*.

events of the Gospel to the "now" nature of redemption. A Gospel that remains in the past, that speaks of disciples who faithfully responded to Christ without indicating how disciples faithfully respond in the present, is no Gospel at all; it is bare history, even if of divine things, and as bare history it may tickle the fancy but it will not move the heart.[24]

Calvin, as many have pointed out, is a theologian of experience,[25] and as such matters of memory alone do not interest him. Maybe it is too much to point out that, in his discussions of the soul, Calvin, while holding on to the traditional notion of reason and will as functions of the soul, leaves out memory. [26] Maybe it is subsumed in some way under the function of reason. While holding to the importance of knowing the past, Calvin emphasized that by itself recollection is not life. [27]

Of course, we have to recognize that, for Calvin, it is not the preachers themselves who make of preaching its importance; it is the Spirit of God. Preaching, like Eucharist, is instrumental; the power to operate the instrument lies outside the instrument, and without that power the instrument is lifeless and void.[28]

---

[24]See Institutes, 3.2.1; CO, 2: 397-398, and note 3 that accompanies it by McNeill; and John Calvin, *The Epistles of Paul the Apostle to the Galatians, Ephesians, Philippians and Colossians*, tr. T. H. L. Parker (Grand Rapids: Eerdmans, 1965), 349-350 (CO, 52: 121), where Calvin comments on Colossians 3:10 and speaks of knowledge as transformation, not as "simple and bare." For more on the relation of gospel history to faith, see Thomas J. Davis, "Historical Knowledge and True Wisdom: Objectivity, Faith and Freedom," *Fides et Historia* 29, no. 3 (Fall, 1997): 20-22. Dawn DeVries sums up nicely *why* the gospel must be more than mere history for Christians, according to Calvin, when she explains that the gospel is not just announcement; it is also the gift of Christ present. See DeVries, *Jesus Christ in the Preaching of Calvin and Schleiermacher*, 16.

[25]For a few examples, see John T. McNeill, "John Calvin: Doctor Ecclesiae," in *Readings in Calvin's Theology*, ed. Donald K. McKim (Grand Rapids: Baker, 1984), 12; Bowsma, "Calvin and the Renaissance Crisis of Knowing," 204, 210; and Ford Lewis Battles, "Calculus Fidei," in *Calvinus Ecclesiae Doctor*, ed. Wilhelm H. Neuser (Kampen: Kok, 1978), 87. Indeed, some have suggested that Calvin is "existentialist" in his thinking; see Gerald J. Postema, "Calvin's Alleged Rejection of Natural Theology," *Scottish Journal of Theology* 24 (1971): 424; and John New Thomas, "The Place of Natural Theology in the Thought of John Calvin," *Journal of Religious Thought* 15 (1958): 108. Calvin speaks of how "each believer experiences within himself" the truth of Scripture. *Institutes*, 1.7.5 Joel Beeke reminds us that when Calvin speaks of experience, however, it is not bare experience of which he speaks but of "experience grounded in the Word." Joel R. Beeke, "Making Sense of Calvin's Paradoxes on Assurance of Faith," in *Calvin Studies Society Papers, 1995-1997*, 13-30, especially p. 19.

[26]*Institutes*, 1.15.7; CO, 2:142.

[27]So, on the one hand, one must have a knowledge of the gospel (*Institutes*, 3.2.29; CO, 2: 421-422), but on the other hand, the gospel is beneficial only if one is joined to Christ (3.2.30; CO, 2: 422).

[28]"This is a noteworthy passage [Romans 10:17] on the efficacy of preaching, for Paul declares that faith is produced by preaching. He has just stated that by itself preaching is profitless, but when the Lord is pleased to work, it is the instrument of His power." Calvin, *Epistles of Paul to the Romans and Thessalonians*, 233; CO, 49:206. In his comment on the next chapter of Romans Calvin states, "Let us, however, understand that preaching is an instrument for effecting the salvation of believers. Although it can accomplish nothing without the Spirit of God, yet through the inward working of the Spirit it reveals His action most powerfully." Ibid., 248; CO, 49:219, commenting on Romans 11:14. In relation to the sacraments, see *Institutes*, 4.14.12; CO, 2: 950.

But, to say this is not to denigrate preaching for Calvin, but simply to understand its working: God uses preaching as an instrument to make known Christ, fully and present. And whereas God may not be bound to use the instrument, Christians are.[29] To speak of instrumentality is simply a way of reckoning with how God works: even Christ's death on a cross is instrumental—in and of itself it has no value. God did not have to use the cross as the means of salvation, but he chose it because it best suited his purpose to show himself as a giving father full of love, or at least so Calvin thought.[30] In like manner, God has chosen preaching, and he invigorates the preaching of ministers by the power of His Spirit so that Christ truly comes in the spoken Word to reside with his people; or, to reverse the direction as Calvin so liked to do, preaching lifted the congregation to Christ, to participate in him and thus gain all the benefits he offers.

The purpose of preaching, in short, is that it is an instrument, along with others such as the Holy Supper, that unites the Christian with Christ. And I would suggest that, if we want to talk about constructing a homiletical legacy for Calvin, this would be the place to start. When and how often preaching takes place, or pedagogy and persuasion in the preaching act, all take a back seat to what is fundamental for Calvin. In preaching, Christ is present. That is the goal, that is the content, that is the raison' d'etre of preaching. Everything else flows from recognition of this experience.

III. Preaching and Presence:
Proclaiming the Heart of the Gospel, Examining the Heart of Calvin

I want to move next to what may seem, on the face of it, to be an odd place: Calvin's exegesis of Ephesians 5. This chapter deals mostly with how Paul directs Christians to conduct themselves in the world, and the latter part of the chapter deals specifically with the relationship between husband and wife (and, at the very end, with the relationship between parents and children).

---

[29]"For, although God's power is not bound to outward means, he has nonetheless bound us to this ordinary manner of teaching." *Institutes,* 4.1.5; CO, 2: 750. In speaking on the same passage, Calvin remarks, "It is a singular privilege that [God] deigns to consecrate to himself the mouths and tongues of men in order that his voice may resound in them." Ibid. This is a common theme in Calvin's sermons.

[30]"[God] was well able to rescue us from the unfathomable depths of death in another fashion [than by Christ's death], but He willed to display the treasures of his infinite goodness when He spared not His only Son." Calvin, *Sermons on the Saving Work of Christ,* 51; CO, 46:833, preaching on Matthew 26: 36-39. Though Calvin held to a version of the satisfaction theory of the atonement (see *Institutes,* 2.17.4-5; CO, 2:388-390, especially), I do not think he is quite as "Anselmian" as some suggest (see, for example, Dawn DeVries, *Jesus Christ in the Preaching of John Calvin and Schleiermacher,* 98) because, for Anselm, there is something of ontological necessity about Christ's sacrifice, whereas for Calvin it is a chosen instrument, not an ontological necessity—an instrument which Calvin thinks best exemplifies God's goodness.

Much used and abused, this passage in Ephesians speaks of wives obeying their husbands and husbands loving their wives. But then Paul brings in the imagery of Christ and the church and speaks of the relationship between Christ and church to be similar to that between husband and wife. The two are one, Paul proclaims, speaking of both husband/wife and Christ/church. An extraordinary thing takes place in Calvin's commentary. For Calvin, often depicted as one devoted when possible to a literal and clear and plain reading of Scripture, takes this passage as an opportunity to speak of the Lord's Supper. And he knows his opponents will fault him:

> In short, Paul [here] describes our union to Christ, a symbol and pledge of which is given to us in the Holy Supper. Some assert that it is a twisting of this passage to refer it to the Lord's Supper, when no mention is made of the Supper, but only of marriage; but they are very mistaken. Although they teach that the death of Christ is commemorated in the Supper, they do not admit a communication such as we assert from the words of Christ. We quote this passage against them.[31]

Why is it that Calvin takes this opportunity to speak of the Supper? It is because, for Calvin, the Supper is the place where union with Christ is most fully pictured; and this passage is about union, as Calvin makes clear when he says, "This is a remarkable passage on the mystical communication which we have with Christ." Furthermore, Calvin states emphatically that the union with Christ that the Christian enjoys is not one simply of a shared humanity; that is, it is not about incarnational likeness or similarity. Rather, staying with the marriage metaphor, Calvin speaks of the prototypical husband and wife, Adam and Eve, and how Eve, in her creation, is bone of Adam's bone and that her life is derived from his flesh. In the same manner, Calvin proclaims, Christians are made into one body with Christ because of communication with his substance. Christians are indeed, Calvin makes clear, flesh of Christ's flesh and bone of his bone. According to Calvin, "this is no exaggeration, but the simple truth." [32]

The Ephesians passage that relates the mystery of the union of Christ with the church to that of husband and wife ends with a declaration that so mirrors Calvin's own feelings about the notion about how the Supper feeds the Christian that it bears repeating in full here, for it is typical of the way Calvin ends discussions of the union of Christ with the Christian:

> 32. *The mystery is great.* He [Paul] concludes with wonder at the spiritual union between Christ and the Church. For he exclaims that this is a great mystery. By which he implies that no language can do it justice. It is in vain that men fret themselves to comprehend, by the understanding of the flesh,

---

[31]Calvin, *Epistles of Paul the Apostle to the Galatians, Ephesians, Philippians and Colossians*, 208-209, commenting on Ephesians 5:30; CO, 51:225-226.

[32]Ibid., commenting on, respectively, Ephesians 5:29, 5:30, 5:31 and 5:30.

its manner and character; for here God exerts the infinite power of His Spirit. Those who refuse to admit anything on this subject beyond what their own capacity can reach, are very foolish. When they deny that the flesh and blood of Christ are offered (*exhiberi*) to us in the Lord's Supper, they say: 'Define the manner or you will not convince us.' But I am overwhelmed by the depth of this mystery.[33]

This passage fits very nicely the pattern that Brian Gerrish has pointed out as the shape of Calvin's theology: there is gift (grace), and then there is grati-tude[34]; or, better stated in this case: there is awe at the mysterious way in which God has joined himself to sinful humanity.

Why this excursus on the Eucharist? First, it is to remind us briefly of Calvin's view that, in the Supper, it is Christ who is given, and given in the fullness of his humanity, which means bodily. Though the Spirit works the mystery of union, it is no mystery what Calvin plainly says: that the union the Christian has with Christ in the Eucharist is not a union of Christ's spirit with the Christian's spirit (or, at least, not just that); rather, it is the sustenance of the Christian's spirit and body with the very substance of Christ's body.[35] With that kept fully in mind, we should keep in mind a second thing: Calvin states that what is received in the sacrament is the same thing that is received in the Word, especially the preached Word.[36]

Dawn DeVries has pictured for us the function of Calvin's preaching as a sacramental word; she makes the point that the function of the preached Word for Calvin is to make Christ present.[37] This is, in my mind, entirely consistent with Calvin's thought: preaching is about the present, not the past, just as the

---

[33]Ibid., 209-210; CO, 51:226-227, commenting on Ephesians 5:32.

[34]Brian A. Gerrish, *Grace and Gratitude: The Eucharistic Theology of John Calvin* (Minneapolis: Fortress Press, 1993).

[35]See especially *Institutes*, 4.17.8-9; CO, 2:1007-1008. In section 9, Calvin does mention that Christ cleaves to us "wholly in spirit and body." The emphasis, however—probably because of the conflict over the "true presence"—is on Christ's body. Also, see Calvin's comments on 1 Corinthians 6:15: "We should note that the spiritual union which we have with Christ is not a mat-ter of the soul alone, but of the body also, so that we are flesh of his flesh etc (Eph. 5:30). The hope of resurrection would be faint, if our union with Him were not complete and total like that." John Calvin, *The First Epistle of Paul to the Corinthians*, tr. John W. Fraser (Edinburgh: Oliver and Boyd, 1960; repr. Grand Rapids: Eerdmans, 1973), 130; CO, 49:398. One of the first contemporary schol-ars to take seriously the idea of Christ's body as a gift was G. P. Hartvelt, *Verum Corpus: Een Studie over een Centraal Hoofd stuk uit de Avondsmaalsleer van Calvijn* (Delft: W. D. Meinema, 1960).

[36]*Institutes*, 4.14.7; CO, 2:945: "It is therefore certain that the Lord offers us mercy and the pledge of his grace [that pledge being Christ] both in his Sacred Word and in his sacraments." Here "Word" refers to preaching; note that 4.14.1; CO, 2: 941-942, sets out the topic of the chapter as relating sacraments to the "preaching of the gospel." See also 4.14.17, cited in note 5 above.

[37]DeVries, *Jesus Christ in the Preaching of Calvin and Schleiermacher,* ix, 16-18, 27.

Eucharist is about the present, not the past. Or, perhaps, we might better say that Word and Sacrament are instruments that bridge past and present so that the grace that originates with the work of Christ in his earthly life—including ministry, passion, death, and resurrection—continues in the present in the life of the believer. But the reason Word and Sacrament work as a bridge is because of Christ himself. Much as the humanity of Christ serves as the mediatorial principle between the righteousness of God and its application to the Christian, so too does the humanity of Christ serve as that which mediates between what happened in the past and how that work becomes present gift and grace.[38]

But over and over again, Calvin asserts that to have these benefits of Christ, one must first have Christ himself.[39] There have been a number of works that deal with what it means to have Christ himself. Calvin himself refers to this experience as participation in Christ, communication in Christ, communion with Christ, union with Christ, and mystical union. Dennis Tamburello has shown how important the notion of union with Christ is for Calvin, and how it relates to Calvin's broader thought on questions like justification and sanctification.[40] Charles Partee, in a fine article, revisits the question of a central dogma in Calvin's theology, and points to union with Christ as being, if not the central dogma, a central dogma.[41] I would like to add my own agreement to these voices, though with a caveat. Tamburello, in particular, with his notion of union, focuses on the spiritual nature of the union. He does not, of course, imply that Calvin thinks there is a mixing of spiritual substances; he is quite right to point out that Calvin thought nothing of the sort. But he does focus on the union of wills as a way to think about the Christian's union with Christ, and while that is involved, he so emphasizes that aspect of union that it tends to spir-

---

[38]On Christ's humanity (body) as the mediatorial principle for righteousness, see John Calvin, *The Gospel According to St. John*, Pt. 1, 1-10, tr. T. H. L. Parker (Edinburgh: Oliver and Boyd, 1961; repr. Grand Rapids: Eerdmans, 1980), 167; CO, 47: 152-153, commenting on John 6:51. Or, as Calvin approvingly quotes St. Augustine, "As God, [Christ] is the destination to which we move; as man, the path by which we go." *Institutes*, 3.2.1; CO, 2: 398. See also his comments on 1 Timothy 3:16: "We cannot know Jesus Christ to be a mediator between God and man, unless we behold him as man." Calvin, *Mystery of Godliness*, 17 (CO, 53: 323). On Christ's past work made present in the Christ who present, see DeVries, *Jesus Christ in the Preaching of calvin and Schleiermacher*, 31, 95.

[39]For example, see *Institutes*, 4.17.11; CO, 2:1010; for a fuller explication and references, see Thomas J. Davis, *The Clearest Promises of God: The Development of Calvin's Eucharistic Teaching* (New York: AMS Press, 1995), esp. 48-50, 80-84, 100-103, 151, 158, 171-172, 215-216. These passages indicate how Calvin moves chronologically from equating Christ with his benefits to distinguishing the two, insisting that reception of Christ is prior to receiving his benefits.

[40]Dennis Tamburello, *Union with Christ: John Calvin and the Mysticism of St. Bernard* (Louisville: Westminster/John Knox Press, 1994).

[41]Charles Partee, "Calvin's Central Dogma Again," *Sixteenth Century Journal* 18, no. 2 (Summer 1987): 191-199. See also Charles Partee, "Calvin's Polemic: Foundational Convictions in the Service of God's Truth," in *Calvinus Sincerioris Religionis Vindex*, 97-122, esp. 114-116.

itualize Calvin's idea of union with Christ—again, spiritualize in the sense of union having to do with a communion of the Christian's spirit with Christ's spirit.[42] Yet, what Calvin makes explicit is that the communion Christians have with Christ is with Christ's body, and that it is Christ's body that feeds first the Christian's soul but also the Christian's body. It is the body of Christ that nourishes the soul unto eternal life, but it is also the body that nourishes the Christian's flesh so that resurrection is assured.[43]

One of the centers of Calvin's thought, therefore, is the body of Christ as the food of the Christian. The body is the place of salvation. Without it, everything else goes. And it is here that David Wright's insight is helpful, I think, for grasping the importance of this concept in understanding Calvin, although I do not claim that Wright himself applies it to this particular assertion. He makes a more general point. Speaking to the International Calvin Congress, Wright said that we miss something important in Calvin if we assume that accommodation—which has received much attention since Ford Lewis Battle's essay on the subject—is only an exegetical tool for Calvin.[44] In other words, the assump-

---

[42]Tamburello, *Union with Christ*, 40, 100-101; but cf. 93.

[43]"Such is the presence of the body that the nature of the sacrament requires: one we say manifests itself here with a power and effectiveness so great that it not only brings undoubted assurance of eternal life to our hearts but also assures us of the immortality of our flesh. Indeed, it is now quickened by his immortal flesh, and in a sense partakes of his immortality." *Institutes*, 4.17.32; CO, 2:1033. Though the above passage is rare in Calvin in its explicitness relating Christ's resurrected flesh to the Christian's, one sees the logic of it at work less explicitly in a number of places. To "eat" Christ's body is to be united to him so that his life flows into the Christian; it is to be in union with him. "We must hold fast to that fellowship which the apostle proclaims: that we arise because Christ arose. For nothing is less likely than that our flesh, in which we bear about the death of Christ himself, should be deprived of Christ's resurrection." *Institutes*, 3.25.7; CO, 2: 738. There is here, it seems, a connection between being united to Christ and the resurrection of the flesh. Also in the same place, in speaking of the resurrection of the flesh, Calvin quotes Paul: "So that the life of Jesus Christ may be manifested in our mortal flesh." CO, 2: 736. When Calvin speaks of the life of Christ being manifested, he usually is speaking of his life in the body. The place Calvin cites is 2 Corinthians 4:11, where Calvin comments, "The best cure for adversity is to know that just as Christ's death was the gate of new life, so we at the end of all our miseries shall come to a blessed resurrection, for Christ has joined us to Himself on condition that if we submit ourselves to die with Him in this world [undergo suffering on behalf of the gospel], we shall share his life." Again, Christ's action in his body (to which Christians are joined and from which they are nourished) is related to resurrection of the flesh. John Calvin, *The Second Epistle of Paul to the Corinthians, and the Epistles to Timothy, Titus and Philemon*, tr. T. A. Small (Edinburgh: Oliver and Boyd, 1964; repr. Grand Rapids: Eerdmans, 1980), 60; CO, 50:55. Calvin also says that Christ's resurrection is the "substance" (hypostasis) of Christian resurrection. Calvin, *First Epistle of Paul to the Corinthians*, 318; CO, 49: 542, commenting on 1 Corinthians 15:12. Thus, Christian resurrection comes about by participation in the body of Christ, which for Calvin, every time he speaks explicitly of such, means a joining bodily to Christ.

[44]David F. Wright, "Calvin's Accommodating God," in *Calvinus Sincerioris Religionis Vindex*, 3-33, esp. 15-16, where Wright argues that accommodation affects not only the form but also the substance of revelation—God accommodates himself, his Word, and his will.

tion often made is that, in reading Scripture, Calvin uses the notion of accommodation to explain a particularly troublesome passage from the Bible—if the passage seems to attribute something to God unworthy of God, for example.[45] More to the point, however, is that accommodation plays a much bigger role in Calvin's thought: it is not just about explaining Scripture; it is the heart of Scripture. More than that, it is the heart of the Gospel, for the Gospel is Christ, and Christ in his humanity is the accommodation par excellence of God.[46]

Accommodation, therefore, is not simply a tool; it is not even primarily about the form of scriptural interpretation and theology; it is about the content of salvation. God reveals Godself to fallen humanity, God redeems fallen humanity, God sustains redeemed humanity through his action and presence in the body of Christ. The body of Christ is the *sine qua non* of Christian life. The Christian experience is nothing more and nothing less than participation in Christ's body. And that, for John Calvin, is how God is to be known. Scripture, Sacrament, and Preaching point to that body and present it; the Holy Spirit joins the Christian to it. Calvin was never able to fully comprehend, much less explain to others, the details of the mode of union. He was content simply to have experienced it, and, having experienced it, to bow down in praise and wonder. And if we miss that in Calvin, we miss everything.[47]

IV. What Now? Constructing a Legacy: Possible Directions

Once we recognize the importance of union with Christ and acknowledge that, for Calvin, such a union is a participation in the true body of Christ, what are we to do with it? One response would be simply to ignore it. One thinks back to the Nevin/Hodge debate of the nineteenth century, and one is reminded that much of the reformed tradition stands with Hodge. Nevin might have been one of the first to bring out Calvin's notion of mystical union, but just because it is in Calvin does not mean that the idea has to be dealt with. Many might agree with Hodge that, after all, the notion is a bit odd and is alien

---

[45]Although Calvin does use this as one way of employing the notion of accommodation, especially when speaking of how God spoke in terms accommodated to the "rudeness" of the ancient Hebrews. See *Institutes*, 1.14.3; CO, 2:199.

[46]See David F. Wright, "Calvin's Pentateuchal Criticism: Equity, Hardness of Heart, and Divine Accommodation in the Mosaic Commentary," *Calvin Theological Journal* 21 (1986): 33-50, esp. 44: "This ... commentary contains some instances of divine accommodation as impressive as any found in Calvin's other writings and pointing forward to the *supreme accommodation of God* to the measure of mankind in the incarnation" (emphasis mine).

[47]Battles, of course, makes much the same point on the "supreme act" of accommodation of God in Christ, in Ford Lewis Battles, "God Was Accommodating Himself to Human Capacity," *Interpretation* 31 (1977): 38, as he looks at Calvin's commentary on 1 Peter 1:20: "In Christ God, so to speak, makes himself little."
See letter to Peter Martyr Vermigli, CO, 15: 722-724; see also Calvin, *Epistles of Paul the Apostle to the Galatians, Ephesians, Philippians and Colossians*, 209; CO, 51: 227.

to Calvin's thought.[48] One is reminded here of the debates over the role of the body in Luther's teaching of the Lord's Supper. It has variously been called alien, left over Catholicism, and a renegade element that is best swept away by the more Protestant principle of justification by faith alone.[49] Yet, one reads essays such as that by Kyle Pasewark and realizes there are riches unrealized if one simply ignores the role of the presence of the body in Luther.[50] It might seem to some the more rational thing to do; it tidies things up a bit. But too much of real insight is lost if wrinkles are simply ironed out of theology.

What are we, then, to gain by taking seriously what Calvin himself took most seriously: the presence of Christ, especially in preaching? In the spirit of an exploratory first word, I will make several suggestions.

A. The Reclamation of Christ's Humanity in Preaching

I will put forward here a suggestion: given Calvin's own use of figures of speech—he knew well and spoke at length on metaphor, metonymy, and synecdoche—I think it not unwarranted to look for the ways figure of speech may help us out, or at least expand the horizon of possibilities, when speaking of the present Christ in Calvin.[51] Calvin himself spoke in one of his sermons about how truth is more forcefully conveyed when figures of speech are used.[52]

Perhaps it would be helpful to think of Calvin's talk of Christ's body as a synecdochal expression for Christ's human life. Synecdoche is, of course, a figure of speech in which a part is used to express the whole. To say I have a roof over my head means I have a house to live in. Roof is used to stand for the notion of house. In like manner, Calvin's insistence that we are saved by our participation in Christ's body and that we are fed by Christ's body can be read as drawing life from Christ's humanity. This is not to dispel the notion that when Calvin speaks of Christ's body he does not mean Christ's body—he means at least that.

---

[48]John Williamson Nevin, *The Mystical Presence: A Vindication of the Reformed or Calvinistic Doctrine of the Holy Eucharist* (Philadelphia: J. B. Lippincott, 1846; repr., Hamden, Connecticut: Archon Books, 1963); Charles Hodge, "Doctrine of the Reformed Church on the Lord's Supper," *Princeton Review* 20 (April 1848): 227, 275-277, 278.

[49] Paul Althaus, *The Theology of Martin Luther,* tr. Robert C. Schultz (Philadelphia: Fortress Press, 1966), 321-322; Adolph Harnack, *History of Dogma,* tr. Neil Buchanan from the 3rd German edition, in 7 vols., bound as 4 (Gloucester, Massachusetts: Peter Smith, 1976), 2: 267.

[50]Kyle Pasewark, "The Body in Ecstasy: Love, Difference, and the Social Organism in Luther's Theory of the Lord's Supper," *Journal of Religion* 77, no. 4 (October, 1997): 511-540.

[51]I take my cue from Calvin himself, as he talks about reading Scripture: "For it is important to know how Scripture uses words. Surely we need not stop simply at words, but we cannot understand the teaching [la doctrine] of God unless we know what procedure, style and language he uses." Calvin, *Sermons on the Saving Work of Christ,* 13; CO, 47: 465, commenting on John 1: 1-5.

[52]See note 17 above.

But the question is, does he mean more? I think that he does. Being human demands having a human body; we see Calvin is insistent on this in his eucharistic teaching, and one can read at length about this in his commentary on the Ascension in Acts.[53] But the reason Calvin demands that Christ's body remain in heaven, even in the eucharistic celebration—hence the requirement of the Christian being lifted up to heaven in mind and spirit to be joined with him there—is because body with its limitations is requisite for true humanity. And, for Calvin, Christ must retain full humanity even after resurrection because it is the humanity of Christ that is the mediatorial principle in Calvin's theology.[53] It is in the humanity of Christ that the Christian sees incarnated the will of God. It is the humanity of Christ to which the Christian has access.[54] Thus, while not denigrating, to be sure, the divine nature of Christ, it is the human nature of Christ and the deeds of the human Christ that serve as the revelation of God's plan of salvation. And it is in the acts of the body—hunger, thirst, pain, suffering, death, resurrection—that Christ is most clearly God's revelation. Any preaching that does not present the drama of Jesus' life, death, and resurrection from the perspective of his human life will not convey the heart of the Gospel.[55]

B. The Reclamation of Christ's Presence in Preaching

Returning to an earlier quote from Calvin, we read: "If the gospel be not preached, Jesus Christ is, as it were, buried."[56] How did Calvin mean this proclamation? Certainly, he did not mean it in an objective sense; the gospel history has a reality apart from the belief or unbelief, knowledge or ignorance, of individuals, groups, nations, and races. But the point for Calvin is that what he calls "bare history" is not of itself salvific. It is the joining to the present Christ that is salvific. And Christ is present, Calvin makes clear, clothed in the gospel, espe-

---

[53] John Calvin, *The Acts of the Apostles,* vol. 1, tr. W. J. G. McDonald (Edinburgh: Oliver and Boyd, 1965; Grand Rapids: Eerdmans, 1965), 21-26; CO, 48: 1-3, commenting on Acts 1: 1-2. See also Thomas J. Davis, "'He Is Outwith the World ... that He May Fill All Things': Calvin's Exegesis of the Ascension and the Eucharist," presented at the October 1998 annual meeting of the Sixteenth Century Studies Conference, Toronto, Ontario.

[54] "We must have recourse to this link [Jesus Christ in the flesh; the French "ceste union" is stronger than the word "link" implies] of God's majesty, and the state of man's nature together." Calvin, *Mystery of Godliness,* 15; CO, 53: 522, on 1 Timothy 3:16. As T. H. L. Parker has said, "when we think of the Word of God, we are not to imagine an unknown being; we are to think of Jesus of Nazareth." T. H. L. Parker, "Calvin's Concept of Revelation," part II: "The Revelation of God the Redeemer," *Scottish Journal of Theology* 2 (1949): 339. See also note 38.

[55] As Calvin says, "Let those who want to discharge the ministry of the Gospel aright learn not only to speak and declaim but also to penetrate into consciences, so that men may see Christ crucified and that His blood may flow." Calvin, *Epistles of Paul the Apostle to the Galatians, Ephesians, Philippians and Colossians,* 47; CO, 50: 202-203, commenting on Galatians 3: 1-5.

[56] See note 19.

cially the gospel as preached. Language, the words the preacher preaches, is the tool by which God makes present the Word, Christ incarnate.[57]

It is of some interest that one of the most innovative homiliticians of our own time has built his career examining the very question under consideration here: the presence of Christ via the Word. David Buttrick, in a remarkable series of books, has done much to educate ministers about the power of words to form consciousness. What is more, Buttrick has detailed how words make reality present to consciousness. In his *Preaching Jesus Christ*, among other works, Buttrick shows how the reality of Christ is tied to our proclamation of him, and how much of that proclamation is tied to concrete metaphors.[58] Much of what he has done can be related to Calvin's sentiment: without preaching, Christ remains buried. Again, this is not to be taken in an absolute sense, but it is indicative of the importance of preaching as an ordained tool for making Christ present with his church.

C. The Reclamation of a Present Faith

Another point at which there is some convergence between Calvin and Buttrick: Christian faith is about the present life. Now, of course, Calvin does speak of the future life; indeed, some have said that the whole of Calvin's theology is a meditation upon the future life.[59] But here is one of those cases where Ford Lewis Battle's *calculus fidei*[60] comes in handy; Calvin does have a concern for the future life, but his concern is not solely about the future life, and to so read Calvin would be to undo the balance he has struck between future and present, between hope and faith.

Another of Buttrick's books speaks of *The New and the Now.* In talking of preaching, he details how one's sermons cannot simply be a dwelling in the past—that is to confine God's activity to the past. That is why, for all the helpfulness of the historical-critical method in biblical exegesis, preaching cannot finally simply be a recapitulation of the findings of the historical-critical method, because that imprisons the message of the gospel in the unreachable past.[61] Antiquarianism can be interesting; it is not the basis for a changed life.

---

[57]Preaching on John 1: 1-5, Calvin says, "When the gospel is proclaimed to us, it is a manifestation of Jesus Christ." Calvin, *Sermons on the Saving Work of Christ*, 14; CO, 47: 466; preaching on 2 Timothy 1: 9-10, Calvin says, "Jesus Christ shows Himself openly to those who have the eyes of faith to look up to Him, when the gospel is preached." Calvin, *Mystery of Godliness*, 48; CO, 54: 61.

[58]David Buttrick, *Preaching Jesus Christ* (Philadelphia: Fortress Press, 1988).

[59]Martin Schulze, *Meditatio futurae vitae: ihre Begriff und ihre Stellung im System Calvins* (Leipzig: Dieterich, 1901).

[60]"Hope of the future life should feed our present life and give it meaning and purpose." Battles, "Calculus Fidei," 105.

[61]David Buttrick, *Preaching the New and the Now* (Louisville: Westminster/John Knox Press, 1998); see also his article that relates some of the problems of preaching to the problems of the historical-critical method in David Buttrick, "Interpretation and Preaching," *Interpretation* 35, no. 1 (January

To speak of a present faith is not simply to believe something once happened; neither is it simply to believe that something will happen. A present faith sees a living Christ working among his elect now, under all the contraries of historical ambiguity, secure enough in the foundations of Christ's historical works and hopeful enough of that work's glorious and universal completion to act now as part of the new creation.[62]

What is more, Christian preaching cannot be about a future that does not impinge on the present. Eschatology is less about the future per se than it is about how God's future works itself into present experience and expression. I think this corresponds well to Calvin's understanding: in the Christ who is present, Christ's past action is wed to his future kingdom, and the Christian finds herself in a community living out God's purpose with Christ as her head.

D. The Reclamation of a Community of Faith

The last sentence points to another way in which a legacy constructed from Calvin's thought on preaching would be helpful: Calvin preached to a community. What is more, he preached to a community with the understanding that through the instrument of preaching Christ himself would be present and, as present, would serve as the head of a body. Christ is not the savior of individuals; he is the savior of the church, to which individuals are joined by the Holy Spirit as members of one body. Christian faith for Calvin is personal and experiential, but it is not individualistic.[63]

Here it would be helpful to remind ourselves about Calvin's understanding of hermeneutics as he went about the task of exegesis and homiletics. Calvin believed figures of speech had their foundation in something real and, if you like, literal. Though he appreciated metaphor and used it, at the root of all metaphor is a literal reality that serves as the guarantee for the truthfulness of figures of speech.[64]

1981): 46-58, esp. 49. The point is not that the historical-critical method cannot be helpful or should not be used; rather, it is that a simple recapitulation of its findings does not make for preaching, because preaching is about *now*. Buttrick also deals with the problem of treating the text like an "object," aping some of the assumptions more appropriate to scientific inquiry.

[62] On the past's relationship to the present, DeVries says, "The sermon does not merely point back to saving events that happened in the life of the Jesus of history, but rather *itself conveys*, or is the medium of, the presence of Christ in the church. DeVries, *Jesus Christ in the Preaching of Calvin and Schleiermacher*, 95. On the future's relation to the present, Paul Fuhrmann is perceptive when he says that "Calvin's works have a *tension toward the future*." Paul T. Fuhrmann, "Calvin the Expositor of Scripture," *Interpretation* 6 (1952): 203. Buttrick seems to me to be a good Calvinist when he says, "We preach from future promise to present tense," and "Our hope is grounded in a sense of God's future purposes that, in a way, are coming to us everyday." Buttrick, *Preaching the New and the Now*, 135, 140.

[63]See note 67 below.

[64]See Robert H. Ayers, "Language, Logic and Reason in Calvin's *Institutes*," *Religious Studies* 16 (1980): 289, where he talks of Calvin's "need for grounding metaphors in something of literal significance."

Thus, it is the body of Christ literally, the integrity of the "continuing flesh of Jesus," as Charles Partee puts it,[65] that is at the heart of all talk of the church as the body of Christ. The church as the body of Christ is tied to the real body of Christ; the union of Christ with Christians in body serves as the foundation for the union of Christians with one another in that holy fellowship of the church. At the base of Calvin's talk of the body as a metaphor for the church is a literal body, and that matches for him the reality of Christian faith; it also is consistent with his exegetical method. One sees this relationship ordered in Calvin's exegesis of 1 Corinthians 11, the passage where Paul exhorts the Corinthians to discern the body of Christ in the Eucharist. Luther, of course, thought this discernment had to do only with Christ's true body; Zwingli said this discernment had to do with the church as the body of Christ. Calvin says it is about both; first, it is about the true body of Christ, and this is primary. But the discernment of the social body of Christ, the church, flows from this first discernment. The church as body rests upon Christ's own body present.[66]

This means, by nature, Christian experience is always experience within the context of the church as the body of believers.[67] This is a message that needs to be grasped, appreciated, and communicated. There is a well-known study of Calvin's spirituality that ends with Calvin as an individualist.[68] He is not. The body of Christ serves as the foundation for the body of the church. And, in a culture that currently sees spirituality as individualistic and anti-church if not

---

[65]Partee, "Calvin's Polemic," 98.

[66]See Thomas J. Davis, "Discerning the Body: The Eucharist and the Social Body in Sixteenth-Century Protestant Exegesis," presented at the October 1996 annual meeting of the Sixteenth Century Studies Conference, St. Louis, Missouri. One might say, just as the eucharistic bread, when presented, must remain bread to be truly significative of Christ's body, so Christ's body, when used significatively of the church, must remain true body according to Calvin's principle of similitude between sign and thing signified. See especially, *Institutes*, 4.17.15; CO, 2: 1015: "Let it therefore remain certain that in the Supper the flesh of Christ is not truly and fittingly promised to us to be truly food unless the true substance of the outward symbol corresponds to it."

[67]Indeed, Calvin seems to equate reception in the church with engrafting into Christ (*Institutes*, 4.15.1; CO, 2: 962). What is more, preaching belongs to the church, because God "deposited this treasure in the church" (*Institutes*, 4.1.1; CO, 2: 745). Also, see Calvin's comments at Ephesians 4:16 on the corporate nature of Christian faith. Calvin, *Epistles of Paul the Apostle to the Galatians, Ephesians, Philippians and Colossians*, 185; CO, 51: 203. As has been observed, "Calvin asserts that God deals not so much with individuals, as with people in community." G. S. M. Walker, "Calvin and the Church," in *Readings in Calvin's Theology*, 220. Tamburello also puts it well: "Thus, Christ's promises are made to individuals, but only insofar as they are members of the community." Tamburello, *Union with Christ*, 97. Thus, there is a nice balance between the personal and the communal. The experience of God is personal, but it has as its context the community of the redeemed. This is not indivdualism.

[68]Lucien Joseph Richard, *The Spirituality of John Calvin* (Atlanta: John Knox, 1974), esp. 17, 180-183.

altogether anti-religion,[69] a reclamation of Calvin's corporate vision of the church is sorely needed.[70]

E. The Reclamation of Love Acting from Faith

Finally, a word about Christian action in the world. Calvin is perceived to be so other-worldly by some that one is certain they have never read his work, or so misread his work because of such strong preconceptions about who Calvin is. An anecdote, with name politely withheld.

I was at a major presentation by someone who is head of a well-known, prestigious school. In talking about religion for the public good, she told a story about serving on a dissertation committee that oversaw a student's work on Calvin's actions on behalf of the poor.[71] She expressed amazement. "Who would have thought Calvin would care anything about this-worldly concerns like food," she exclaimed. Of course, many of us know quite well, thanks to the work of a number of scholars, that Calvin was interested in the way the church was to care for the poor. But think of that assumption! This scholar had an image of Calvin as so other-worldly that she had a hard time reconciling her preconceptions (misconceptions) about Calvin with the textual evidence in the dissertation.

To reclaim Calvin's notion of the bodily presence of Christ in preaching is to reclaim a Christ whose presence as human demands attention be paid to humanity. Calvin saw flowing from faith in Christ and him crucified a love that

---

[69]See Robert Wuthnow, *After Heaven: Spirituality in America since the 1950s* (Berkeley: University of California Press, 1998), 2: "Most Americans say their spirituality is private—that it must develop without the guidance of religious institutions." See also 74, 76-77.

[70]See again note 67 and Calvin's comments of Ephesians 4: 16, which are stunning in the way they understand the interconnectedness of body. As one would expect, his vision and concern comes out in sermons as well. For example: "Let us be so united [to Christ], that it may be not only for each one of us that such a thing may be said, but for all in general. Let us have mutual concord and brotherhood together, since He has sustained and borne the condemnation which was pronounced by God His Father upon us all. So let us aim at that, and let each one come here not only for himself (as I have said), but let him try to draw his companions to it, and let us so urge one another on to walk steadfastly, noticing always that our life is a road which must be followed to the end, and that we must not grow weary in the middle of the journey, but let us profit so much day by day and let us take trouble to approach those who are out of the road; let this be all our joy, our life, our glory and contentment, and let us so help one another until God has fully gathered us to himself." Calvin, *Sermons on the Saving Work of Christ*, 65; CO, 46: 846, commenting on Matthew 26: 36-39. On the notion of individual spirituality outside the church: "We shall not have access to God by prayer, unless we be joined together; for he that separates himself from his neighbors shuts his own mouth, so that he cannot pray to God as our Lord Jesus Christ has commanded." Calvin, *Mystery of Godliness*, 189; CO, 53: 190, commenting on 1 Timothy 2:8.

[71]See Jeanine E. Olson, *Calvin and Social Welfare: Deacons and the Bourse Française* (Cranbury, New Jersey: Susquehanna University Press, 1989); and Elsie Anne McKee, *John Calvin: On the Diaconate and Liturgical Almsgiving* (Geneva: Librairie Droz, 1984).

cared for neighbors in not only spirit but also body. And a faith that proclaims Christ present bodily cannot be accused of being anti-body, and a faith that announces Christ's presence announces God's presence as well, as one who dwells near unto God's people.[72]

V. Conclusion

It has been argued that "the uneasy relations between presence and absence . . . are the dialectical conditions of Western metaphor."[73] If, at root, language about God must be accommodated, as Calvin thought, then we are left with that unforgettable phrase from the works of the poet W. S. Merwyn: "Language [is] a vehicle of the unsayable."[74] Presence and absence. Christ is in heaven bodily—absence. You are joined to Christ bodily by the Spirit's work—presence. God is transcendent—absence. God is near; look at Christ bodily—presence. Christians are engaged in the work of mystery, of declaring the hidden and revealed God.[75] Calvin's work teaches that the proclamation of that mystery comes through the humble instrument of preaching. Language is, indeed, the vehicle of the unsayble. No wonder the Holy Spirit must bless the words and work their outcome. And that, as Calvin also teaches, is not a cause for resignation, but a call to preparation.[76]

---

[72]"Let us remember that the Word of God is preached to us, that God dwelleth among us, and is present with us." Calvin, *Mystery of Godliness*, 118; CO, 53: 309, commenting on 1 Timothy 3: 14-15.

[73]Ed Folsom and Carey Nelson, "Introduction" to W. S. Merwyn, *Regions of Memory: Uncollected Prose, 1949-1982* (Urbana: University of Illinois Press, 1987), 1. Battles says something similar of Calvin, though in a more positive way: "Our grasp of all Christian truth has this dynamic polarity—between absence and presence, between nothing and infinity." Battles, "Calculus Fidei," 104.

[74]Merwyn, *Regions of Memory*, 199. It is interesting to relate this to Alister McGrath's statement that "Calvin does not, and does not believe that it is possible to, reduce God or Christian experience to words." He goes on to talk of the way he perceives Calvin to view the relationship between the experience of the risen Christ to the words that channel that experience. See Alister D. McGrath, *A Life of John Calvin: A Study in the Shaping of Western Culture* (Oxford: Blackwell, 1990), 132.

[75]A nice entry into the notion of the hidden God in Calvin's thought is Brian A. Gerrish, "'To the Unknown God': Luther and Calvin on the Hiddenness of God," in *The Old Protestantism and the New: Essays on the Reformation Heritage* (Chicago: University of Chicago Press, 1982), 131-149.

[76]As note 28 indicates, Calvin thought preaching powerless without the work of the Holy Spirit. From a human perspective, however, one must prepare to be used by the Spirit, especially if one is to preach. As Calvin states in a sermon on Deuteronomy 5: 23-27, "No one will be a good minister of the word of God unless that one be first of all a scholar." CO, 26: 406. This is said by Calvin in the context of stating (a) that God has set up the ministry of the Word to announce God's teachings unto salvation; and (b) that such an office is obviously different than that performed by the prelates of the Roman church.

A Response to "Preaching and Presence:
Constructing Calvin's Homiletical Legacy"

Randall C. Zachman

Thomas Davis has rightly noted that the legacy of John Calvin has in large part been dominated by the idea of the incomprehensible transcendence of God. This of course is no accident, since Calvin frames his understanding of the self-revelation of God in terms of the immense magnitude and altitude of God, due to God's infinite and spiritual essence. However, Calvin always juxtaposes the transcendence of God with the real presence of God among us and for us in Jesus Christ and our intimate union with Christ by faith and the Holy Spirit. This leads Davis directly to his thesis, namely, that the legacy which Calvin wished to hand on to subsequent generations is the real presence of Christ among us, both in preaching and in the sacraments, and that this is precisely the legacy which has been dropped by the subsequent Reformed tradition. Hence, according to Davis, the task at hand is not to describe the legacy which Calvin left to us, since that has been dropped, but rather to construct such a legacy, and to do so around the centrality of union with Christ, and especially union with the body of Christ, as the center of Christian faith and life. Davis writes, "The body of Christ is the sine qua non of Christian life. The Christian experience is nothing more and nothing less than participation in the body. And that, for Calvin, is how God is to be known. Scripture, Sacrament, and Preaching point to that body and present it; the Holy Spirit joins the Christian to it. . . . And if we miss that in Calvin, we miss everything."

Davis is to be commended for stressing so strongly the centrality of union with Christ for Calvin. I am in complete agreement with him when he claims that Calvin describes the preaching of the gospel as the self-representation and the self-presentation of Jesus Christ himself with all his benefits, to be received by faith through the power and illumination of the Holy Spirit. Since Calvin equates the purpose of preaching with the purpose of the sacraments, Davis is also correct to use what Calvin says about the Holy Supper of the Lord to reinforce the centrality of the self-presentation of Christ in preaching. If Nevin, Gerrish, and Davis are correct in claiming that the Reformed tradition abandoned this theme of the self-presentation of Christ in the gospel, then it would seem that Davis's thesis is correct, at least when it comes to Calvin's description of the goal of preaching.

Davis also wants to counter certain spiritualizing interpretations of Calvin which so stress the role of the Holy Spirit in uniting us to Christ that they miss the centrality of the actual body of Christ as the locus of our union with him. Davis uses to great effect the way Calvin, in his comments on Ephesians 5:32, appeals to the mystery of our communion with the body and blood of Christ in his description of the mystery of our union with Christ himself: "In short, Paul [here] describes our union to Christ, a symbol and pledge of which is given in the Holy Supper." Davis is right to stress the central role that the body of Christ plays for Calvin. Even though, as he notes, Calvin can use the body of Christ as a *synechdoche* for the humanity of Christ, and even though it is the Spirit which is the bond of our union with Christ, and not the Incarnation itself, Davis is nonetheless correct that the gospel and the Holy Spirit unite us especially to the body of Christ, which is the source of all we need for eternal life. Thus when Calvin comments on the statement in Ephesians that "they two shall become one flesh," he says, "Such is the union between us and Christ, that in a sense he pours himself into us. For we are not bone of his bone, and flesh of his flesh, because, like ourselves, He is human, but because, by the power of his Spirit, He engrafts us into His Body (*in corpus suum inserit*), so that from him we derive life."[1]

However, I think that Davis overstates the role of our communion with the Body of Christ when he says, "It is the body of Christ that nourishes the soul unto eternal life but it is also the body that nourishes the Christian's flesh so that resurrection is assured." I do not recall Calvin ever saying this. To the contrary, in his description of the analogy of the sign to the thing signified in the Holy Supper, Calvin always says that just as the bread and wine nourish our bodies with life, so also the body and blood of Christ nourish our souls to eternal life. The body of Christ is the spiritual food of our souls, not of our bodies. The position Davis puts forth was one justification Luther gave for the oral eating of Christ's body and blood.

If Davis is right in stating that the main purpose of preaching is our incomprehensible spiritual union with the body of Christ, then the primary gulf which preaching bridges is not, as Davis often suggests, the past and the present, but rather Christ's ascended humanity and his members on earth. The problem which preaching addresses is not the making present of a past event, but rather the making present of an absent person. Davis hits the nail on the head when he says that by the Holy Spirit Christ truly comes in the spoken word in order to lift his people to himself in heaven, and again in the conclusion, where he addresses the dichotomy between absence and presence; but the rest of the paper uses a past-present dichotomy which does not fit Calvin. Ironically, because of the ascension, the same body of Christ which mediates between the transcendent God and humanity must itself be mediated to us by the power of

---

[1] CO 51:226C; CNTC 11:209.

the Holy Spirit through the instruments of preaching and the sacraments, since it is now in heaven, not on earth.

Although Davis focuses on union with the body of Christ as the primary legacy of Calvin's preaching, he also discusses Calvin's actual method of preaching, both as studied historically by T. H. L. Parker, and as studied rhetorically by scholars such as Millet and Bouwsma. Davis rightly notes that Calvin's method of preaching built on his exegetical practice, which had as its goal revealing the mind of the author by a contextual reading of Scripture. Hence the commentaries on Scripture and the weekday sermons both follow the method of *lectio continua*, since such a reading best reveals the meaning from the context. Davis also notes that the commentaries were primarily pedagogical and written with lucid brevity, whereas the sermons were both didactic and persuasive, with their persuasive force coming from the use of metaphorical speech: "This seems to be an extremely important principle in Calvin's preaching; though he does, in fact, for pedagogical reasons, want to make the things of Scripture clear, he also wants to make those things clearly present to the heart of believers."

It seems to me that Davis could clarify his interpretation of Calvin if he substituted "doctrine" for "things." In both his commentaries and his sermons, Calvin seeks to draw fruitful doctrine from Scripture, but unlike the lucid brevity of the commentaries, in his sermons Calvin goes to great lengths to apply this doctrine to the lives of the members of his congregation, so that it takes root in the inmost affection of their hearts, and transforms their lives. One can see this difference simply by looking at the passage from Paul to which Davis refers, Ephesians 5:28-33. Calvin's comments on this passage take up less than three columns in the *Corpus Reformatorum*, whereas his sermons on the same passage take up two full sermons, and fill over 23 columns.

However, as important as teaching and persuasion are to Calvin's actual sermons, Davis claims that Calvin's method of preaching is secondary to the goal of preaching, i.e., union with the body of Christ. This brings me to the central question which Davis's paper raises for me. If it is true that the goal of preaching is the self-presentation of Christ, so that we might be united to the body of Christ by faith through the power of the Holy Spirit, then the method which Calvin consistently adopted in his preaching cannot be secondary to that goal, but must be the right way to reach that goal. In other words, the legacy which Calvin wished to hand on was both the goal and the right way to reach that goal, and he did not think a person could have one without the other. The fact that Christ was not present in power in the Roman Church was for Calvin directly related to the way they treated Scripture in their teaching and in their sermons, in tandem with their prohibition of the private reading of Scripture by ordinary Christians. Christ will only be present anew with power if sermons clearly and persuasively present the doctrine of Scripture to the congregation, and if the congregation reads Scripture for itself. It is therefore not accurate to say, as Davis does, that for Calvin Christ comes to us primarily in the gospel proclaimed, for this sounds more like Luther. Calvin insists that Christ is known with power only when preachers preach doctrine drawn from Scripture, and the congregation reads Scripture for itself, under the guidance of godly pastors.

Calvin thought the main problem preachers of his day confronted was not the bridging of the past and the present, but rather bridging the gap between doctrine and life in evangelical congregations. Calvin insisted that the gospel "is a doctrine not of the tongue but of life. It is not apprehended by the understanding and memory alone, as other disciplines are, but it is received only when it possesses the whole soul, and finds a seat and resting place in the inmost affection of the heart" (*Institutes*, 3.6.4). Calvin does not mean that the understanding and memory do not play a central role in the transformation of life, as Davis himself suggests when he says that matters of memory do not interest Calvin. In his sermons, Calvin repeatedly claims that the lives of the members of the congregation are disordered because they fail to keep in mind and remember the doctrine taught them by God in Scripture. A constant refrain in the sermons is the formulaic phrase, "That is what we must bear in mind (*a retinir*) in this passage."

Moreover, Calvin's favorite method of seeking to move the congregation is not, as Davis suggests, the metaphor, but rather the interior dialogue which reveals the thoughts of the heart, first when one does not have the doctrine of Scripture in mind, and then by contrast when one does. Hence when he preaches on Ephesians 5:28-30, he imagines the interior conversation of a husband who is unmindful of the doctrine taught by Paul. He says of his wife, "I cannot live with her, she is a mad beast, there is nothing in her but pride and haughtiness and rebelliousness." He then imagines the interior monologue of the husband who remembers the doctrine of Paul. Even though he is not blind to her faults, he thinks thus with himself, "Yet I am bound to her; yes, and I am not only bound to my wife but also to God, who presides over marriage, and to Jesus Christ, who is like a mirror and living image of it to us."[2] Hence in his sermons Calvin wants us always to remember and keep in mind the doctrine of Scripture, so that we think differently in our hearts about one another and ourselves, and thereby transform our lives.

In conclusion, I am not sure that Calvin has only one understanding of the gospel, as Davis suggests, i.e., the instrument God uses to unite us to the flesh of Christ. Calvin also understands the gospel as edifying doctrine that should build up the repentance and faith of the congregation, and as the scepter of Christ whereby he establishes the kingdom of God on earth. Both of these understandings of the gospel emphasize our obedience to and transformation by the gospel. It seems to me that these are the goals to which Calvin primarily attends in his actual preaching. For Calvin, the pastor "is to proclaim the Word of God, to instruct, admonish, exhort and censure, both in public and in pri-

---

[2] *Sermons on Ephesians* (Edinburgh: Banner of Truth Trust, 1973; revision of trans. by Arthur Golding), 596-7.

vate, to administer the sacraments and to enjoin brotherly corrections along with the elders and colleagues" (*Draft Ecclesiological Ordinances, 1541*). In this regard, Calvin left a rather potent legacy in the preaching of those who came to be called the pietists, for they, like Calvin, devoted most of their efforts to bridging the gap between the doctrine their congregations professed, and the lives they actually led.

Calvin's Socio-Political Legacy: Collective Government, Resistance to Tyranny, Discipline

by Robert M. Kingdon

There are three aspects of Calvin's socio-political legacy upon which I would like to dwell: first is a commitment to collective government; second is an endorsement of resistance to tyrannical government; and third is an insistence upon the maintenance of discipline in any community that claims to be Christian.

I. Collective Government[1]

In a celebrated passage in his *Institutes*, Calvin declares a special preference among all the various types of government for "aristocracy, or a system compounded of aristocracy and democracy" (*Institutes*, 4.20.8). For Calvin this was not solely a matter of theory. It was also a guiding principle for governments in which he became personally involved. The shape of Calvin's preference for collective government can be more fully discerned if one looks at the constitutions Calvin drafted for the Reformed community in Geneva. One was the set of ecclesiastical ordinances he drafted alone in 1541, soon after his return from Strasbourg to take over general direction of the Genevan church. It was to serve as the constitution for the local church for generations. The other was the set of ordinances on offices and officers he helped draft in 1543, as the most talented member of a small committee appointed to codify the rules governing the Genevan state. It was to serve as the constitution for the Genevan state for generations.[2]

---

[1]In developing this first theme, I turn to a topic I have discussed in lectures in Geneva, at Harvard, and in a seminar at the International Calvin Research Congress held in Debrecen, Hungary, in 1986. Robert M. Kingdon, "Calvin et la constitution genevoise," in *Actualité de la Réforme: vingt-quatre leçons présentées par la Faculté de théologie de l'Université de Genève à l'Auditoire de Calvin dans le cadre du 450e anniversaire de la Réformation, 1536-1986*, no. 12 in *Publications de la Faculté de Théologie de l'Université de Genève* (Geneva: Labor et Fides, 1987), 209-219; "Calvinus Legislator: the 1543 'constitution' of the City-State of Geneva," in Wilhelm H. Neuser, ed., *Calvinus Servus Christi: die Referate des ... International Congress on Calvin Research, vom 25 bis 28 August 1986 in Debrecen* (Budapest, 1988), 225-232.

[2]*Les Sources du droit du Canton de Genève*, vol. 2, published by Emile Rivoire and Victor van Berchem (Arau: Sauerländer, 1930), 2: 377-390: "Ordonnances ecclésiastiques," 20 nov. 1541; 2:409-434: "Ordonnance sur les offices et officiers," 28 jan. 1543.

Calvin thus deserves credit for writing two constitutions, one ecclesiastical and the other secular. Both of these constitutions display a strong preference for collective government. Neither of them incorporates any trace of the preference for monarchic or one-man government that most thinkers of the sixteenth century preferred, that most, indeed, felt was the only really natural way of organizing a society.

The ecclesiastical ordinances provided that the church be governed by a Company of Pastors, including all those formally hired for preaching service in that church. It further provided that this Company would meet once a week for discussing Scripture, in order to maintain a unified theological front before the entire community. One of its members was supposed to serve as secretary and to keep Registers of the Company's meetings. In the early years, those Registers were not kept regularly, and the surviving records of them are patchy.[3] There are enough of them, however, to give us some idea of how the Company functioned. They suggest that the Company took responsibility for the joint planning of the routine of local services and other measures designed to keep the local church healthy. They reveal that it could, on occasion, become deeply involved in local theological controversy, most notably in the trials of Jerome Bolsec, focused on the doctrine of predestination, and of Michael Servetus, focused on the doctrine of the Trinity. They suggest that it regularly included sessions of mutual criticism, in which its members frankly pointed out the shortcomings of their colleagues and admitted their own shortcomings. In later years, the Company also spent a certain amount of time in discussing strategies for spreading Reformed Christianity to other communities, especially in selecting pastors for new churches in France. These Registers reveal that the Company of Pastors always took action as a body. The sentences condemning Bolsec and Servetus, for example, were signed by every member of the Company.

It is true that Calvin became the Moderator of this Company. There was no provision in the ordinances for the office of Moderator and little in the Registers to indicate what he did. In practice it seems to have meant that Calvin called meetings of the Company, that he presided over those meetings, and that he represented the Company in negotiations with the city government. Even in this capacity, however, he often did not act alone. He was often accompanied in appearances before the governing Small Council of the city with some of his fellow pastors. He was always careful to explain that he spoke for the Company as a whole, that he was never expressing a purely personal opinion. When Calvin died, Theodore Beza became his successor as Moderator, but from the beginning there was some resentment within the Company at his preeminence. His continuing role as Moderator seems to have been as much the

---

[3] *Registres de la Compagnie des Pasteurs de Genève au temps de Calvin*, edited by Jean-François Bergier and Robert M. Kingdon, 2 vols. (Geneva: Droz, 1962-1964).

city government's preference for Beza as a spokesman with whom they felt comfortable negotiating as the preference of the other ministers. Finally in 1580, Beza refused to continue as Moderator.[4] From then on the position rotated from one minister to another, sometimes as often as once a week, in more recent times for terms of one or more years. It has generally been felt that any minister has the ability to serve as Moderator, to meet the obvious practical needs of providing someone who can take responsibility for presiding over meetings and negotiating on the Company's behalf with the outside world. It has generally been felt that it would be unwise to delegate these responsibilities to any one person for extended periods of time, to ask any minister to become a specialist in things administrative.

This preference for collective government of the church spread to other countries. It became particularly strong and obvious in France. There the church came to be governed by a hierarchy of collective bodies: a consistory within the local community, made up of pastors, elders, and deacons; a colloquy within an area containing several communities; a provincial synod within each one, if possible, of the provinces into which France was divided for administrative purposes; a national synod charged with defining the faith and regulating discipline for the Reformed within the entire kingdom. In all of these bodies, rule was collective. In none was supreme power delegated to any one person. Even the national synods elected a Moderator only to serve as the presiding officer during the meetings at which they assembled every few years. When the synod adjourned, the position of Moderator ended. There was no one person charged with implementing the decisions of a synod in succeeding months. Only the collective bodies at lower levels held any powers of enforcement.[5]

These institutions were all overtly and consciously anti-monarchic. None of them, however, can really be called democratic. The members of the Geneva Company of Pastors were chosen in this way: the city government would first authorize a search, the existing pastors would then examine a potential candidate and decide if he was qualified to join them, their recommendation would be reviewed and normally ratified by the city government, the proposed new candidate would finally be presented to the parish in which he was to serve. If everyone involved in this process was in agreement the new candidate would finally be put on the city payroll. Of these steps, the crucial one was the examination by the Company of Pastors. It alone normally identified candidates. Its

[4]Olivier Labarthe, "En marge de l'édition des Registres de la Compagnie des pasteurs de Genève: le changement du mode de présidence de la Compagnie, 1578-1580," in *Revue d'histoire ecclésiastique suisse*, vol. 67 (1972), 160-186.

[5]Glenn S. Sunshine, "From French Protestantism to the French Reformed Churches: the Development of Huguenot Ecclesiastical Institutions, 1559-1598," Ph.D. dissertation, University of Wisconsin-Madison, 1992.

approval was essential before the process could go any further. The system, therefore, was basically one of co-optation. One may discern a kind of popular check upon the selection of pastors, particularly in the final presentation of a candidate to his parish. But there is never any question of a pastor being elected by or being a representative of the community as a whole.

Similarly the delegates to colloquies and synods in France were chosen by virtue of office, because they were already pastors or elders or deacons in local churches. They were never elected to represent a local constituency. If one wants to apply a label to this form of government, the obvious one is the classic term "aristocracy," although not, of course, an aristocracy of birth, rather one of talent.

These forms of ecclesiastical government often find parallels in secular government within Calvinist communities. In the city of Geneva, power was vested in a hierarchy of councils. At the top of the hierarchy was the Small Council of about twenty-five members, from old citizen families, elected once every year, but in times of stability generally re-elected year after year. From that Council four members were chosen every year to be syndics, executives who presided over meetings of both the Council and of some of its most important committees, and who represented Geneva to the general population and the outside world. One of them was entitled to carry a baton which was a symbol of sovereignty. But no man could serve as syndic for more than a year. Each syndic had to return to the ranks of the Council at the end of his term, and was normally not re-elected for a period of several years.

Below the Small Council in Geneva, there was a Council of Sixty that met periodically to consider certain kinds of important issues, often in foreign policy, and a Council of Two Hundred that met periodically to consider other kinds of important issues, for example appeals of judicial decisions by the Small Council. The Council of Two Hundred was a comparatively new institution, created in the sixteenth century in imitation of a similar council in Bern. The Small Council and the Council of Sixty (or earlier Fifty) had been created centuries earlier by the ruling prince-bishop who was then Geneva's sovereign, to give residents of the city some measure of local autonomy. Below these three councils there was a Grand Council, of all the citizens and bourgeois of the republic, all the men of property and reputation. It met at least once a year to engage in the annual elections that renewed the government. It also met on occasion to act on particularly important matters, for example to adopt the act that severed all connection with Catholicism and made of Geneva a Protestant republic in 1536. [6]

The functions of all of these councils, and of the agents they elected to carry out various duties, are described in detail in the edict on offices and officers

---

[6]*Encyclopédie de Genève*, vol. 4: *Les institutions politiques, judiciaires, et militaires* (Fribourg, 1985), 86-87, 200-203, and works there cited.

Calvin helped draft in 1543. It may be fairly called Geneva's new constitution, replacing the earlier ecclesiastical government in which a single person, the prince-bishop, held ultimate sovereign powers, with a new government in which all powers were exercised collectively. This new government was really an aristocracy, with sovereign power vested in a group of twenty-five men. It might be called an aristocracy compounded with democracy, in that each of these men was required to stand for re-election every year, and in times of crisis a few might be replaced. It might also be called a government compounded with democracy in that a few crucial decisions were made not by the Small Council alone but by subordinate councils, including the General Council made up of all the citizens and bourgeois. But there was no role in this government for men without property, a tightly restricted role for men who had immigrated from other countries, and no role at all, of course, for women. Real power was exercised most of the time by a small group of twenty-five men.

Calvin cannot be said to have created this secular government, in the way that he had created the ecclesiastical government of Geneva. Still he had played a significant role in its consolidation by helping to codify the laws that gave it shape. And he was clearly more comfortable in working with a government of this type than with a monarchic government. The government of Geneva, to be sure, was much like the government of free city-states all over Europe, most notably in Germany and Switzerland, but to a degree in parts of Italy and other countries. All were committed to collective rule; none encouraged rule by single individuals. All were sensitive to public opinion; none provided enough direct participation in government to deserve the label of democracy.

Calvinists did not insist on working with secular governments that were collective. They were prepared to work with monarchies that supported their religious policies. In Scotland they worked with a monarchic government. In Germany, they often worked with governments run by single hereditary princes. In eastern Europe, they also worked with monarchic governments. But the correlation with collective secular government was common, in Switzerland, in the Netherlands, in certain imperial cities of the Holy Roman Empire. I think it fair to say that a preference for collective government is a significant part of the socio-political legacy of Calvinism, that Calvinists almost always preferred collective government for their churches and that they often preferred collective government for the states in which they lived.

II. Resistance to Tyranny

In developing this second theme, I turn to a topic which I discussed at more length at the International Congress on Calvin Research in Seoul, Korea, last August, in 1998. From the very beginning, French Protestants were convinced that there was one thing that they must resist. That was participation in the Catholic Mass. They had persuaded themselves that the Mass was a form of idolatry, that it involved the worship of manmade objects, specifically pieces of bread and cups of wine. They believed that it was one of the forms of idolatry the Old Testament reveals is despised by the Lord God. They believed that the continuing practice of this form of idolatry may well bring down divinely commanded disaster on any community that permits it. That is the clear message of the notorious placards of 1534, posted all around France by a group of radical Protestants, provoking violent reactions and bitter persecution from authorities, persuading many Protestants to leave the kingdom and to go into exile abroad. The message of these placards is summarized neatly by their title: "Articles veritables sur les horribles, grand & importables abuz de la Messe papalle: inventes directement contre la saincte Cene de Jesus Christ (True articles on the horrible, great, and insupportable abuses of the papal Mass, invented directly against the holy Supper of Jesus Christ)."[7] That is a message that was surely shared by John Calvin, when he went into exile during the wave of persecution provoked by these placards, before he even began to study theology systematically in Basel, before he had even written the first edition of the *Institutes of the Christian Religion.*

In any event, throughout his career, Calvin objected to participation in the Catholic Mass. He frequently railed against the "Nicodemites," Christians who accepted his interpretations of their faith, but who nevertheless for prudential reasons attended Mass rather than facing persecution. He insisted that any true Christian must avoid the Mass, even if it meant savage persecution, including death, even it meant going into exile. He was certain that Christians must never obey any authorities, whether they be ecclesiastical or governmental, who required attendance at Mass. In this he no doubt felt he was only obeying the rule adopted by the apostle Peter as reported in Acts 5:29, "We must obey God rather than men."

This led Calvin frequently to speak with contempt of governing authorities. He was always willing to extend them respect if they accepted his interpretation of Christianity, and at times he had hopes that they might. The first edition of his *Institutes*, after all, is dedicated to King Francis I of France, to demonstrate to him that the Protestant position is reasonable, in the hope, no doubt, that Francis I might be persuaded to adopt it. But when kings proved obstinate, when they supported active persecution of his fellow believers, Calvin was quite capable of turning on them with vitriolic comment. Max Engammare of Geneva has recently uncovered about a dozen attacks on governing authorities by Calvin in his sermons, some of them published, some of them not yet published. Let me give two examples:(1) In 1550, in his sermons on Acts, Calvin says that if princes "wish to turn us from the honor of God, if they wish to force us to idolatries and superstitions, they then have no more authority over us than frogs and lice." (2) In 1560, in his sermons on Genesis, Calvin says, "if kings wish to force their subjects to follow their superstitions and idolatries . . . ,

---

[7] Robert Hari, "Les Placards de 1543," in *Aspects de la propagande religieuse* (Geneva: Droz, 1957), 79-142, for a full text and extensive analysis.

they are no longer kings" and their subjects must be prepared to "die a hundred times rather than abandon the true service of God. They must render to God that which belongs to him and denounce all edicts and menaces, all commandments and all traditions, holding them all for filth and dirt produced by earthworms in the face of Him to whom alone obedience belongs."[8]

This is rather strong language. It was formulated in a period when rulers, particularly kings, were regarded as agents of God, who some would say ruled by divine right, who were to be treated with the greatest deference, who were normally described in obsequious language. Yet Calvin is now calling them frogs, lice, and earthworms, deserving no respect or obedience whenever they stoop to idolatry. In many of the monarchies of that day language like this could have gotten Calvin into serious trouble.

It clearly shocked some of his listeners. We can find a striking example of one such reaction in a polemical pamphlet published in 1556, apparently by a French Franciscan named Antoine Cathelan, after his return to his native country following a visit of more than a year to French Switzerland. This pamphlet contains fascinating if hostile descriptions of the Protestant rituals he had observed. It provides more detailed information about early Calvinist rituals than we can find in any other source that has come to my attention. It contains descriptions of communion ceremonies, baptisms, weddings, burials, and sermons. Max Engammare has pointed out that Cathelan in his description of Protestant sermons reported that he had been particularly horrified by the atrocious insults he had heard in them thrown against the pope, the emperor, and all Christian kings and princes. He had been offended that local governments made no attempt to control this kind of speech.[9] Cathelan does not finger Calvin as the preacher who particularly horrified him, and, indeed, it is quite possible that he heard more of the sermons of Pierre Viret than those of Calvin, since Cathelan seems to have spent most of his time in Lausanne, at a time when Viret was that city's principal preacher. Viret seems to have been even more vitriolic than Calvin in both his writing and his preaching. But it is perfectly clear from the texts of Calvin's sermons that he joined in this type of villification.

How does this connect to resistance? It means most obviously that Calvin felt there were some laws that must be resisted, even though they were legitimately enacted by legitimate governments in legitimate ways, since they violated the commands of the supreme God. There is an eloquent summary of this argument at the very end of the *Institutes of the Christian Religion*, in 4. 20. 32. Of these laws that must be resisted, the most obvious were those that required attendance at Mass and adoration of a host that had been consecrated in a

---

[8]Max Engammare, "Calvin monarchomaque? Du soupçon à l'argument," *Archive for Reformation History*, vol. 89 (1998), 207-226. For these quotations, see pp. 213, 210.

[9]Ibid., 214.

Mass, for example in a Corpus Christi procession. In most cases it seems that Calvin thought this resistance should be passive, a form of civil disobedience. He recognized that it could lead to terrible punishment, including even torture and death, on charges of sacrilege and blasphemy. But he saw no alternative for the committed Christian but resistance to this extent. Like true Christians in all centuries, the Christians of his period were expected to face the distinct possibility of martyrdom. Some of Calvin's most eloquent letters are written to prisoners of the Reformed religion, facing the near certainty of agonizing death, urging them to stand firm in their faith.

In normal circumstances, Calvin did not contemplate or authorize resistance more active than this. He did, however, lay open the possibility of more active resistance, even armed resistance, in a celebrated passage towards the end of his *Institutes*, in 4. 20. 31. There he said that while no private persons could engage in active resistance there might be subordinate authorities in governments, "inferior magistrates," to use the language of the period, who could take action to restrain a ruler. Examples that occurred to him included the ephors in Sparta, the tribunes in Rome, and the demarchi in ancient Athens. They might also include in his own time, he added, the "three estates . . . in every realm when they hold their chief assemblies."

Through most of his career, however, Calvin resisted attempts in practice to exercise this right. In 1560, for example, when King Francis II of France was firmly under the control of the rabidly Catholic Guise family of his wife, a group of young nobles led by a man named La Renaudie, plotted to kidnap the king, dispose of his regents, and put him under the tutelage of relatives more sympathetic to the Protestant cause. La Renaudie came to Geneva to solicit Calvin's moral support for this conspiracy. Calvin's immediate reaction was that this was a hare-brained scheme unlikely of success and he flatly refused to give it his support. Two years later, however, Louis of Condé, a prince of the French blood royal, organized an open revolt against royal authority, seized the city of Orleans as his headquarters, and asked Protestants throughout France to send troops to his support. He again proposed to rescue a young king, now Charles IX, from wicked advisers. Calvin gave this enterprise unqualified and vigorous support. He even helped the armies of Condé to raise money and recruit mercenary troops in other countries. He apparently had decided that Condé, as a prince of the blood royal and thus normally entitled to a position in the king's privy council, was an "inferior magistrate" to whom the power of resistance could be granted, even if he did not directly represent the assembled three estates. He had also decided, I suspect, that Condé had some chance of success, unlike La Renaudie. Calvin always had an acute sense of political realities.[10]

---

[10]Robert M. Kingdon, *Geneva and the Coming of the Wars of Religion in France, 1555-1563* (Geneva: Droz, 1956), especially chapters 7 and 11.

Calvin's acceptance of the demands of Condé and his supporters for moral support helped launch the wars of religion in France. Those wars ripped France apart and brought desolation to many parts of the kingdom between 1562 and 1598, when the Edict of Nantes finally brought them to a provisional and unsatisfactory end. Throughout those wars, Calvin's successors, most notably Theodore Beza, developed more and more sophisticated arguments for resistance. Those arguments were picked up and restated and applied to local circumstances by Calvinists in other countries, including primarily Scotland and the Netherlands in the sixteenth century and England in the seventeenth century. They became an integral part of Calvin's socio-political legacy.

III. Maintenance of Discipline

In developing this third theme, I turn to a topic I have often discussed in connection with the edition of the Registers of the Consistory of Geneva in the period of Calvin's ministry in which I have been involved for more than ten years, most fully in my preface to the first volume in that series, published by the Librairie Droz in 1996.[11]

Discipline, it seems to me, was an essential part of Calvin's socio-political legacy. He insisted that Christians must not only accept true doctrine but also behave in a proper way. During the negotiations that led to his definitive return to Geneva in 1541, after his expulsion from the city in 1538 and a period of service to the church of French refugees in Strasbourg, Calvin demanded above all two things: the creation of an institution that would establish discipline and provision for regular instruction with a catechism. The institution that would establish discipline was called the Consistory. Its shape is described in the ecclesiastical ordinances that, as we have already noted, Calvin drafted after his return from Strasbourg. It began functioning almost immediately after the adoption of those ordinances, although the earliest surviving registers of its weekly meetings date from early 1542.

The Consistory legally was a standing committee of the city government. It was made up of all the pastors on the city payroll and twelve lay commissioners or elders, elected every year for this purpose in the elections that renewed the entire Genevan government. Its presiding officer was one of the four syndics elected for the year as Geneva's chief executives. The Registers of the Consistory make it clear that Calvin attended its weekly meetings faithfully, that if he was not present it meant he was either out of town on business or ill. Records also make it clear that he played an important part in the Consistory's activities. Each case heard before the Consistory normally involved a charge, a response by the person summoned, a judgment by the Consistory of what

---

[11] *Registres du Consistoire de Genève au temps Calvin*, ed. Thomas A. Lambert and Isabella Watt (Geneva: Droz, 1996), vii-xi.

should be done with the person summoned, and finally an "admonition" or "remonstrance," a kind of public scolding, normally including citation of relevant texts from Scripture, that concluded the proceedings. The "admonition" or "remonstrance" was normally administered by one of the ministers then present, and a high percentage were administered by Calvin himself. After Calvin's death, one of his biographers claimed that Calvin administered *all* of these public scoldings.[12] A close reading of the registers reveals this to be an exaggeration, but it is probably true that he administered most of them.

Calvin also fought for the powers of the Consistory. He insisted above all that it be vested with the power to excommunicate people who had committed serious sins or were unrepentant, without any possibility of appeal to the city government to reverse or lift a sentence of excommunication. That was a power that the ordinances did not clearly grant to the Consistory. But Calvin and the other ministers insisted upon it, and threatened to leave the city if it were not granted. They simply would not serve communion to anyone who had been excommunicated and who had not persuaded the Consistory that he or she had repented to a point that justified readmission to communion. After years of acrid controversy over this matter, Calvin finally won his way in 1555, and from then on the powers of the Consistory to excommunicate and to lift sentences of excommunication were absolute. Only in the seventeenth century did the city government finally reclaim some right to control this process.

Consistorial discipline became an important feature of life in Calvin's Geneva. We estimate that between 6 and 8% of the entire adult population were summoned to appear before the Consistory every single year. That made it a remarkably intrusive institution. Consistorial discipline also had a perceptible effect on life in Geneva. People either shaped up or moved out of town. Observers often remarked on the dramatic changes in the behavior of the Genevan population over the sixteenth century, on how sober and responsible Genevans became during these years.

Discipline, furthermore, becomes an important feature of Calvinism wherever it spread. In only a few places did Calvinists win the full measure of government cooperation they finally gained in Geneva, but they invariably tried to take steps in that direction. In almost every area that adopted the Calvinist version of the Reformation, consistories or equivalent institutions were established. In countries like France, where Calvinists were persecuted minorities, or in countries like the Netherlands, where Calvinists were privileged but still in the minority, consistories obviously had to operate in different ways and could not have had as great an overall impact. But everywhere that Calvinism went, discipline went as well. [13]

---

[12]Nicolas Colladon, *Vie de Calvin*, in CO, 21: 66.

[13]Raymond A. Mentzer, ed., *Sin and the Calvinists: Morals Control and the Consistory in the Reformed Tradition*, vol. 32, *Sixteenth Century Essays and Studies* (Kirksville, Missouri: Sixteenth Century Journal Publishers, 1994).

This creates in my mind an important distinguishing characteristic of Calvinism, one that separates it from such other forms of Protestantism as Lutheranism. Lutherans insisted on the primacy of faith. Calvinists always joined order to faith. One index of the relative importance of these elements can be found in the confessions of faith adopted in the sixteenth century. Most of them included a section describing the *notae* or marks of a true church, of how one can recognize a true church in the welter of competing institutions each then claiming to contain the essence of Christianity. The classic statement of the Lutheran position on this issue is to be found in article VII of the Augsburg Confession, which defines the true church as the "congregation of the saints, in which the Gospel is purely taught and the sacraments rightly administered."[14] But this was not enough for many Calvinists. They felt it necessary to add a third defining mark, the mark of discipline. There is a classic statement of this position in the Scotch Confession of Faith of 1560, which in its article XVIII, declares that the "notes" or marks of the true church are: "the true preaching of the Word of God, . . . the right administration of the sacraments of Christ Jesus . . . [and] ecclesiastical discipline uprightly ministered, as God's Word prescribes, whereby vice is repressed and virtue nourished."[15] There is another in the Belgic Confession of 1561, which similarly states in its article XXIX: "The marks by which the true church is known are these: if the pure doctrine of the gospel is preached therein, if she maintains the pure administration of the sacraments as instituted by Christ, if church discipline is exercised in the punishing of sin. . .," there we can be certain we have a true church.[16]

What is curious is that Calvin himself did not adopt this three-mark definition of the true church in his own most widely distributed writings. In edition after edition of his *Institutes*, including several revised and published well after the successful outcome of his battle for discipline in Geneva, he consistently uses a formula which sounds Lutheran: "Wherever we see the Word of God purely preached and heard, and the sacraments administered according to Christ's institution, there, it is not to be doubted, a church of God exists" (4.1.9). We find, in other words, that Calvin acted as if he believed in a three-mark definition of the true church but wrote as if he believed in a two-mark definition of the true church.

This poses a problem that needs to be resolved. One friend of mine suggests that Calvin was so committed to a doctrine of justification similar to Luther's that he wished to limit discipline and the entire realm of Christian ethics to the sanctification that follows justification, rather than to give it parity with preach-

---

[14] *The Creeds of Christendom*, ed. Philip Schaff, vol. 3 (Grand Rapids, Michigan: Baker, 1966; reprint of 1877 edition), 11-12.

[15] Ibid., 3: 461-462.

[16] Ibid., 3: 419.

ing and the sacraments. Another friend of mine suggests that Calvin for political reasons wanted to be able to say that he could still accept the Confession of Augsburg, at least in one of its versions, and thus avoid breaking ranks with Lutherans within the Holy Roman Empire. It occurs to me that another political reason might be that he did not want to offend Bullinger and the other leaders of the Zurich Church, who feared that any emphasis on discipline would encourage Anabaptists. I do not pretend to have resolved this problem. I present it for further consideration.

Much of Calvin's legacy, moreover, was the work not of Calvin himself but rather of his followers. To a degree, that is true of all three of the components of his socio-political legacy I have discussed. Whatever their precise source, I think I am right in arguing that commitments to collective government, to resistance against tyrannical government, and to discipline are important parts of the Calvinist legacy.

A Response to "Calvin's Socio-Political Legacy: Collective Government, Resistance to Tyranny, and Discipline"

Jeannine E. Olson

Professor Kingdon has highlighted the importance of Calvin's socio-political legacy in this well-organized paper, and, of course, I am of the same conviction. There is little with which to disagree and much to praise in this excellent paper.

In the first place, Dr. Kingdon focused on Calvin's commitment to collective government in church and in state and gave examples in the church of Geneva and in the government of the city, examples that have become precedents down to the present day in church polity in Reformed and Presbyterian circles and in city governments. Without stating it overtly, Kingdon dismissed the stereotype that still exists of Geneva as a theocracy under the thumb of Calvin.

In the second place, the paper highlighted the resistance of Calvin and Calvinists to the Mass and to governments that insisted on their subjects attending the Mass.

In the third place, Professor Kingdon suggested that insistence upon "discipline" was characteristic of Calvin and the Reformed churches, but he questioned why Calvin had failed to make "discipline" a mark of the true Church.

Let us take each of these aspects of Calvin's socio-political legacy in turn, starting with Calvin's commitment to collective government:

The presentation made it clear that Calvin was not an absolutist nor was he a democrat. He favored neither rule by one person nor rule by everyone. This position between absolutism and democracy was not unique to Calvin, of course. It was a common position in the sixteenth century when there were no democrats and when even monarchists felt that kings should rule in council.

As for democracy, although Geneva was not democratic (no government was in the sixteenth century), Geneva did have a Grand Council of all the citizens of the republic. Geneva was not necessarily unique in that regard. The existence of a Grand Council did not make Geneva democratic. The Council was limited in its power and decisions came down to the citizens from above.

I have two questions of clarification: who were the citizens of Geneva? Who was on the Grand Council? I would have thought that the citizens of Geneva were all those who had been born in the republic rather than only those of property and reputation. Those of property and reputation were likely to have been the bourgeois of the city, although the bourgeois were not necessarily Genevan-born. Please clarify more precisely who the citizens were and who the members of the Grand Council were.

It is easier to determine that Calvin was not a democrat than to ascertain his position on monarchy. Certainly, living in Geneva with a city government run by councils composed of members from prosperous and influential families, Calvin was not a monarchist. I would call Geneva an "oligarchy" rather than an "aristocracy of birth," however, especially since oligarchy implies a certain amount of self-interest.

What Calvin would have been under a ruler who was favorable to the Reformation we do not know. What if he had been under an Elector of Saxony or a Jeanne d'Albret, Queen of Navarre, for instance? Also, we do not know what Calvin would have been under a King of France who favored a Reformation. There never was such a king of France, of course, for when Henry IV, King of Navarre, came to the French throne in 1589, his options were severely limited by the powerful Catholic League, and, in order to bring peace to France, on July 25, 1593, he abjured his Reformed faith and became Catholic.

In the sixteenth century in the secular realm there were reformers or liberals who favored strong monarchs. These liberals lived in countries where reform was being blocked by nobles and position-seekers. Michel de L'Hôpital was one such liberal. He was chancellor of France from 1560-68, during the regency of Catherine de Médicis and the reigns of her sons, Francis II and Charles IX. Although Michel de l'Hôpital never joined a Reformed Church (how could he as chancellor to a Catholic monarch?), his wife was Reformed as was his daughter, his son-in-law, and his grandchildren. Michel de L'Hôpital was a secular reformer who favored more power to the monarchy in France in order to override resistance to the administrative, financial, and judicial reforms which de L'Hôpital favored and which Frenchmen with vested interests resisted.[1]

What Calvin would have been under a reforming monarch we will never know, but like most sixteenth-century thinkers, he supported government as God-given, whatever the form of that government was, so long as it did not limit Reformed worship. That he could not condone.

In the area of Church government, our insights into Calvin's world of thought are clearer since there Calvin had a freer hand to form a church as he saw fit. In Geneva he formed a collective style of church government, but again,

---

[1]Seong-Hak Kim. *Michel de L'Hôpital: The Vision of a Reformist Chancellor during the French Religious Wars.* Sixteenth Century Essays & Studies 36 (Kirksville, Missouri: Sixteenth Century Journal Publishers, 1997), 216.

not a democratic style, and despite his preference for a collective style of church government, he did not oppose bishops, at least in churches that already had them such as England. Nevertheless, in general, Reformed churches were ruled by pastors, elders, and sometimes deacons, and pastors were particularly important in selecting other pastors, as Professor Kingdon has pointed out in Geneva. We can safely say that Calvin preferred a collective form of church government but not a congregational form of church government, that is, not a form of church government in which every congregation picked its own pastor.

As to the collective nature of Calvin's actions, I would go even further than Professor Kingdon to state that Calvin seems to have acted collectively in almost every life situation, from his search for a wife, in which he had the help of friends, especially Martin Bucer, although he made the final decision for Idelette de Bure by himself, to the publication of his works, for which, after the initial years, he had to rely on his friends and countrymen as Jean-François Gilmont has so intelligently pointed out. For someone who, in some circles, has such a reputation as a loner, Calvin was very congenial indeed and seemed almost to shy away from acting unilaterally. He much preferred the support of others, and although one suspects that decisions made collectively while Calvin was around were often made in accordance with Calvin's preference, we do not always know that. It is entirely possible that Calvin was influenced by other people's advice, although one is hard pressed to find an example.

Do we have examples of Calvin having changed his mind on something because of someone else's opinion? I can think of one such example: In the matter of his publications, he let others take notes on his lectures and sermons. Then, when he was too overburdened and ill in the late 1550s to do everything that he wanted to do, after initially dragging his feet, he allowed his friends to publish, under his name, biblical commentaries and sermons that they had copied down. The publication of Calvin's sermons and lectures was generally consigned to those who were responsible for writing them down. Calvin did not have time to provide a prepared text, and he expressed some reticence in having published what he had not himself written down.[2]

For Calvin's sermons, the *Bourse française*, or French Fund for poor foreigners who had come to Geneva, was responsible for most of the sermons. The administrators of that Fund hired one Denis Raguenier, who began as early as 1549 to copy down the sermons, and after his death they employed Paris Prostat.[3] In 1554 and 1555, Jean Girard published an edition of Calvin's sermons based on Raguenier's transcriptions. In 1557, Conrad Badius took up the

---

[2]Jean-François Gilmont, "Les sermons de Calvin: de l'oral à l'imprimé," *Bulletin de la Société de l'Histoire du Protestantisme Français* 141 (1995): 153, 158.

[3]Jeanine E. Olson, *Calvin and Social Welfare: Deacons and the Bourse française* (Selinsgrove: Susquehanna University Press; London: Associated University Presses, 1989), 48.

publication of Calvin's sermons in Geneva, probably with the support of Laurent de Normandie. After Badius, the publication of Calvin's sermons diversified to a number of publishers.[4] The proceeds of Calvin's sermons were intended for the poor, specifically for the *Bourse française* that had paid to copy them down. There is no record in the surviving account books of the *Bourse française* that this happened. The account books do not reveal everything, however.

As for Calvin's lectures, Jean Budé, Charles de Jonvilliers, and Nicolas Des Gallars took notes while Calvin lectured, beginning in 1552. Indeed, Des Gallars had already been taking notes for some time. Again Calvin was reticent to publish his oral work, but he overcame that by 1557 with the publication of his lectures on Hosea. After that, Calvin accepted that Budé and de Jonvilliers would continue to take notes of his lectures and publish them, which they did.[5]

That is enough for Calvin acting collectively and with the help of others. It is time to move on to the second point in Calvin's socio-political legacy, and that is his endorsement of resistance to tyrannical government.

On this issue, the paper begins at an interesting point, and I think at the correct point, with French Protestant resistance to the "Mass." Resistance did not begin with resistance to government per se. It began with resistance to idolatry. Resistance to government within Reformed circles began not as a theoretical position, but rather in reaction to governments repressing Reformed worship. One cannot say that Calvinists favored religious liberty, however. What they favored was the true church, of which they were a part. They did not want religious liberty for everyone as an abstract principle. They did not want religious liberty for Anabaptists, for instance.

As French kings became more adamant in their opposition to Reformed Christianity, as persecution picked up, and especially as Reformed congregations began to form and organize into a Reformed Church in France, Calvinists were resistant to what they considered "tyrannical government" and especially the government in France. The development of the Wars of Religion in France (1562-1598), made resistance a fact, and the Massacre of St. Bartholomew's day, August 23-24, 1572, gave resistance theory an additional boast. Theory provided a rationalization for the resistance that was already taking place. Clearly Calvinists resisted what they defined as tyranny, and they developed resistance theories to justify their actions in an age when government was thought of as God-given and, therefore, to be obeyed.

The third social-political legacy of Calvin is "discipline," by that meaning not so much self-discipline, although there was plenty of that, but the discipline of the Christian community and the institutional structures put into place to

---

[4]Gilmont, "Comment Calvin choisissait-il ses imprimeurs?" 302-303.

[5]Gilmont, "Les sermons de Calvin," 157-160.

insure a disciplined community, that is, chiefly the institution of the Consistory. This discipline became a mark of Reformed communities and a defining characteristic. Clearly Calvin thought it was important.

Why, then, did Calvin not make discipline a third defining mark of the church alongside the preaching of the Word of God and the right administration of the sacraments? The First Scottish Confession of 1560 does make discipline a defining mark of the church, as does the Belgic Confession of 1561.

I must confess that for all the emphasis on discipline in Reformed Churches and despite the importance of the Consistory as an institution, it had never occurred to me that Calvin would consider discipline a necessary mark of the true church. He was too Augustinian for that. For St. Augustine, the true Church on earth consisted of both the "wheat" and of the "tares." How could an established church, a state church, such as that of the Roman Empire in which Augustine lived in the fourth and the fifth centuries have been otherwise when every citizen was supposed to be a Christian. The winnowing of the wheat and the tares in the Church would come later. As an Augustinian, Calvin was no Donatist. Donatists wanted to exclude from their churches and from the priesthood Christians who had aposticized under persecution. For Calvin, God left room for repentance, even for those who attended the Mass after having become Reformed. Excommunication in the Genevan church was, for Calvin, a means of bringing people to repentance, not a means of excluding them forever.

On a larger scale, at what the modern world would consider the level of the Christian denomination, if Calvin had wanted to exclude denominations from the true church, surely it would not have been on the basis of discipline but rather on the basis of their practice of idolatry.

One could argue also, I suppose, that Calvin wanted, in the interest of being inclusive, to support Protestant churches that did not have Reformed discipline. Also, Calvin relied on and did not wish to diverge from Martin Luther, in whose footsteps he followed, and Luther's marks of the Church were the preaching of the Word and the rightful administration of the sacraments. Calvin's position on Luther is described well in Brian Gerrish's article, "John Calvin on Luther," in *Interpreters of Luther: Essays in Honor of Wilhelm Pauck.*[6]

Nevertheless, discipline was important to Calvin, perhaps in part because of his thorough personality, his efficiency, and his desire to pull together the loose ends of any argument or theological statement. Calvin's *Institutes* were, after all, a systematic theology, asking the questions that medieval theologians asked. Calvin wrote the *Institutes* and developed it throughout his lifetime, whereas Luther's closest approach to a systematic theology could be said to have been his smaller and larger catechisms. Luther wrote biblical commentaries, trea-

---

[6]Jaroslav Pelikan, ed., *Interpreters of Luther: Essays in Honor of Wilhelm Pauck* (Philadelphia: Fortress Press, 1968), 67, 87.

tises, pamphlets, and letters. In addition, Calvin finished law school, whereas Luther was about to begin law school when he entered the monastery. That too might have made a difference in their respective attitudes toward the organization of the Church. Finally, Calvinists historically were often in the position of being a minority church, struggling for survival and growth, in France and in the Low Countries, for instance. Minority churches needed discipline and cohesiveness for survival.

One would not want to stretch this point of discipline among the Reformed too far, however, since Germans, among whom Lutheranism developed, have historically been a disciplined people. Their church must have contributed to that.

These comments are by way of continuing the conversation. I agree with this paper. It gives us much to think about on Calvin's Socio-Political Legacy.

Images and Themes in Calvin's Theology of Liturgy:
One Dimension of Calvin's Liturgical Legacy

John D. Witvliet

My first reaction to my assigned topic was one of puzzlement. What would be Calvin's *liturgical* legacy? As Elsie Anne McKee, in her inaugural address at Princeton Seminary, quipped, "It is common knowledge that Calvin and worship are incongruous topics, and that, whatever the strengths of those who are predestined to the glory of God, they are hopeless failures when it comes to liturgy."[1] But then I remembered my first day as a graduate student at the University of Notre Dame, where I was welcomed to the theology department by Fr. Regis Duffy with these words: "Well, it certainly is good to have another Calvinist around here."

Fr. Duffy was a connoisseur of Calvin. He was what we might call a book four Calvinist. His seminars on sacramental theology featured lectures on Augustine and Rahner, to be sure; but his courses pivoted around book four of Calvin's *Institutes.* He was attracted to Calvin's vision of sacramental worship that was

---

[1]Elsie Anne McKee, "Context, Contours, Contents: Towards a Description of the Classical Reformed Teaching on Worship," *Princeton Theological Seminary Bulletin* 16 (1995): 172; also printed in *Calvin Studies Society Papers, 1995, 1997,* ed. David Foxgrover (Grand Rapids, Michigan: Calvin Studies Society/CRC Product Services, 1998). Studies of Calvin's theology of liturgy prior to McKee's are relatively few in number. The primary titles, presented chronologically, include J. S. Whale, "Calvin," in *Christian Worship: Studies in its History and Meaning,* ed. Nathaniel Micklem (London: Oxford University Press, 1936), 154-171; Bernhard Buschbeck, *Die Lehre vom Gottesdienst im Werk Johannes Calvins* (Marburg: Phillipps-Universiteit Inaug. Diss, 1968); Kilian McDonnell, O.S.B. "Calvin's Conception of Liturgy and the Future of Roman Catholic Liturgy," in *The Crisis of Liturgical Reform,* vol. 42 of *Concilium* (New York: Paulist Press, 1969), 87-97; Bruno Bürki, "Jean Calvin avait-il le sens liturgique?" in *Communio sanctorum. Mélanges offerts Jean-Jacques von Allmen* (Geneva, 1982), 157-172; Teunis Brienen, *De Liturgie bij Johannes Calvijn* (Kampen: de Groot Goudriaan, 1987); Pamela Moeller, "Worship in John Calvin's 1559 Institutes with a View to Contemporary Worship Renewal" (Ph.D. dissertation, Emory University, 1988); Hughes Oliphant Old, "John Calvin and the Prophetic Criticism of Worship," in *John Calvin and the Church: A Prism of Reform,* ed. Timothy George (Louisville: Westminster/John Knox Press, 1990); and Rodolphe Peter, "Calvin and Liturgy, according to the Institutes," in *John Calvin's Institutes: His Opus Magnum. Proceedings of the Second South African Congress for Calvin Research.* July 31-August 3, 1984 (Potchefstroom: Potchefstroom University for Christian Higher Education, 1986).

mystical, but not magical. This suggests the dimension of Calvin's legacy in the area of worship that I will explore in this paper.

In many ways, Calvin's liturgical legacy is difficult to assess. For one, it is as complex as worship itself. An exhaustive study would need to address the influence of each of his particular rites (particularly on John Knox and worship in Scotland), his approach to preaching, his particular approach to iconoclasm, and his various liturgical preferences for each element of public worship, including at least preaching, prayers, Baptism, the Lord's Supper, marriage, funeral pratices, and music. Undoubtedly, one of the most enduring aspects of Calvin's legacy is his promotion of vernacular psalmody in Geneva—but I have already addressed this society on that subject.[2] Another complicating factor is that some aspects of his legacy were short-lived. With respect to sacramental practice, for example, Zwingli (or at least Zwingli's views) won the battle to guide the practice of most Reformed congregations. Yet, at any meeting of the North American Academy of Liturgy, a mention of Zwingli's name elicits mild chuckles, while Calvin's name generally evokes appreciative nods of respect. Why is that? The answer, I would guess, is not because of Calvin's liturgical texts, but rather his highly sacramental (small "s") view of worship.

In this paper I will address this one dimension of his liturgical legacy, the aspect of his thought that was attractive to Fr. Duffy: Calvin's theology of worship, or more narrowly, his theology of liturgy (that is, his understanding of what takes place in the "stated assemblies of the church").[3] More specifically, I will explore some basic themes and images in Calvin's theology of liturgy. This cannot be done comprehensively in this space. But I hope to begin, and on the basis of familiarity with many individual trees, to draw a map of the forest; that is, to sketch the conceptual cartography of Calvin's theology of liturgy. Then, second, I will offer a series of concluding comments, hoping to suggest several historical and theological questions that have significant interest for future academic discussions and for the life of the church today.

---

[2]John D. Witvliet, "Spirituality of the Psalter: Metrical Psalms in Liturgy and Life in Calvin's Geneva," *Calvin Studies Society Papers, 1995, 1997,* ed. David Foxgrover (Grand Rapids: Calvin Studies Society/CRC Product Services, 1998), 93-117.

[3]This topic is broader than his theology of any particular element of worship (e.g., preaching, common prayer, Baptism, etc.). This topic is narrower than worship in the broad sense of the worship Christians offer in all of life. There are numerous studies of specific elements of worship. In this category, I would include Bryan D. Spinks, "Calvin's Baptismal Theology and the Making of The Strasbourg and Genevan Baptismal Liturgies 1540 and 1542," *Scottish Journal of Theology* 48 (1995): 55-78; and B. A. Gerrish, *Grace and Gratitude: The Eucharistic Theology of John Calvin* (Minneapolis: Fortress, 1993), 175. The best study of worship in the broad sense is Elsie McKee's "Context, Contours, Content." These are very helpful studies, yet few of them discuss the categories and topics that I highlight in this paper. I would argue that we need all three levels of analysis to grasp Calvin's thought clearly: studies of each element of liturgy, studies of liturgy as a whole, and studies of worship broadly defined.

At the outset, let me state two methodological premises. First, I am convinced that any study of this topic is bound to be successful only insofar as it takes into account the full range of Calvin's writings on the subject—not only the *Institutes* and liturgical texts, but also the commentaries, sermons, letters, and other ecclesiastical documents of various kinds. Generally speaking, this paper is commentary-heavy, a corrective move in response to the heavy emphasis on the *Institutes* in prior studies of Calvin's theology of liturgy. Second, I am less interested in exploring Calvin's understanding of worship *in se* than in exploring his understanding of the experience of the worshiper. Calvin, like his medieval forebears, did write about the theological status of the elements of worship, most significantly the elements of the Lord's Supper. But he also wrote about the dimensions of the worshiper's experience of worship. It is this theme that I will highlight in the following explication.

I. "Four Liturgical Sins"

I begin, *via negativa,* with a section that I will give the attractive title, "Calvin's theology of liturgical sin." Calvin's writings on worship, particularly the commentaries, return time and time again to what I will call four primary "liturgical sins," that is, four sins that have to do with the practice of public worship.

Sin number one is disobedience. Given that Calvin's primary liturgical criterion was that liturgy should be executed according to the Word of God, it is no surprise that a first abuse he identified was that of disobedience to God's explicit commands regarding worship. Degenerate rites are those "when every one invented something new for himself," those "not based upon His Word."[4] Calvin understood many of the prophetic critiques of the worship of Israel as injunctions against the subversion of God's explicit command for worship. His comment on Zephaniah 1:5 is typical:

> What then was it that the Prophet condemned? That they were not content with what the law simply and plainly prescribed, but that they devised for themselves various and strange modes of worship; for when men take to themselves such a liberty as this, they no longer worship the true God . . . He shows that all kinds of worship are abominable to him whenever men depart in any measure from his pure Word. For we must hold this as the main principle—that obedience is more valued by God than all sacrifices.[5]

Significantly, the text on which he is commenting does not explicitly raise the issue of disobedience. That Calvin introduces the notion of disobedience to exegete this text indicates how this functions as a "root sin" in Calvin's thought.

Sin number two is hypocrisy. Commenting on Joel 1, Calvin provides a succinct description of this sin:

---

[4]CO, 24:489 (Commentary on Exod. 29:38-46).

[5]CO, 44:10 (Commentary on Zeph. 1:5).

The priests did not rightly worship God; *for though their external rites were according to the command of God, yet as their hearts were polluted,* it is certain that whatever they did was repudiated by God, until, being touched with the fear of his judgement, they fled to his mercy, as the Prophet now exhorts them to do.[6]

Notice here that this false worship passed the first test, the one regarding obedience to God's Word, but failed a second, a test of the heart.

So Calvin's emphasis falls on inner worship, the worship of the heart. Without it, external liturgy is meaningless. Calvin's commentary on Micah 6 summarizes: "Hypocrites place all holiness in external rites; but God requires what is very different; for his worship is spiritual."[7] Thus, Cain is an archetypal hypocrite as one who "wished to appease God, as one discharging a debt, by external sacrifices, without the least intention of dedicating himself to God."[8] Perhaps the classic statement on this theme is found in Calvin's commentary on Isaiah 1:11:

But hypocrites observe them [cultic instructions] with the most scrupulous care, as if the whole of religion turned on this point, and think that they are the most devout of all men, when they have long and anxiously wearied themselves in observing them. And that they may be thought more devout, they likewise add something of their own, and daily contrive new inventions, and most wickedly abuse the holy ordinances of God, by not keeping in view their true object.[9]

Here especially, Calvin is less interested in the actions of worship than in the people who offer them.

Sin number three is superstition. Superstition is the failure to perceive the proper relationship between the external acts of worship and the spiritual reality of God. Thus Calvin comments on Isaiah 66:1, "Yet, as the minds of men are prone to *superstition,* the Jews converted into *obstacles* to themselves those things which were intended to be *aids,* and *when they ought to have risen by faith to heaven, they believed that God was bound to them,* and worshiped him only in a careless manner, or rather made sport of worshiping him at their own pleasure."[10] Again, one could avoid the abuses of both disobedience and hypocrisy and still suffer from superstition. That is, one could perform rites according to scripture and with a pure heart, but with a misguided notion of how those rites and symbols related to God. What was needed was not only obedience to God's com-

---

[6]CO, 42:527 (Commentary on Joel 1:13-15). Another example of this more subtle abuse was Jereboam (see commentary on Hosea 3:2-5).

[7]CO, 23:86 (Commentary on Mic. 6:6-8).

[8]CO, 23:86 (Commentary on Gen. 4:5).

[9]CO, 36:38-39 (Commentary on Isa. 1:11).

[10]CO, 37: 437 (Commentary on Isa. 66:1). See also *Institutes,* 1.4.1,4.

mands and a pure heart, but also right understanding, a right knowledge of the spiritual character of God. Calvin, here on Genesis 33: "For as *superstitious* men foolishly and wickedly *attach God to symbols*, and, as it were, *draw him down from his heavenly throne* to render him subject to their gross inventions: [in contrast] so the faithful, piously and rightly, ascend from earthly signs to heaven."[11] And here, on Isaiah 1: "[Superstition is] In the disposition of the mind, when men imitate those services which are lawful and of which God approves, but keep their *whole attention fixed on the outward form, and do not attend to their object or truth.*"[12] Note carefully: superstition here is not pagan reliance on a wooden god. It is a sin of the mind or spirit. It is mis-placed attention in regard to its object of contemplation; it is the failure to attend to the spiritual significance of physical action. Tongue-in-cheek, we might call it something like a "Liturgical Attention Deficit Disorder." It is sin to which even orthodox Christians are prone.

Sin number four is idolatry. Calvin, like the other Reformers, was an iconoclast. He lamented what he labeled "grosser idolatry," which occurs "when idols are worshiped openly." In this category, Calvin placed the mass, which he believed amounted to the worship of a physical entity. But Calvin was as concerned about idolatry that emerged in a more subtle form: "The other kinds of idolatry, although more hidden, [are] abominable before God, namely, when, under the disguise of a name, men *boldly mingle whatever comes into their minds, and invent various modes of worship.*"[13] Calvin's concern was for what we might call "intellectual idolatry," this mingling of ideas about God in the mind.

For Calvin, this is a concept that is intimately linked with the knowledge of God, that large concept that is central to the structure of the *Institutes* and many significant passages throughout his corpus. In Calvin's words, here on Malachi 1:11: "We must bear in mind that God cannot be rightly worshiped except as he is known."[14] Thus, a typical phrase from Calvin's biblical commentaries records that "So he [Paul] makes a beginning with the definition of God, so that he might prove from that how he ought to be worshiped, because the one thing depends on the other."[15] In the classic *Institutes* passage on this point, he argues:

> . . . in seeking God, miserable men do not rise above themselves as they should, but measure him by the yardstick of their own carnal stupidity, and neglect sound investigation; thus out of curiosity they fly off into empty speculations. They do not therefore apprehend God as he offers himself, but imagine him as they have fashioned him in their own presumption. When

---

[11]CO, 23:454 (Commentary on Gen. 33:21).

[12]CO, 36:60 (Commentary on Isa. 1:14).

[13]CO, 40:497 (Commentary on Ezek. 20:27).

[14]CO, 44:420 (Commentary on Mal.1:11).

[15]CO, 48:410 (Commentary on Acts 17:25).

this gulf opens, in whatever direction they move their feet, they cannot but plunge headlong into ruin. Indeed, whatever they afterward attempt by way of worship or service of God, they cannot bring as tribute to him, but they are worshiping not God but a figment and a dream of their own heart.[16] In other words, most idols—most graven images—are chiseled out not by a hammer and pick, but rather by our mental faculties.

In sum, Calvin identifies four particular abuses of worship: disobedience, hypocrisy, superstition, and idolatry. Though undoubtedly related, each can be clearly distinguished. Calvin uses these terms in technically precise ways: disobedience consists of ignoring God's commands for worship, hypocrisy is the separation of external from internal worship, superstition is the confusion regarding how external rites relate to the presence of God, and idolatry is fixation on the wrong object of worship. Like the detailed Eskimo vocabulary for snow, Calvin's detailed vocabulary points to a nuanced understanding of the broad category of false worship. And this vocabulary—*via negativa*—provides clues to the positive, constructive comments Calvin offers at other points. It serves as a limit to mark off the parameters of right and true worship—a fence around the playground.[17]

II. Metaphors and Images in Calvin's Theology of Liturgy

And that is where we move next, to a playground of images, metaphors, visions, pictures, and illustrations that describe what Calvin called the "inestimable privilege of the stated assemblies of the church."

Scottish, Barthian theologian Thomas Torrance, early in his career, once argued that Calvin rejected "pictorial thinking pertaining to God."[18] Yet, there is much evidence to suggest this is not correct. Although Calvin is reputed to have been an enemy of the visual arts, his prose is distinguished by the pervasive and gripping use of visual images, which he called figures or similitudes. Calvin was self-conscious about his visual rhetoric, and—as several recent studies of Calvin's rhetoric have reminded us—he extolled the virtues of such rhetorical flourishes. In his words (here from one of his treatises on the Lord's Supper), "figures are called the eyes of speech, not because they explain the

---

[16]OS, 3:41 (*Institutes*, 1.4.1).

[17]Despite this prophetic critique, Calvin insisted on the value of liturgical action. Thus, even in his comment on the most acerbic prophetic critiques, Calvin argued: "We now see that God does not simply reject sacrifices, as far as he has enjoined them, but only condemns the abuse of them. And hence what I have already said ought to be remembered, that the Prophet here sets external rites in opposition to piety and faith, because hypocrites tear these things asunder which are, as it were, inseparable: it is an impious divorce, when anyone only obtrudes ceremonies on God, while he himself is void of piety" (CO, 42:330-331; Commentary on Hos. 6:6-7). For Calvin, the abuses in public liturgy must be rooted out, but not liturgy itself.

[18]Torrance, "Calvin and the Knowledge of God," *Christian Century* 81 (1964): 697.

matter more correctly than simple, proper language, but because they win attention by their propriety, arouse the mind by their luster, and by their lively similitude so represent what is said that it enters more effectively into the heart."[19] What follows is a survey of nine such metaphors or figures.

A. Spatial Metaphors

The most pervasive metaphor for Calvin is that of bidirectional movement between God and humanity: in and through the assembly, God moves down toward humanity so that humanity might rise to God. God descends that we might ascend. This was true, Calvin believed, already for the worship Israel rendered to God under the terms of the Old Covenant. Concerning the ancient cult of temple and ark of the covenant, Calvin wrote: "as [God] was not tied to one place, so the last thing He intended was to tie down His people to earthly symbols. *On the contrary He comes down to them, in order to lift them up on high to Himself*. . . . He merely uses symbols as intermediaries with which to introduce Himself in familiar ways to slow men until, step by step, they ascend to heaven."[20] In this pictorial way, Calvin describes the inner dynamic of public worship, as it were, on a cosmic vertical axis.

The first movement in this dynamic sweep is always God's move toward humanity. Here we are thrust into a central and distinctive feature of Calvin's thought: God's accommodation to human capacity. In Calvin's view, God is fundamentally a being who condescends, who deigns to move down toward humanity. Such a view presupposes the great contrast Calvin draws between God's greatness and human weakness: "for God, who fills the heavens and earth, is yet said to descend to us, though he changes not his place, whenever he gives us any token of his presence; a mode of expression adopted in accommodation to our littleness."[21] This divine accommodation is accomplished in many ways: in Old Testament theophanies, in the incarnation, and in his provision of scripture. But another instance of accommodation, not often noted in studies on this theme, is the divine provision for the liturgical life of the church.

In the Old Covenant, according to Calvin, God provided ceremonies by which the people of Israel could render right worship: "God [was] accommodating himself to their weaker and unripe apprehensions by the rudiments of ceremony."[22] In the New Covenant, the age of the church, preaching and espe-

---

[19]CO, 9: 514. For recent discussion of this point, see Philip W. Butin, "John Calvin's Humanist Image of Popular Late-Medieval Piety and Its Contribution to Reformed Worship," *Calvin Theological Journal* 29 (1994): 419-431; and Serene Jones, *Calvin and the Rhetoric of Piety* (Louisville: Westminster John Knox Press, 1995).

[20]CO, 48:412 (Commentary on Acts 17:24).

[21]CO, 23:471 (Commentary on Gen. 35:13).

[22]CO, 31:502 (Commentary on Ps. 50:14).

cially the sacraments are God's gift of accommodation to the church. For example, in his 1541 *Short Treatise on the Lord's Supper*, Calvin argued:

> For seeing we are so foolish, that we cannot receive him [Christ] with true confidence of heart, when he is presented by simple teaching and preaching, the Father, of his mercy, not at all disdaining to condescend in this matter to our infirmity, has desired to attach to his Word a visible sign, by which he represents the substance of his promises, to confirm and fortify us, and to deliver us from all doubt and uncertainty.[23]

In this way, the external rites of the church, including preaching, prayer and sacraments, are possible because of God's gracious condescension or accommodation.

This first downward movement of worship is mirrored by the upward movement of God's people, the *sursum corda*, the lifting of one's heart. The language of ascent is a refrain that echoes throughout Calvin's *corpus*, echoing earlier writings by Guillaume Farel.[24] Nearly every one of Calvin's texts on public prayer, preaching, and the sacraments enjoins Christians to use these means to *rise* to God. Calvin's sermon on 2 Samuel 6:1-7 is a typical example:

> Thus, we must note that when God declares himself to us, we must not cling to any earthly thing, but must elevate our senses above the world, and lift ourselves up by faith to his eternal glory. In sum, God comes down to us so that then we might go up to him. That is why the sacraments are compared to the steps of a ladder. For as I have said, if we want to go there, alas, we who not have wings; we are so small that we cannot make it. God, therefore, must come down to seek us. But when he has come down, it is not to make us dullwitted; it is not to make us imagine that he is like us. Rather, it is so that we might go up little by little, by degrees, as we climb up a ladder one rung at the time.[25]

Public worship is like a ladder. Perhaps no image crystallizes so concretely this aspect of Calvin's liturgical vision.[26]

---

[23]OS, 1:505 (1541 *Short Treatise on the Lord's Supper*).

[24]In 1533, Farel wrote the following liturgical formula: "Therefore, lift up your hearts on high, seeking the heavenly things in heaven, where Jesus Christ is seated at the right hand of the Father; and do not fix your eyes on the visible signs which are corrupted through usage." (Old, *Patristic Roots of Reformed Worship* [Zurich: Theologischer Verlag, 1975], 75). See also *Institutes*, 1.11.3, 2.7.1.

[25]SC 1:135 (Sermon on 2 Sam. 6:1-7). Calvin is commenting here on the ark of the covenant in Old Testament worship, but his application applies directly to the New Testament age: "The sacraments are like this, and the ark was like a sacrament—at least in principle. The people have been moved to seek God in a very tangible manner." He then goes on to speak specifically about preaching, the Lord's Supper, and Baptism. In his Old Testament commentaries Calvin cited nearly every liturgical practice as an occasion for ascending to heaven, including the ark of the covenant (see commentary on Is. 56:2) and the temple (see commentary on Is. 66:1).

[26]For other references to this ladder image, see his commentary on Ps. 42:1-2, Gen. 3: 23, Gen. 28:13, Acts 17:23 and obliquely in *Institutes* 4.1.5.

But what does ascent entail? What does it mean? And how does one accomplish it? The key to answering these questions lies in Calvin's frequent use of the term "spiritual worship." For Calvin (as it was for Erasmus, among others) the ascent toward God is a purely spiritual ascent—here from commentary on Psalm 95: "the worshipers were to lift their eyes to heaven, and serve God in a spiritual manner."[27] The basis for this was simple: God's spiritual nature required that worship be spiritual. So Calvin comments: "it is certain that God would never be worshiped except agreeably to His nature; from which it follows, that His true worship was always spiritual, and therefore by no means comprised in external pomp."[28] Calvin's privileged text on this point is certainly John 4:21-24, which he cites copiously throughout his commentaries, sermons, and polemical writings on liturgical matters. In his commentary on this text, Calvin notes:

> But here we must ask first, why and in what sense the worship of God may be called spiritual. To understand this we must note the antithesis between the Spirit and external figures, as between the shadow and the substance. The worship of God is said to consist in the Spirit because it is only the inward faith of the heart that produces prayer and purity of conscience and denial of ourselves, that we may be given up to obedience of God as holy sacrifices.[29]

The ascent to God that Calvin described consists of the attentive direction of the mind and heart away from external forms toward God.

This emphasis on "spiritual worship" introduces a second important pair of metaphors for Calvin: inward and outward, internal and external. Spiritual worship, by which we rise to God, is most fundamentally "inside" the human person: "When they [the prophets] speak of the worship of God they describe it by outward acts, such as altars, sacrifices, washings, and such like; and indeed, the worship of God *being within the soul, there is no way in which it can be described but by outward signs,* by which men declare that they worship and adore God."[30] External worship of God is insufficient: "for it is not enough for our outward acts to be applied to God's service,"[31] and again "when we have to deal with God nothing is achieved unless we begin from the inner disposition of the heart."[32]

At the same time, internal authenticity is also not sufficient. External expression is necessary. In his commentary on Genesis 12, Calvin develops a horti-

---

[27]CO, 32:31 (Commentary on Ps. 95:6). See also *Institutes,* 1.11-13; 4.10.14, and commentary on Is. 56:2, John 4:24, and Acts 15:9. As Alexandre Ganoczy observes, this theme was prominent in the writings of the humanists, especially Erasmus (*The Young Calvin,* trans. David Foxgrover and Wade Provo [Philadelphia: Westminster Press, 1987], 365, n106).

[28]CO, 24:43 (Commentary on Exod. 25:8). See also his commentary on Is. 66:1.

[29]CO, 47:88 (Commentary on John 4:23). See also commentary on Psalm 50:14, James 1:17, Isaiah 1:13, 11:4.

[30]CO, 36:326 (Commentary on Isa. 18:7).

[31]OS, 5:431 (*Institutes,* 4.18.16).

[32]OS, 4:73 (*Institutes,* 3.3.16).

cultural image to make his point: "the inward worship of the heart is not suffi-cient, unless external profession before men be added. Religion has truly its appropriate seat in the heart; but from this root, public confession afterwards arises, as its fruit."[33]

Notice how this spatial language of up/down and in/out fits with the "litur-gical sins" discussed above. *Hypocrisy* is an abuse that violates the inward/out-ward relationship. *Superstition,* in contrast, violates the upward movement of worship. To summarize thus far: Calvin's theology of worship is, in part, revealed in his use of simple prepositions: up, down, in, out. God comes down, accommodating to human capacity by making provision for liturgical expres-sion. Worshipers rise to God, by offering spiritual worship, elevating their mind to God. This occurs most fundamentally within the human person, and is given expression externally through tangible, public means. Notice the pervasive use of this language in his commentary on Psalm 9:11:

> It was not enough for the faithful, in those days, to depend upon the Word of God, and to engage in those ceremonial services which he required, unless, aided by *external* symbols, they *elevated* their *minds* above these, and yielded to God *spiritual* worship. God, indeed, gave real tokens of his pres-ence in that visible sanctuary, but not for the purpose of binding the senses and thoughts of his people to earthly elements; he wished rather that these external symbols should serve as *ladders,* by which the faithful might *ascend* even to heaven. The design of God from the commencement in the appointment of the sacraments, and all the outward exercises of religion, was to consult the infirmity and weak capacity of his people. Accordingly, even at the present day, the true and proper use of them is, to assist us in seeking God *spiritually* in his heavenly glory, and not to occupy our *minds* with the things of this world, or keep them fixed in the vanities of the flesh.[34]

This vivid account of up, down, in, and out, is a convenient summary of the building blocks for Calvin's understanding of worship.

B. Sensory Metaphors

Beyond the prepositions we have already addressed, a second set of metaphors depicts liturgical action in terms of human sensory experience. Of these, the most pervasive are metaphors of speaking and hearing.[35] Worship is

---

[33]CO, 23:181 (Commentary on Gen. 12:7). See also his commentary on Daniel 6:10 and Isaiah 19:18.

[34]CO, 31:102 (Commentary on Ps. 9:11).

[35]In the use of the speech metaphor, Calvin was, of course, expressing his preference for a favored Renaissance category. See William J. Bouwsma, "Calvin and the Renaissance Crisis of Knowing," *Calvin Theological Journal* 17 (1982): 204, and "Calvinism as *Theologia Rhetorica*," in Wilhelm Wuellner, ed., *Calvinism as Theologia Rhetorica* (Berkeley: Center for Hermenuetical Studies in Hellenistic and Modern Culture, 1986).

God's speech to humanity. Commenting on Jeremiah 7, Calvin argues, "the main part of true and right worship and service is to hear God speaking."[36] God's speech is realized, in part—to no one's surprise—through the preaching of the Word. Commenting on Isaiah 11:4, Calvin asserts, "When the prophet says 'by the breath of his lip,' this must not be limited to the person of Christ. For it refers to the Word which is preached by His ministers. Christ acts by them in such a manner that He wishes their mouth to be reckoned as His mouth, and their lips as His lips."[37] Yet even in visual and sacramental signs, God speaks: "although we must maintain the distinction between the Word and the sign; yet let us know, that as soon as the sign itself meets our eyes, the Word ought to sound in our ears."[38] Thus, in worship, through word and sign, God speaks. And so do we. Prayer and praise are our speech to God, so much so that Calvin speaks of prayer as an "intimate conversation of the pious with God."[39]

Worship is also an image or mirror: "the Word, sacraments, public prayers, and other helps of this kind, cannot be neglected, without a wicked contempt of God, who manifests himself to us in these ordinances, *as in a mirror or image.*"[40] This metaphorical, spiritual seeing is in some way tied to the physical, literal sight of the external forms of worship.[41] Old Testament forms were intended "so that under the external image the spiritual truth *might meet their eyes.*"[42] Physical sight of external forms should lead to correct spiritual perception. The same is true of sacraments: "the believer, when he sees the sacraments with his own eyes, does not halt at the *physical sight of them,* but by those steps (which I have indicated by analogy) rises up in devout contemplation to those lofty mysteries which lie hidden in the sacraments."[43] And again, a sacrament "represents God's promises as painted in a picture and sets them before our sight, portrayed graphically and in the manner of icons."[44] Like the seventh century iconoclasts, Calvin saw the Lord's Supper as the "only true icon" of Christ.

---

[36]CO, 37:693 (Commentary on Jer. 7:21).

[37]CO, 36:240 (Commentary on Isa. 11:4).

[38]CO, 23:240 (Commentary on Gen. 17:9).

[39]OS, 4:320 (*Institutes,* 3.20.16).

[40]CO, 31:274 (Commentary on Ps. 27:4).

[41]On this point, see T. H. L. Parker, *Calvin's Old Testament Commentaries* (Louisville: Westminster/ John Knox Press, 1986), 116-121, and Serene Jones, *The Rhetoric of Piety,* 77, 102-103. On the one hand, both the seeing and the hearing, for Calvin, are metaphorical. It is ascent of the mind to heaven that he is describing in metaphorical terms. But, on the other, Calvin retains a surprisingly literal sense of actual seeing and hearing in the act of worship. On visual sense, see his commentary on Ez. 18:5-9.

[42]CO, 24:513 (Commentary on Lev. 3:1).

[43]OS, 5:262 (*Institutes,* 4.14.5).

[44]OS, 5:263 (*Institutes,* 4.14.6). Calvin's depiction of the Eucharist as the true icon of God is strikingly similar to the seventh century iconoclast doctrine of the Eucharist as the only true icon of Christ. Significantly, Calvin leaves the word icon in Greek in this passage.

Both physical sight *and* spiritual perception thus are bound up with the inward, outward, downward, upward movement of worship described earlier. Because God has descended toward humanity and provided external forms for worship, humanity can rise to God through correct internal perception of God and God's works. The mirror or image metaphor is particularly apt for the sacraments, which are experienced in part through sight: "Yet those ancient sacraments looked to the same purpose to which ours now tend: to direct and almost lead men by the hand to Christ, or rather, as images, to represent him and show him forth to be known."[45]

Calvin frequently combined metaphors of speech and sight. In the memorable Augustinian mixed metaphor, also adopted by other sixteenth century theologians like Peter Martyr Vermigli, the sacraments are, for Calvin, visible words: "a sacrament is nothing else than a *visible word*, or sculpture and image of that grace of God, which the words more fully illustrate."[46] Elsewhere, he called them a *vocal sign*.[47]

Calvin's gallery of sensory images is completed by metaphors of taste or eating. Worship is also nourishment, the giving and receiving and tasting of spiritual food. This metaphor is certainly most naturally applicable to the Lord's Supper. Passage after passage of Calvin's writing on the holy meal features this metaphor prominently:

> from the physical things set forth in the Sacrament we are led by a sort of analogy to spiritual things. Thus, when bread is given as a symbol of Christ's body, we must at once grasp this comparison: as bread nourishes, sustains, and keeps the life of our body, so Christ's body is the only food to invigorate and enliven our soul. When we see wine set forth as a symbol of blood, we must reflect on the benefits which wine imparts to the body, and so realize that the same are spiritually imparted to us by Christ's blood. These benefits are to nourish, refresh, strengthen, and [!] gladden.[48]

Yet spiritual nourishment is in no way limited to the Lord's Supper. Both the giving of the gospel and the Lord's Supper are instances of spiritual nourishment: "daily he gives it [his body as spiritual food] when by the word of the gospel he offers it for us to partake . . .[and] . . . when he seals such giving of himself by the sacred mystery of the Supper."[49]

---

[45]OS, 5:278 (*Institutes*, 4.14.20).

[46]CO, 23:240 (Commentary on Gen. 17:9). See also his commentary on Gen. 17:9, Jer. 27:1-5, and Ezekiel 2:3. The notion of sacraments as the visible word of God is thoroughly Augustinian and was common in sixteenth century Reformation thought. See Joseph McClelland, *The Visible Words of God: An Exposition of the Sacramental Theology of Peter Martyr Vermigli* (Edinburgh: Oliver and Boyd, 1957), 128-138. Thus, sound and sight, mind and body, understanding and will are all brought to bear in the lifting of the heart of the believer to the Lord in worship.

[47]See his commentary on Gen. 9:12.

[48]OS, 5: 344-345 (*Institutes*, 4.17.3).

[49]OS, 5: 346 (*Institutes*, 4.17.5).

The metaphor of spiritual nourishment is particularly important in order to complement and balance the mental and cognitive nature of the others. As B. A. Gerrish has observed: "sometimes, to be sure, the spatial language appears to stand for a mental or cognitive operation: invited by the symbols, we are lifted up to heaven *oculis animisque* ("by our eyes and minds"), and this fits well with the *Sursum corda* of the liturgy. But it cannot possibly be taken to negate everything Calvin says, here and elsewhere, about feeding on the body, which is not a purely mental or cognitive operation."[50]

Note also how all three sensory images function on at least two levels, both literally and metaphorically. That is, we hear God speaking through preaching. We see and are nourished by God's grace in the Lord's Supper. But we also hear God speaking through the Supper, and are fed through preaching.

C. Additional Images

These spatial and sensory metaphors are complemented by another set of metaphors, most drawn from biblical narratives. First, the metaphor of *sacrifice*. This metaphor is inevitably significant in Calvin's thought because of his careful attention to and high view of the Hebrew scriptures. The fundamental continuity Calvin perceived in God's revelation in both testaments led him to take seriously the patterns of the Old Testament cult for understanding the worship of the Christian church. In Calvin's words:

> It then follows that this mode of speaking ought to be so taken, that we may understand the analogy between the legal rites, and the spiritual manner of worshiping God now prescribed in the gospel. Though then the words of the Prophet are metaphorical, yet their meaning is plain enough—that God will be worshiped and adored everywhere. But what are the sacrifices of the New Testament? They are prayers and thanksgivings, according to what the Apostle says in the last chapter of the epistle to the Hebrews.[51]

That the people of God should render sacrifices to God is a matter of continuity between Old and New Testaments. Christian worship, like the worship of Israel, is a sacrifice rendered to God.

But there is also discontinuity. As this last passage suggests, the discontinuity consisted in part of the fact that in the new dispensation the people of God followed a "spiritual manner of worshiping God." What had been a literal, physical exercise, i.e., the burning of an animal, was now less literal and more metaphoric. In other words, it is spiritual—the same term we encountered earlier to express the human ascent to God. Calvin expressed this forcefully in his treatise *The Necessity of Reforming the Church:*

---

[50]Gerrish, *Grace and Gratitude*, 175.

[51]CO, 44:421 (Commentary on Mal. 1:11). See also commentary on Heb. 13:15.

In short, as God requires us to worship him in a spiritual manner, so we with all zeal urge men to all the spiritual sacrifices which he commends. . . .This, I say, is the sure and unerring form of divine worship, which we know that he approves, because it is the form which his Word prescribes. These are the only sacrifices of the Christian Church which have attestation from him.[52]

Further, there was discontinuity for Calvin in that Christ had fulfilled the meaning and purpose of the Old Testament sacrifices once and for all. On this basis, Calvin repudiated any impression that the sacrament either repeated or effected this sacrifice anew. He was steadfastly opposed to understanding the Eucharist as the self-offering of the Church. He reserves the strongest polemic language to counter the sacrificial interpretation of the Eucharist:

Though the papists should shout a thousand times that the sacrifice which Christ made once for all on the cross and which they themselves make today is not different but one and the same, I shall still maintain from the apostle's own mouth that if the sacrifice of Christ availed to please God it not only put an end to other sacrifices but that it is impossible to repeat it.[53]

Worship is a sacrifice, but a sacrifice of praise and not propitiation. Worshipers are priests: "For we who are defiled in ourselves, yet are priests in him, offer ourselves and our all to God, and freely enter the heavenly sanctuary that the sacrifices of prayers and praise that we bring may be acceptable and sweet-smelling before God."[54]

Along with sacrifice, covenant-making was central in Calvin's biblical theology. Calvin's exegesis of the Old Testament highlighted the significance of the various covenants between God and humanity. Calvin saw these covenants as examples of the primary bond that was made possible by God between God and humanity. The act of external worship served to ratify or enact the covenant bond between God and humanity. Thus, Old Testament sacrifices were means toward union with God as expressed in the covenant: "In like manner, the design with which sacrifices were instituted by God was to *bind* his people more closely to himself, and to ratify and confirm his covenant."[55]

This emphasis on covenant bond is but one part of a much larger conceptual category for Calvin, that of the union of humanity with God. Calvin spoke of the service of the sanctuary as "the sacred bond of intercourse with God."[56] In the New Testament age, such union is particularly realized in the Eucharist, which Calvin spoke of as "the sacrament of the Supper, by means of which our

Covenant-making

---

[52]CO, 6:460 (*The Necessity of Reforming the Church*).

[53]CO, 55:122 (Commentary on Heb. 10:2).

[54]OS, 3:481 (*Institutes*, 2.15.6); see also *Institutes*, 4.18.16.

[55]CO, 31:498 (Commentary on Ps. 50:45).

[56]CO, 31:246 (Commentary on Ps. 42:1).

Lord leads us to communion with Jesus Christ."[57] Recalling our spatial images, Calvin described the sacraments as being "like a ladder to us so that we may seek our Lord Jesus Christ, and so that we may be fully convinced that he lives in us and we are united to him."[58] Just as the Old Testament cult was a bond between God and Israel, so too the worship of the Christian church serves to unite God and the worshiping church.

Next, Calvin described public worship as a *school of faith:* "Whenever true believers assemble together at the present day, the end which they ought to have in view is to employ themselves in the exercises of religion, to call to remembrance the benefits which they have received from God, to make progress in the knowledge of his Word, and to testify the oneness of their faith."[59] The purpose of ceremonies was to assure that the faithful were "*trained to godliness,* and might make greater and greater progress in faith and in the pure worship of God."[60] Thus Calvin glowingly describes how the worship of Israel was useful for teaching the people lessons in theology. Such lessons were offered on the subject of the atonement: "the ancient people were exercised in these ceremonies, *to teach them that God can only be appeased by the payment of a ransom*";[61] the mediation of Christ: "besides, it was right that they should always have before their eyes symbols, by which they would be *admonished,* that they could have no access to God but through a mediator";[62] about how one can please God: "the rite of ablution reminded the ancient people that no one can please God, except he both seek for expiation in the blood of Christ, and labour to purify himself from the pollutions of the flesh";[63] and about the judgement of God: "for when an animal was killed at the altar, all were reminded that they were guilty of death."[64] Ceremonies and symbols were, in Calvin's words, useful for encouraging and stimulating faith. He frequently referred to them as "props," "stimulants," and "exercises."[65] Ceremonies and signs have value for teaching, stimulating, and assuring the believer in faith:

> But here we ought also to observe the usefulness of outward signs of repentance; for they serve as spurs to prompt us more to know and abhor sin. In this way, so far as they are spurs, they may be called *causes of repentance;* and as far as they are evidences, they may be called *effects.* They are *causes,*

---

[57]OS, 1:505 (1541 *Short Treatise on the Lord's Supper*). See also *Institutes,* 4.17.33.

[58]CO, 51:750 (Sermon on Eph. 5:25-27).

[59]CO, 31:760 (Commentary on Ps. 81:1-3).

[60]CO, 36:38 (Commentary on Isa. 1:11).

[61]CO, 24:523 (Commentary on Lev. 5:6).

[62]CO, 23:138 (Commentary on Gen. 8:20).

[63]CO, 24:199 (Commentary on Exod. 19:10).

[64]CO, 37:391 (Commentary on Jer. 7:21).

[65]See also commentary on Gen. 8:20, 33:20, 35:7, Dan. 9:1-3, Jer.7:21, and *Institutes,* 4.1.1 and 4.10.31, where Calvin discusses the sacraments in terms of their value for edification.

because the marks of our guilt, which we carry about us, excite us the more to acknowledge ourselves to be sinners and guilty; and they are effects, because, if they were not preceded by repentance, we would never be induced to perform them sincerely.[66] Worship in public ceremonies arises out of genuine faith, to be sure, but it also causes, confirms, and stimulates it.

Finally, Calvin describes worship as a *testimony to the world*. In addition to these tangible benefits for the life of the individual Christian believer and community of faith, Calvin also observes that cultic activity has a particular purpose beyond the gathered church. This purpose for the world is, in turn, two-fold: Christian worship both testifies to the goodness of God before the world and is an act of separation, signaling a clear delineation between the world and the worshiping community. Both themes are expressed in Calvin's analysis of Isaac's sacrifice:

> From other passages we are well aware that Moses here speaks of public worship; for inward invocation of God neither requires an altar, nor has any special choice of place; and it is certain that the saints, wherever they lived, worshiped. *But because religion ought to maintain a testimony before men,* Isaac, having erected and consecrated an altar, professes himself a worshiper of the true and only God, and *by this method separates himself from the polluted rites of heathens.*[67]

Calvin was not content with only the benefits of testimony and separation, but also wished that these acts would in turn lead others to call on the Lord: "and when each recites the personal benefits which he has received, let all be animated unitedly and in a public manner to give praise to God. We give thanks publicly to God, not only that men may be witnesses of our gratitude, but also *that they may follow our example.*"[68] Christian worship then not only resulted in the greater union of God and his people and the edification of the church, but also in a witness to the world.

In sum, Calvin paints an entire gallery of images to depict the meaning and purpose of public liturgy: worship is like a ladder, a fruit tree, a conversation, a mirror or image, a feast, a sacrifice, a ratification of a treaty, a master teacher, a testimony. Calvin spoke about public worship with rhetoric that was imaginative and full of high expectations.

III. Theological Framework: Trinitarian Understandings of Divine Action

These images convey the energy, force, and imagination of Calvin's view of worship. But to gain full force, they need to be set in their larger theological

---

[66]CO, 36: 374 (Commentary on Isa. 22:13).

[67]CO, 23:366 (Commentary on Gen. 26:25). See also commentary on Gen. 33:20.

[68]CO, 31:337 (Commentary on Ps. 34:3). See also commentary on Ps. 22:22, 23.

context. If we were to go back over all the descriptions and images of worship I have outlined, and were to diagram Calvin's sentences, we would find that the nominative case or subject of many of those sentences is not the gathered congregation, but God. We the people warrant the dative or objective case, not the nominative.

At the heart of Calvin's vision is the notion that worship is charged with divine activity: "Wherever the faithful, who worship him purely and in due form, according to the appointment of his Word, are assembled together to engage in the solemn acts of religious worship, *he is graciously present, and presides in the midst of them.*"[69] Regarding the sacraments, Calvin argued that they "are not strictly the works of men but of God. In Baptism or the Lord's Supper we do nothing; we simply come to God to receive His grace. Baptism, from our side, is a passive work (*respectua nostri est opus passivum*). We bring nothing to it but faith, which has all things laid up in Christ."[70] As Hughes Oliphant Old has repeatedly argued, "What Calvin has in mind is that God is active in our worship. When we worship God according to his Word, he is at work in the worship of the church. For Calvin the worship of the church is a matter of divine activity rather than human creativity."[71] Similarly, John Leith contends: "The sense of the reality of the Creator and Source of all things, the feeling of the objective presence of God, a sensitivity to the activity of God in life in general and in worship in particular, left an imprint on everything Calvin did or wrote."[72]

Calvin's theocentric view of worship is thus more fully and accurately described as a Trinitarian vision. Each divine person is described as having a particular role in the inner movement or nature of worship. God the Father is agent, giver, initiator. God the Son is mediator, particularly in the office of priest. God the Spirit is prompter, enabler, and effector. In short, to use Philip Butin's phrase, worship is "Trinitarian enactment," in which

> . . . the initiatory "downward" movement of Christian worship begins in the Father's gracious and free revelation of the divine nature to the church through the Son, by means of the Spirit. In more concrete terms, this takes place in the proclamation of the Word according to scripture, by the empowerment and illumination of the Spirit. . . . [T]he "upward" move-

---

[69]CO, 31:102 (Commentary on Ps. 9:11).

[70]CO, 50:245 (Commentary on Gal. 5:3).

[71]Old, "The Prophetic Criticism of Worship," 234, and again, "If there is one doctrine which is at the heart of Reformed worship it is the doctrine of the Holy Spirit. It is the belief that the Holy Spirit brings the Church into being, that the Holy Spirit dwells in the Church and sanctifies the Church. Worship is the manifestation of the creation and sanctifying presence of the Holy Spirit" (*The Patristic Roots of Reformed Worship* [Zurich: Theologischer Verlag, 1975], 341).

[72]John Leith, "Calvin's Doctrine of the Proclamation of the Word and Its Significance for Today," in *John Calvin and the Church: A Prism of Reform*, ed. Timothy George (Louisville: Westminster/ John Knox Press, 1990), 208.

ment of human response in worship—focused around prayer and the celebration of the sacraments . . . is also fundamentally motivated by God. Human response—the "sacrifice of praise and thanksgiving"—arises from the faith that has its source in the indwelling Holy Spirit. In that Spirit, prayer, devotion, and obedience are offered to God the Father, who is the proper object of worship, through the Son Jesus Christ, who being fully divine and fully human is the mediator of the church's worship.[73]

In sum, as Calvin saw it, the weekly assembly of the church for public worship was no ordinary gathering. It was an event charged with divine activity, an arena in which the divine-human relationship was depicted and enacted. In public worship, God was not only the One to whom worship was directed, but also the One who was active in the worship of the church. Through public worship— that is, through public prayers, preaching, and the celebration of Baptism and the Lord's Supper—God actively worked to draw human beings into divine fellowship. Only the most exalted language could convey the significance of this event. As Calvin himself expressed it: "it is an instance of the inestimable grace of God, that so far as the infirmity of our flesh will permit, we are lifted up even to God by the exercises of religion. What is the design of the preaching of the Word, the sacraments, the holy assemblies, and the whole external government of the church, but that we may be united to God?"[74]

Thus far, my exposition.

IV. Concluding Observations

Now for six concluding observations: three that are historical, and three theological. Each of these could be a paper in itself; in this paper, a few paragraphs must suffice.

Observation 1: Calvin is not necessarily an innovator when it came to anything I have mentioned.

I hasten to disavow any suggestion in this exposition of Calvin's thought that his contribution is singular, unique, or independent (which can be a danger of this genre). The next step in this analysis will necessarily be to compare these themes with the likes of Bucer, Erasmus, Farel, Vermigli, as well as Calvin's patristic sources.[75] Calvin was widely dependent on a host of sixteenth century conversation partners, as well as several patristic sources. The danger with my approach is to abstract Calvin from his historical context.

---

[73]Philip W. Butin, *Revelation, Redemption, Response: Calvin's Trinitarian Understanding of the Divine-Human Relationship* (New York: Oxford University Press, 1995), 102.

[74]CO, 31:248 (Commentary on Ps. 24:7).

[75]Here I have in mind the kind of work so well exemplified in David C. Steinmetz, *Calvin In Context* (New York: Oxford University Press, 1995).

In fact, in the main themes—the use of biblical images of sacrifice and covenant renewal, the acute sense of divine activity in worship—Calvin was recapitulating several ancient biblical and patristic motifs. Indeed, the language of "inward ascent of the soul" is a very Augustinian theme, and expertly surveyed in Bernard McGinn's *History of Western Mysticism*.[76] No wonder Hughes Oliphant Old did his dissertation on "the patristic roots of Reformed Worship." No wonder Calvin entitled his liturgy, "according to the custom of ancient church." Calvin's theology of liturgy is a remarkably catholic theology of liturgy—trinitarian, christocentric, evangelical, orthodox.

Why then is Calvin's legacy significant in this area? Consider three reasons. First, Calvin had the ability to crystallize this heritage in rhetoric that was picturesque, forceful, and memorable. Second, Calvin's legacy on this topic is significant because of the sheer volume of his writing on this subject. Arguably, Calvin has written as much about the theology of liturgy as almost any other major figure in the history of the church. This becomes especially apparent when his commentaries and sermons are taken seriously. Third, Calvin's legacy is also due to publishing practices that have kept Calvin's writings on countless preachers' bookshelves for 400 years, relegating the writings of his contemporaries to the dusty shelves of rare book rooms.

Observation 2: Both the extent and nuance of Calvin's writing on this topic have typically not been acknowledged in broader Calvin scholarship.

After a modestly comprehensive program of reading through the commentaries, I am amazed at how often Calvin comments on public, cultic liturgy, even speaking about it when the link between this topic and his text is a stretch. In fact, Calvin frequently referred to any number of cultic acts—including oath-taking, invocation, and praise and prayer—as *synecdoche* for all of worship, and thus an excuse to write about "the stated assemblies of the church." For all of this, the bibliography of works on Calvin's theology of liturgy is rather modest.

I could provide any number of examples of the scholarly community's lack of attention to this topic. Many liturgical scholars virtually ignore Calvin's theology of liturgy, acknowledging only the simplicity of his written rites, his preference for weekly communion, and his promotion of vernacular metrical psalmody. But this lack of attention is also found among Calvin scholars. One interesting example has been discussions on Calvin's theology of divine accommodation. The classic study on this theme remains that of Ford Lewis Battles. Battles notes that the created universe and the human body are forms of accommodation, and he discusses in greater detail scripture and the incarnation as the examples *par excellence* of God's accommodation. Strikingly, he

---

[76]McGinn begins his explanation of Augustine with a description of "his account of the soul's ascension to contemplative and ecstatic experience of the divine presence." *The Foundations of Mysticism*, 231 ff.

devotes little attention to visual signs and liturgical acts as signs of accommodation, including only a few paragraphs on the sacraments as such.[77] David Wright has given us some brilliant additions to the literature on divine accommodation, but again with few references to the liturgical actions of the church.[78] Suzanne Selinger does observe the sacraments as a sign of accommodation, but this only a passing reference in work on a much larger subject.[79] Our understanding of Calvin's concept of divine accommodation can be enriched by taking into account his understanding of public worship.

Observation 3: Calvin scholarship on this topic suffers from the genre problem.

That is, we have been blinded to much of this imagery in Calvin because people looking at Calvin's theology of liturgy generally have not read much beyond the *Institutes*. Both a major dissertation, completed at Emory University, and a major scholarly article, completed by a South African historian, have recently attempted to address Calvin's theology of worship with the limiting rubric "as seen in the *Institutes*." The *Institutes* do include many of Calvin's positive statements about liturgy, but they are often overwhelmed by his extended polemics.[80] When we liturgy types have gotten beyond the *Institutes*, we probably only make it as far as the liturgical texts and rites themselves. Yet, as Bryan Spinks once noted, [generally speaking] "Calvin's rich doctrine was not given adequate liturgical expression because he was so dependent upon the liturgies of others."[81] May it be that a future Calvin-liturgy scholar would be inadvertently locked in the Meeter Center with a stack of Calvin's sermons and commentaries to continue this work.

---

[77]Ford Lewis Battles, "God Was Accommodating Himself to Human Capacity," *Interpretation* 31 (1977): 19-38, reprinted in *Readings in Calvin's Theology*, ed. Donald K. McKim (Grand Rapids: Baker Book House, 1984), 21-42. For a broader study of this theme, see Stephen D. Benin, *The Footprints of God: Divine Accommodation in Jewish and Christian Thought*, SUNY Series in Judaica: Hermeneutics, Mysticism, and Religion (Albany: State University of New York Press, 1993).

[78]David F. Wright, "Calvin's 'Accommodation' Revisited," in *Calvin As Exegete: Papers and Responses Presented at the Ninth Colloquium on Calvin and Calvin Studies*. Ed. Peter De Klerk (Grand Rapids: Calvin Studies Society, 1995), 171-190, and "Calvin's Accommodating God," in *Calvinus Sincerioris Religionis Vindex*, ed. Wilhelm H. Neuser and Brian G. Armstrong (Kirksville, Missouri: Sixteenth Century Journal Publishers, 1997), 3-19.

[79]Suzanne Selinger, *Calvin Against Himself: An Inquiry in Intellectual History* (Hamden, Connecticut: Archon Books, 1984), 67.

[80]In the *Institutes* (and in his various treatises on the sacraments), Calvin tends to treat the sacraments as discreet subjects or loci, topics—as we might expect from him, given the tradition of seeing the sacraments as discreet topics in nearly every catechism or theological system. In the commentaries, Calvin often writes about the worship service as a whole. He writes about prayers, preaching, Baptism, and the Lord's Supper all as part of what causes us to be lifted up to heaven.

[81]Bryan Spinks in a book review of James F. White, *Protestant Worship*, in *Scottish Journal of Theology* 46 (1993): 406.

Observation 4: A full-orbed view of Calvin's theology of liturgy demonstrates how the structure and logic of a theology of liturgy mirrors the structure and logic of other more traditionally prominent theological loci.

A case in point is the notion of divine agency in worship, which bears an exact correlation with Calvin's soteriological structure. Like other theological loci that attempt to relate divine and human action (e.g., the doctrine of faith, the doctrine of providence), a theology of liturgy must explain how worship is *both* a free act of human beings, and also one which is inspired and enabled by God. If we were to ask Calvin about the main agent in worship, he would respond—as he would regarding faith—by answering "The Holy Spirit." The Holy Spirit effects the proclamation of the Word in our hearts, unites us to Christ in the Supper, and inspires our praise and prayer. The Holy Spirit makes the whole up-and-down parabola of worship work.

Generally speaking, every first-rate theologian in the history of the church has approached theology of liturgy as a correlate of their larger theological system. Liturgy is an icon of life before God. For Calvin, this is true not only with respect to the doctrine of faith, but also with respect to the doctrine of the knowledge of God, the doctrine of the work of Christ, and any number of other doctrines. Part of the enduring appeal of Calvin's theology of liturgy is that his position is carefully worked out in conversation with and in terms of an entire theological system. Future studies could well analyze the points of correspondence between Calivn's theology of liturgy and several of his other main theological themes.

Observation 5: The pervasive imagery of ascent and descent raises the specter of unwanted dualism in Calvin's thought—but perhaps unnecessarily.

All of this up/down imagery can quickly invite the charge that Calvin is replicating a Neoplatonic world in which—to be maddeningly simplistic, and purposely provocative—Gothic architecture, Gregorian chant, and mystical prayer all help the worshiper escape from earthly reality into heavenly repose. Indeed, Suzanne Selinger speaks of the fact that "historians have so often thought it necessary to rescue him from the charge [of dualism]."[82]

And probably there are some pretty direct connections. Calvin's Platonist leanings are well-known. And then there is this ladder image, which may also indicate dependence on the influence of the long Christian tradition of spiritual writings on the ascent of the soul to God. The image had patristic origins, but was also prevalent in the sixteenth century, perhaps most significantly in the poems of Marguerite of Navarre, with whom Calvin corresponded. (The most recent work on Marguerite is entitled *Celestial Ladders: Readings in Marguerite of*

---

[82]Selinger, *Calvin Against Himself*, 3.

Navarre's Poetry of Spiritual Ascent.) The historical connections and inclination toward these Neoplatonic constructions are not hard to find.

At the same time, I suspect that the issue is more complex than might first be admitted. This is especially true if we remember that when we ascend to heaven we find there, according to Calvin, Jesus Christ, who, *in his humanity*, is seated at the right hand of the Father. The presence of the human Jesus there hardly squares with a celestial, otherworldly vision of eternal repose associated with Neoplatonism.

There are also these dandy little passages every once in a while in Calvin that highlight the physical materiality of liturgical action. In a description of preaching, for example, Calvin notes that "God himself appears in our midst . . . an inestimable treasure is given us *in earthen vessels.*"[83] The same is true of the sacraments:

> First of all, we ought to believe that the truth must never be separated from the signs, though it ought to be distinguished from them. We *perceive and feel* a sign, such as the bread which is put into our hands by the minister in the Lord's Supper; and because we ought to seek Christ in heaven, *our thoughts ought to be carried there.* By the hand of the minister he presents to us his body, that it may be actually enjoyed by the godly, who rise by faith to fellowship with him.[84]

Here, the sense of touch is important, such that the very feel of the bread aids the faithful in their contemplation of heavenly reality.

I suggest, along with Philip Butin, that it is Calvin's Trinitarian language that ultimately allows him to escape the grossest errors of dualism. Butin argues that Calvin's view is "not Neoplatonic, as if the flesh or the world were to be avoided because they are material or tangible. Rather, the sense is Pauline. Calvin wants to stress the freedom of spiritual worship in contrast to the strictures of humanly devised and required ceremonies. Spirit stands in contrast, not to matter, but to the law, and to human attempts to please God by regulated liturgical conformity which misrepresents its object."[85]

Observation 6 is actually a series of questions.

As historians, we need not ask anachronistic questions like "what would Calvin say to the church today?" Nevertheless, for those of us who, in addition to our roles of historians, are also theologians of the church, let us ask: how do our discussions of worship stack up against the measuring stick of Calvin's the-

---

[83]OS, 5:8 (*Institutes,* 4.1.5).

[84]CO, 36:133 (Commentary on Isa. 6:7).

[85]Butin, "Constructive Iconoclasm: Trinitarian Concern in Reformed Worship," *Studia Liturgica* 19 (1989): 133-142. See also Butin, "Calvin's Humanist Image," 422.

ology of liturgy? How many of our current discussions about worship are really theological? That is, how often do we ask, whether or not our worship portrays and depicts the God of Abraham and the God of Jesus Christ or whether it depicts some other kind of god? How many of our discussions focus not on the mechanics of worship, but on its inner meaning? How often do we line up our programs for liturgical reform with scriptural teaching; or, if we do, how hard do we really work at it? How often do we ask whether our minds and hearts are focused on the proper relationship between our actions and our God? Have we given an account of the nature and purpose of what we are doing when we gather for liturgy? How many focus not on mechanics or method, but on meaning? How many of our conversations move beyond what we deplore in worship to our constructive, theological vision for worship? How have we done in providing instructive images for our assemblies that "win attention by their propriety, arouse the mind by their luster . . . so that they enter effectively into the heart"? In comparison to the consommé of Calvin's rhetoric, ours is often a motley bowl of porridge.

To conclude, let me suggest that honest answers to these questions provide us with a large challenge. They throw us back to Calvin's own instruction and they demand our common resolve to echo this advice:

> [Let us] engrave this useful lesson upon our hearts, that we should consider it the great end of our existence to be found numbered among the worshipers of God; and that we should avail ourselves of the inestimable privilege of the stated assemblies of the Church, which are necessary helps to our infirmity, and means of mutual excitement and encouragement. By these, and our common sacraments, the Lord who is one God, and who designed that we should be one in him, is training us up together in the hope of eternal life, and in the united celebration of his holy name.[86]

---

[86]CO, 31:529 (Commentary on Ps. 52:8).

A Response to "Images and Themes in Calvin's Theology of Liturgy"

Ward Holder

John Witvliet's paper is rich in both thematic structure and supportive content. He is offering some new ways to consider and organize our thinking about Calvin's approach to liturgy, as well as drawing our attention to particular texts of great import. In doing so, he is already helping the process of scholarly appropriation of Calvin's work. As I seek to further that goal in my response, I shall consider the paper at several points to offer congratulations and suggestions, and reflect more deeply on a smaller number of issues.

One of the great strengths the paper brings is the rejection of the normal "polite indulgence" of Calvin's place in the history of liturgy. In the same way that Calvin notes that the "spectacles of scripture" (*Institutes*, 1.6.1) allow us to see items that reveal God in the whole of creation that we had previously missed, so too does Witvliet's consideration of Calvin as a liturgical theologian. From the outset of his paper, Witvliet challenges the validity of our myopia (dare I say "presbyopia"?) concerning Calvin's consideration of liturgy. Calvin's contributions in the history of liturgy represent a significant theme in his overall work. Further, the importance of Calvin's thought here cannot be exhausted by noting that it was not always highly original or innovative. Indeed, the construction of a theology of liturgy that is truly "catholic," drawing together the trinitarian schemes more familiar to us from his doctrinal treatises and the *Institutes*, is a major accomplishment. Further, to find that the connections normally found within Calvin's more prominent theological points are mirrored in his liturgical theology is pedagogically satisfying. As the principal in the Genevan *schola fide*, Calvin maintained a single curriculum, and re-enforced it wherever possible.

The myopia challenged by Witvliet touches upon his second point as well, that "both the extent and nuance of Calvin's writing on {the theology of liturgy} have typically not been acknowledged in broader Calvin scholarship." As Calvin scholars, we tend to see that which we seek. Armed with Witvliet's admonitions, I returned to consider again some of Calvin's New Testament commentaries. Again and again, passages which I had seen as general admonitions now seemed to apply more particularly to the construction of a sound worshipping community. Witvliet points out that the consideration of the theme of accommodation, so well known to Calvin scholars, has ignored the category of liturgy. He points out that classical and later studies have not granted consideration to how liturgical acts and visual signs might further develop the theme of accommodation. This is a significant observation, and I shall return to this theme at greater depth presently.

Witvliet's discernment of a *via negativa* in Calvin's theology of liturgy and his placement of that material at the beginning of his treatment deserves some applause. By beginning with liturgical sins, of course, Witvliet plays to our own knowledge. If we do not really know what Calvin says constructively about the liturgy, we are absolutely certain what he rejects! I found the presentation to be particularly clear and concise, and that alone would have won my gratitude. But after pointing out the pitfalls which are to be avoided, such as disobedience, hypocrisy, superstition, and idolatry, Witvliet goes further. These liturgical sins do not "hang" in the air, but are closely integrated into the theory behind the exposition of the spatial metaphors. Hypocrisy violates the relationship between the inner and outer aspects of true worship, and superstition, the upward movement of genuine worship. Thus, the hypocrites confuse the external rites with the true, inner spiritual worship; and the superstitious remain at an earthly level, unwilling to be raised up to God.

Another issue to which Witvliet alludes, and one which deserves fuller consideration, is that of placing Calvin's contribution's more firmly in context. For instance, I am anxious to see the paper, which Professor Witvliet promises, that links this material to authors such as Bucer, Erasmus, Farel and Vermigli. As the history of exegesis school has argued, the essential way to understand historical figures is situated within the contexts in which they appeared.[1] This holds true for Calvin's work on the liturgy. Making explicit what Calvin has borrowed also allows one to consider those items which Calvin eschewed, giving a fuller picture of the mind at work in generating this liturgy and the type of worshipping community he wished to form.

Critically, I have three questions to pose to Professor Witvliet. First, he has chosen to consider Calvin's theology of liturgy. But the breadth of topics and texts addressed in his paper suggests that he is far more frequently speaking about worship, and the proper attitudes toward and preparation for worship. Is there a significance in using the more narrow term?

The second question is a query of clarification. Witvliet urges in his methodological caution that "study of this topic is bound to be successful only insofar as it takes into account the full range of Calvin's writings on the subject—not

---

[1] See for instance, David C. Steinmetz, *Calvin in Context* (Oxford: Oxford University Press, 1995), 209. "The principal thesis of the book is, after all, methodological; namely, that the best and most productive way to study Calvin is to place him in the context of the theological and exegetical traditions that formed him and in the lively company of the friends and enemies from whom he learned and with whom he quarreled."

only the *Institutes* and liturgical texts, but also the commentaries, sermons, letters, and other ecclesiastical documents of various kinds." He notes further that at present, the move is "commentary-heavy." Certainly, he is correct, his material does depend on the commentaries, and especially upon the commentaries from the Old Testament. My question would be to ask whether that is a research conclusion, or an as-yet-unfinished research filter? Is the material to be found most often in the Old Testament comments,[2] or did those simply make the case better under time constraints of this paper?

The final question has to do with Professor Witvliet's second methodological premise. He states that he is interested "in exploring Calvin's theology of worship primarily from the point of view of the worshipper." Bluntly, I must ask: what does this mean? If it means that this is to be taken as an exercise in social history, then the sources, which all come from Calvin's pen, are wrong. If his point instead is to consider the type of worshipping consciousness or worshipping community that Calvin wished to form, I think that this way of describing the issue obfuscates rather than clarifies.

Finally, I wish to engage at somewhat more depth with Prof. Witvliet's consideration of the metaphors that Calvin uses to elucidate the acts of God and the worshiping community. He writes convincingly about Calvin's use of metaphors, such as ladder, a fruit tree, a conversation, a mirror, a feast, a sacrifice, a ratification of a treaty, and the master teacher in the *schola fide*. I am intrigued by this, and wonder whether this bacchanalia of images might begin to suggest an approach to Calvin's aesthetic, and an answer to Torrance's characterization of Calvin's thought. To bolster this notion, I offer up another text from Calvin's commentary on Galatians. Through a consideration of the text, several of Witvliet's points about Calvin's theology of liturgy are illustrated, and the significance of his comments are made clearer.

Commenting on Galatians 3.1, Calvin writes that

[Paul] suggests that the actual sight of Christ's death could not have affected them more than his preaching. … Paul's doctrine had taught them about Christ in such a manner that it was as if He had been shown to them in a pic-

---

[2]This could be a problem for another reason than simple balance in Calvin's corpus. David F. Wright has written about the characters of peoples, that Calvin could see God's accommodation to the rudeness and barbarity of the Israelite people in the Old Testament. This opens the question of whether the New Testament communities, as people, were more advanced, and needing less accommodation. If such were the case, naturally, the New Testament worship texts would make better models for later worship practices. See Wright, "Calvin's Pentateuchal Criticism: Equity, Hardness of Heart, and Divine Accommodation in the Mosaic Harmony Commentary," *Calvin and Hermeneutics*, Articles on Calvin and Calvinism, v. 6, edited by Richard J. Gamble (New York: Garland Publishing Co., 1992), 213-230; and "Accommodation and Barbarity in John Calvin's Old Testament Commentaries." In *Understanding Prophets and Poets: Essays in Honor of George Wishart Anderson*, edited by A. Graeme Auld (Sheffield: Journal for the Study of the Old Testament Press, 1993).

ture, even crucified among them. Such a representation could not have been effected by any eloquence or tricks of oratory, had not that power of the Spirit been present, of which he spoke in both the epistles to the Corinthians.

Let those who want to discharge the ministry of the Gospel aright learn not only to speak and declaim but also to penetrate into consciences, so that men may see Christ crucified and that His blood may flow. When the Church has such painters as these she no longer needs wood and stone, that is, dead images, she no longer requires any pictures. And certainly images and pictures were first admitted to Christian temples when, partly, the pastors had become dumb and were mere shadows, partly, when they uttered a few words from the pulpit so coldly and superficially that the power and efficacy of the ministry were utterly extinguished.[3]

Calvin propounds a surprisingly earthy picture for those who have already consigned him to the scrap-heap saved for cold intellectuals. The point of preaching is to make Christ's blood flow in the sight of men, bringing forth fresh blood from the wounding of their consciences. The gory sight of the crucified Lord, rather than the sanitized Christ, must be taught through mental images to the Christians. Of course, this is too tall an order for even the most skilled rhetorician. Only the fulfillment of the Holy Spirit makes this possible. Here, we see again that God is the actor in worship. Not even Paul's powers of persuasion would be sufficient if the Spirit were absent.

So, too, one can see Prof. Witvliet's point on the nature of worship as accommodation. It is the choice of the Holy Spirit to act in this manner, making pure declamations into powers that can penetrate consciences. Certainly Calvin makes clear that the words, and skills, and beauty of the words fall short of the necessary material power. Further, he does not suggest that they are grand enough to "fit" the divine power. Rather, the Spirit condescends to make preaching a holy ministry, a true preaching of the Gospel, a "Word of God" as Bullinger would say.

To conclude this section of my consideration, I must note that this text beautifully portrays Witvliet's point on the close correlation of the spatial metaphors with the liturgical sins, as well as his difference with Torrance about Calvin's use of imagery. For Calvin, the idolatry of icons or images comes as a direct result of the lack of inner spiritual worship. When the preachers could no longer provide the necessary rhetorical images for the Spirit to enliven so as to sustain true worship, false and external images were brought in to supply the lack. Calvin has, in point of fact, a rich aesthetic vocabulary, ready to be brandished at moments of need. What he refuses is to do is to externalize that aesthetic in frozen visual moments which grant a preference to seeing over hearing.

---

[3]Commentary on Galatians, 3.1, *Calvin's New Testament Commentaries*, vol. 11, edited by David and Thomas Torrance, translated by T.H.L. Parker (Grand Rapids: Eerdmans, 1965), 47. *Commentarii in Pauli Epistolas, Ad Galatas*, edited by Helmut Feld (Geneve: Librairie Droz, 1992), 59-60.

In conclusion, I get to comment upon Prof. Witvliet's final observation, his question of "how do our discussions of worship stack up against the measuring stick of Calvin's theology of liturgy?" He asks this to those who would not only claim the titles of professor and instructor, but also of pastor and doctor. He asks, "How many of our current discussions about worship are really theological?" This is a significant theme, as Calvin himself never separated the tasks of Church and Academy. I can only bring one pastor's voice to this discussion. But this pastor can say that in his connections with congregations, very little rises to the level of theological urgency in these liturgical discussions. Too often lost —in the discussions of whether the choir should process, or whether we should pass the peace when the service is already too long, or whether the candles should be lit before or after the preacher walks in— are questions of whether our worship is scriptural, God-inspired and motivated, and pointing toward the God who has saved us? I suspect that Dr. Witvliet has an answer, in his comparison of Calvin's "rhetorical consummé to our motley porridge." If so, I share it.

Can Calvin's thought be lifted bodily out of its sixteenth century context? Can we grasp his theology of liturgy and drop it into the end of the twentieth century? We cannot. However, that inability does not leave us at a dead-end. Perhaps, in our deliberations on forming a theologically authentic liturgy, Calvin's model can inspire us to greater efforts, as this paper has sparked our imaginations about Calvin's place in the history of liturgy.

CONSTRUCTING TRADITION:
SCHLEIERMACHER, HODGE, AND THE THEOLOGICAL LEGACY OF CALVIN

B. A. Gerrish

I have offspring by thousands all over Christendom.— *Calvin*

On 25 April 1564, shortly before his death, Calvin dictated his last will and testament to a Genevan notary, who certified that the Reformer, though sick in body, was of a sound mind. Calvin first reaffirmed his faith in the gospel: he had no other refuge, he said, than God's gratuitous adoption, on which alone his salvation depended. He then went on to specify how his slender patrimony was to be assigned. The boys' school, the fund for impoverished aliens, and the daughter of Calvin's half-sister, Marie, were each to receive ten crowns (*escus*). Next, Calvin designated unequal sums of money for the children born from his brother Antoine's two marriages: for two of the boys 40 crowns each, for the three girls 30 each, and for their brother David only twenty-five, to chastise him for his frivolousness. Calvin added the proviso that should the sale of his books and other personal effects raise a larger amount than he expected, the surplus was to be distributed equally among the children—including David, if through the goodness of God he had returned to good behavior.[1] The testator thus exercised full control over his legacy, discriminating as he saw fit among his several beneficiaries: the girls received less than two of the boys, but David received less than the girls. Though Calvin would not be in a position to supervise the way the children spent their inheritance, he alone determined how much each of them had to spend.

Quite different from a monetary bequest is a theological legacy. It is not only possible for Calvin's theological heirs to spend their inheritance in ways he might not approve; even what they receive is pretty much what they decide to take. In this sense, tradition is not simply a gift but a construct—something we make rather than passively receive.[2] Bickering over the inheritance is likely. Not

---

[1] Calvin's will is reproduced in French in CO, 20:298-302. It is also given in Latin in the third version of Beza's life of Calvin: Theodore Beza, *Ioannis Calvini vita* (1575), CO, 21:162-164.

[2] Strictly speaking, Calvin's theological "legacy" is the *Opera omnia*. It is what is *taken* from this legacy that constitutes a theological "tradition."

that everyone will want the same things from the treasure chest; the argument will be over the value of the things chosen. There are certainly limits to what one may reasonably claim as Calvin's theological legacy. It is always possible to protest, "Calvin never said that," or, "That's not what he meant," or, "Well, he did say that, but it's not *all* he said." Still, appropriating Calvin's theological legacy is not the same as getting him right, or setting the historical record straight; the difference between his time and ours makes it impossible to take him just as he was, and we are deluding ourselves if we think otherwise. An appeal to Calvin's legacy as a theological warrant, even if it presupposes historical knowledge, is not a historical procedure. What he said may have a certain *prima facie* weight among those who locate themselves in a Calvinist tradition. For the theologian, however, the appeal to Calvin must be subjected to the same theological norms as everything else. The preeminent norm will naturally be the one to which he himself pointed his readers in the preface to the 1541 French *Institutes*: "Above all, they will be well advised to resort to Scripture, in order to ponder the testimonies I advance from it."[3] And precisely because our time is not his time, most theologians will recognize in the present state of knowledge *outside* the Scriptures a second norm, whether as part of a full-blown method of correlation or simply in recognition of the need to adapt and apply whatever we receive from the past.

It is not my intention in this essay to make a case either for or against Calvin's legacy, or any part of it. For now, I am interested in a third task that falls between determining what his theology was and appropriating his theology today: I mean the quest for examples of how Calvin's theological legacy has, as a matter of fact, been perceived or assimilated by others in other times. The quest may well be undertaken for the sake of the properly theological task, but it is itself strictly historical. Obviously, there is more than enough material out there to fill an entire book on the reception of Calvin's theological legacy from the sixteenth to the twentieth century. I am not aware of any attempt to write such a comprehensive study. If the attempt were made, the result would not be just a history of Calvin scholarship, and it would not be a book quite like McNeill's classic *History and Character of Calvinism*, in which the precise connection of Calvinism with Calvin is not the focus of inquiry.[4] Neither, incidentally, would it be a book like Bornkamm's *Luther im Spiegel der deutschen Geistesgeschichte*, which traces the changing images of Martin Luther reflected in the successive phases of German intellectual history.[5] The eagerness of the Germans to claim Luther's authority for their various programs has made him the patron of an astonishing number of mutually exclusive causes.

---

[3] *Institution de la religion chrestienne* (1541), "Argument du présent livre," in OS, 3:8. Trans. mine.

[4] John T. McNeill, *The History and Character of Calvinism* (New York: Oxford University Press, 1954).

[5] Heinrich Bornkamm, *Luther im Spiegel der deutschen Geistesgeschichte, mit ausgewählten Texten von Lessing bis zur Gegenwart* (Heidelberg: Quelle & Meyer, 1955).

The Reformed, by contrast, despite one or two attempts at hagiography, have not discovered in John Calvin good material for a personality cult, and in modern times they have not always turned instinctively to his theology as the touchstone of pure doctrine. But at no time has he been without his beneficiaries, and for now I want to think about just two of them: Friedrich Schleiermacher (1768-1834) and Charles Hodge (1797-1878). Then I will offer one or two concluding comments about Calvin's theological legacy. To anticipate: I want to show, first, that Schleiermacher and Hodge exemplify two quite different views of faithfulness to a tradition and, second, that Schleiermacher's view could well be regarded as akin to Calvin's own understanding of the Reformation tradition.

I

Schleiermacher was the greatest theologian of the Reformed church between Calvin and Barth. Only Jonathan Edwards comes close. I have made more than one previous attempt to explore the question of Schleiermacher's relation to Luther, the Reformation, and especially Calvin, always concluding that much more needs to be done.[6] The most obvious reason for neglect of the question is that since the 1920s the canonical narrative of Protestant history has represented Schleiermacher's thought as a disastrous break with the heritage of the Reformation. Karl Barth's famous declaration of 1922 set the pattern. Speaking of the line that runs back through Kierkegaard to Luther and Calvin, and so to Paul and Jeremiah, Barth added: "And to be absolutely clear, I would like to point out expressly that in the ancestral line I am commending to you the name *Schleiermacher does not appear.*"[7] The most detailed and comprehensive critique of Schleiermacher from what we commonly call the "neo-orthodox" camp was written not by Barth, but by his associate Emil Brunner. In *Die Mystik und das Wort* (1924), Brunner passionately accused his adversary of replacing biblical-Reformation faith with a mystical religion; taking this hermeneutic key in hand, he exposed the alleged flaws in a wide range of Schleiermacher's doctrines.[8] A few years later, an article by Wilhelm Niesel dealt specifically with Schleiermacher's relation to the Reformed tradition. His negative conclusion

---

[6]See especially "Schleiermacher and the Reformation: A Question of Doctrinal Development" (1980), reprinted in B. A. Gerrish, *The Old Protestantism and the New: Essays on the Reformation Heritage* (Chicago: University of Chicago Press; Edinburgh: T. & T. Clark, 1982), chap. 11, and "From Calvin to Schleiermacher: The Theme and the Shape of Christian Dogmatics" (1985), reprinted in Gerrish, *Continuing the Reformation: Essays on Modern Religious Thought* (Chicago: University of Chicago Press, 1993), chap. 8.

[7]Karl Barth, "Das Wort Gottes als Aufgabe der Theologie" (1922), *Karl Barth Gesamtausgabe*, 3,19 (Zurich: Theologischer Verlag, 1990), 158. Barth's emphasis; my trans.

[8][H.] Emil Brunner, *Die Mystik und das Wort: Der Gegensatz zwischen moderner Religionsauffassung und christlichem Glauben dargestellt an der Theologie Schleiermachers* (Tübingen: J. C. B. Mohr [Paul Siebeck], 1924; 2d ed., 1928).

was stated as an ironical question: Did Schleiermacher's supposedly Reformed makeup consist only in the fact that he possessed a Reformed certificate of baptism?[9]

Brunner and Niesel considered the matter closed; Barth was never quite so sure.[10] But it must be added that the way the neo-orthodox theologians construed the story found some support from German historians, who professed disappointment with Schleiermacher's strange failure to display much warmth in speaking of Martin Luther.[11] And here one must note another reason for the state of the secondary literature: in Germany the assumption, sometimes tacit, sometimes spoken, has always been that the Reformation means Luther. Hence the question of Schleiermacher's connection with the Reformation is presumed to have been answered when his rare and somewhat restrained remarks about Luther have been duly noted and lamented. But the obvious next step would be to see if he spoke more approvingly either of the Reformation in general or of John Calvin in particular, the reformer most esteemed in Schleiermacher's own church. Though German, Schleiermacher was not a Lutheran, and even after the union of the Lutherans and the Reformed in 1817, which he supported, he continued to profess his allegiance to what he called "the Reformed school."[12]

It must be said, to begin with, that one should not expect much more warmth in Schleiermacher's references to Calvin than in his references to Luther. He understood history to be everywhere the collective work of a "common spirit" and was unwilling to attribute too much to individuals.[13] He hoped that when the dividing names "Lutheran" and "Reformed" disappeared in the Church of the Union, it would no longer seem as if the Reformed were less respectful than the Lutherans of the man after whom the Lutherans were named, nor yet as if the Lutherans were less concerned than the Reformed to avoid glorifying any one man too much.[14] He viewed Luther's achievement as

---

[9]Wilhelm Niesel, "Schleiermachers Verhältnis zur reformierten Tradition," *Zwischen den Zeiten* 8 (1930): 511-25.

[10]See Barth's review of Brunner's *Die Mystik und das Wort*: "Brunners Schleiermacherbuch," *Zwischen den Zeiten* 2 (1924): 49-64; see p. 60. The apparent uncertainty—despite some heady rhetoric—continued to the year of Barth's death, when he admitted he was not so sure of his own cause that his "yes" entailed a "no" to Schleiermacher's cause. Heinz Bolli, ed., *Schleiermacher-Auswahl mit einem Nachwort von Karl Barth* (Munich and Hamburg: Siebenstern Taschenbuch Verlag, 1968), 307.

[11]I mentioned some of the pertinent literature in the articles referred to in n. 6 above.

[12]See, for example, Schleiermacher, *An Herrn Oberhofprediger Dr. Ammon über seine Prüfung der Harmsischen Sätze* (1818), in *Friedrich Schleiermachers sämmtliche Werke* (hereafter *SW*, cited by division, volume, and page), 31 vols. (Berlin: Georg Reimer, 1834-64), 1, 5: 341.

[13]He applies this view of history expressly to the Reformation in *Geschichte der christlichen Kirche, aus Schleiermachers handschriftlichem Nachlasse und nachgeschriebenen Vorlesungen herausgegeben* (1840), *SW*, 1, 11: 576.

[14]*An Ammon*, *SW*, 1, 5: 396-397.

part of a larger, unfinished Reformation that could not be the work of any single individual, but in which several individuals—Erasmus, Luther, Zwingli, Calvin, and others—have all played their essential roles.[15] No belittling of any one of them, nor of the Reformation itself, was intended. Schleiermacher believed that he still lived and did his theology in the period of the Reformation, which was likely to endure for a good many more years; no comparable epoch separated him from the first generation of Protestants.[16] For the Reformation was not merely a correction of abuses; much less was it simply the restitution of the apostolic age. It brought into existence a new and distinctive formation of the Christian spirit, which for the foreseeable future will stand over against the Catholic type of Christianity.[17] Although he was certain that the work of theology, or more exactly the work of dogmatic theology, had to be determined by the antithesis of Catholic and Protestant, Schleiermacher had some difficulty defining the exact nature of the antithesis. Sometimes he located it in the contrast between symbolic action and the word; sometimes in the different ways the two communions represent the relation of the individual to the church.[18] But there is no need to pursue the problem here. The point is simply that if we are to understand his references to Calvin, we have to read them in the context of what he made of the Protestant Reformation. Then we will not be disappointed if we find little inclination to venerate Calvin, or even to elevate him above the other evangelical Reformers.

This leads me to a second contextual point, closely related to the first. If the Reformation is the collective work of a common spirit, collective expressions of the Reformation will naturally be assigned dogmatic precedence over the opinions of individual theologians. With this in mind, no one need be surprised that Schleiermacher's great dogmatic work, *The Christian Faith* (2d ed., 1830-31), especially the second part, bristles with quotations from the Protestant confessions; often, he introduces a new theme with a long catena of passages. At the time of his writing, the authority of so-called symbolic books was the center of a heated theological controversy, in which he was obliged more than once to take a public stand. Ironically, the formation of the united church coincided

---

[15] *Gespräch zweier selbst überlegender evangelischer Christen,* etc. (1827), *SW,* 1, 5: 542-548, 625; *Geschichte der Kirche, SW,* 1, 11: 582-583 (on the role of Erasmus).

[16] *Kurze Darstellung des theologischen Studiums zum Behuf einleitender Vorlesungen* (hereafter *KD*), 3d, critical ed., ed. Heinrich Scholz (1910; reprint, Darmstadt: Wissenschaftliche Buchgesellschaft, 1961), §§ 71-93, 186, 212; cf. *Geschichte der Kirche, SW,* 1, 11: 36, 612.

[17] *Der christliche Glaube, nach den Grundsätzen der evangelischen Kirche im Zusammenhange dargestellt* (hereafter *CG,* cited by section), 7th ed., based on the 2d (1830-31), ed. Martin Redeker, 2 vols. (Berlin: Walter de Gruyter, 1960), § 24. Eng. trans. of the 2d German ed.: *The Christian Faith,* ed. H. R. Mackintosh and J. S. Stewart (Edinburgh: T. & T. Clark, 1928).

[18] The ecclesiological contrast appears in *CG,* § 24. For the contrast between word and symbolic action in worship, see *Die christliche Sitte, nach den Grundsätzen der evangelischen Kirche im Zusammenhange dargestellt* (1884), *SW,* 1, 12: 212; cf. *Geschichte der Kirche, SW,* 1, 11: 45-46.

with the rise of Lutheran confessionalism and even intensified it. Many Lutherans feared that association with the Reformed might further dilute the purity of Lutheranism, already threatened by rationalism, and they called for strict adherence to their Reformation creeds.

In response, Schleiermacher pointed to a middle way between rationalism and inflexible confessionalism. He professed astonishment that there were those who would have erased so many years of church history, demanding subscription to a document from the sixteenth century. But if this set him firmly against the Lutheran confessionalists, it did not align him with the opposing rationalist party, which held that precisely because the Reformation confessions were written for their own time, they were mere historical documents and had no claim to present-day attention. This view too in its own way, he argued, betrayed a lack of historical sense. For there is always a difference between the first decisive moments and the subsequent course of a historical phenomenon, and between a merely personal statement and one that represents a widespread conviction. Although we are not forever bound to the letter, the confessions have their unique worth as the first public expressions of the Protestant spirit, which is identical in both the Lutheran and the Reformed churches.[19] The difference between the two communions that trace their lineage back to the Reformation is only a difference of "school"—not, that is, a divergence in the religious affections, but in the way they are represented.[20]

It is against the background of these fundamental principles that Schleiermacher's attitude to Calvin and his theological legacy are to be understood. He could not confer on Calvin the value reserved for the Reformation confessions, both Lutheran and Reformed, and he was not tempted to make him a denominational hero. Within these limits, his judgments on Calvin are generous. He did not claim to be a Calvin scholar with a broad knowledge of the *Opera omnia*, but he was well acquainted with the *Institutes*. When a theological opponent attributed a dubious sentiment to Calvin, Schleiermacher's reaction was confident: "I cannot find this principle anywhere in my Calvin; rather, as I consider the matter more closely, I find grounds enough in my slight knowledge of Calvin to assert that he cannot have written that." The expression "my Calvin" is intriguing. By his "slight knowledge of Calvin" he evidently meant his limited acquaintance with other works of Calvin besides the *Institutes*. For when the opponent supplied a reference, it turned out that he had misrepresented a passage on election from the third book of the *Institutes*, with which Schleier-

---

[19] *Über den eigenthümlichen Wert und das bindende Ansehen symbolischer Bücher* (1819), in Schleiermacher, *Kleine Schriften und Predigten* (hereafter *KS*), ed. Hayo Gerdes and Emanuel Hirsch, 3 vols. (Berlin: Walter de Gruyter, 1969-70), 2: 143-44, 159-62. Nevertheless, against any temptation to exaggerate the perfection of the old confessions, Schleiermacher points out that their authors were men and theologians like us (*An die Herren D.D.D. von Cölln und D. Schulz: Ein Sendschreiben* [1831], *KS*, 2: 237-238).

[20] *CG*, § 24, *Zusatz*.

macher was perfectly well acquainted. "And I thought the proof would come," he remarks, "from who knows what more seldom read commentary of Calvin!"[21] We can safely infer that he had not spent much time reading Calvin's commentaries. But he seems to have been at home in the *Institutes*, which he admired for two main reasons. First, he judged it a priceless work because it never loses touch with the religious affections, not even in the most intricate material. Second, it is distinguished by sharpness of method and systematic compass.[22] Though he regretted the fact that in Calvin the systematic impulse was hindered by a polemical tendency, it is obvious that Schleiermacher admired most in the *Institutes* exactly what he himself strove for in his own systematic work, *The Christian Faith*.[23] But it does not necessarily follow that he actually *owed* his methodological ideals to Calvin's theological legacy. The next question is whether he was indebted to Calvin for the content he gave to some of his dogmatic themes.

There are a number of points at which a comparison between the 1559 *Institutes* and the second edition of *The Christian Faith* proves very interesting. Some of them I have taken up elsewhere.[24] But resemblances, if and when they emerge, do not establish debts; and the comparison just as often uncovers differences, whether or not they reflect conscious modifications or corrections of the Calvinist heritage. For this reason, I want to confine my attention to the passages in *The Christian Faith* in which Calvin is expressly named. There are sixteen references to Calvin[25]—more than to Zwingli (7) or Luther (13), but fewer than the references to Johann Gerhard (19), Melanchthon (21), Reinhard (25), or Augustine (33). Obviously, I cannot take a close look at all Schleiermacher's Calvin citations, but I can at least make a start. All the references, without exception, are to the *Institutes*: six to book 1, two to book 2, five to book 3, and three to book 4. It is not always certain whether Calvin is being cited to confirm Schleiermacher's argument, or to exemplify a position he is

---

[21] *Zugabe zu meinem Schreiben an Herrn Ammon* (1818), *SW*, 1, 5: 409-410.

[22] *An Ammon*, *SW*, 1, 5: 345; *Geschichte der Kirche*, *SW*, 1, 11: 602.

[23] *Geschichte der Kirche*, *SW*, 1, 11: 615-616; cf. *CG*, §§ 17, 27-28.

[24] See in particular "Theology Within the Limits of Piety Alone: Schleiermacher and Calvin's Notion of God" (1981), *The Old Protestantism*, chap. 12, and "Nature and the Theater of Redemption: Schleiermacher on Christian Dogmatics and the Creation Story" (1987), *Continuing the Reformation*, chap. 9.

[25] Sixteen is the number given in the index to the English translation (see n. 17 above). Redeker's index lists fifteen, but that is because he takes as one reference the two citations from Calvin in *CG*, § 119.3. (Neither index includes the third mention of Calvin, without quotation, in this same section.) In Redeker's first reference, § 37 is apparently a slip for § 38. There are also slips—no doubt errors of transcription—in Schleiermacher's own citations from the *Institutes:* in the footnote reference to Calvin in *CG*, § 108.4 the Roman numeral IX should of course be IV; the second Calvin quotation in *CG*, § 119.3 is from the *Institutes,* book three, chapter 21 (not chap. 23); the quotation at the head of § 141 is from book four, chapter 17 (not chap. 7).

criticizing. He tells us, for instance, it is questionable (*bedenklich*) to teach that angels bring outside protection to us, and he adds a footnote reference to the *Institutes*.[26] Now, in the place cited Calvin does assert that angels are our protectors, though he hesitates to say that each of us has a personal guardian angel; but he warns us against transferring to the angels what belongs to God and Christ.[27] So, is he cited disapprovingly for his assertion, or approvingly for his warning? Perhaps both, since Schleiermacher thinks the hazard is great enough to warrant the complete exclusion of angel talk from dogmatics, allowing it only a limited private and liturgical use.[28] Similarly ambivalent is a passage in which Calvin is described as acute (*scharfsinnig*), but unable to put together a consistent account of the Devil's activity from the different strands in the biblical allusions to him.[29]

Schleiermacher can of course quote what Calvin says, without either endorsing or criticizing it, simply as one of the views held on the theme under discussion. This is the point of his quotations from Calvin on the Lord's Supper: we have to distinguish the Lutheran, the Zwinglian, and the Calvinistic views, but none of them is free from difficulties.[30] Mostly, however, he refers to Calvin to indicate their agreement. The list of approving references is interesting. Calvin's reading of the Mosaic creation narrative rules out the use of Genesis to construct an actual theory of creation. Calvin asserted that God foresees future events because he decreed them. (A good point, Schleiermacher thinks, but John Scotus Erigena [810-877] put it better when he said "God sees," not "God foresees," what he willed to make.) Again, Calvin refused to say that the contagion of original sin is transmitted through the substance of either the flesh or the soul. He rightly distinguished God's will from his precept (that is, the efficient from the commanding will of God). Whereas some deny the necessity for the baptized to be converted, Calvin represented baptism precisely as the "seed" of future repentance and faith. And he held it to be beyond controversy that no one is loved by God outside of Christ.[31] On all of these six points, then, Calvin gives expression to thoughts that Schleiermacher shares with him. He is drawing on the theological legacy of Calvin—whether to confirm his own thoughts or to acknowledge a formative influence on them is hard to say. But I have saved until last the most instructive of his attempts to see himself in

---

[26] *CG*, § 43.1.

[27] *Institutes*, 1.14.6-11.

[28] *CG*, § 43.2.

[29] *CG*, § 45.2 (with reference to *Institutes*, 1.14.17-18).

[30] *CG*, § 140.4. At the beginning of the following section (§ 141), Schleiermacher quotes Calvin—among others—on the effects of the Lord's Supper, but without subsequent comment.

[31] *CG*, §§ 40.2, 55.1 n., 72.4 n., 81.1 n., 108.4, 109.4 n. Calvin is also cited (with implicit approval) for his assertion that belief in providence, no less than creation, distinguishes Christians from unbelievers (*CG*, § 38).

Calvin's lineage: his adherence to the doctrine of election, which led his contemporaries to characterize him as a "bold and resolute disciple of Calvin."

Schleiermacher defended election in the long, 119-page article that launched the *Theologische Zeitschrift* in 1819.[32] He stated expressly that he wished to take up the doctrine in its original presentation in Calvin's *Institutes*, avoiding the later Canons of Dort (1618-19). The argument of the article is carried over into *The Christian Faith*, only there, as one would expect, in the form not of an apology for Calvin but of a constructive statement, followed as usual by an assessment of the official church teachings (*kirchliche Lehrsätze*). Schleiermacher's key thought is very simple: the kingdom of God established by Christ is a phenomenon of history, and it is therefore impossible that the whole of humanity should be taken into it at one time. What proceeds from a single point can spread only gradually. This "law" is so plainly a part of the divine governance of the world that we must judge the antithesis between those who are, and those who are not, members of the church to be grounded solely in the divine good-pleasure. But it is a *vanishing* antithesis, and the Christian consciousness cannot suppose that because some die outside the kingdom, a part of the human race is intended to be finally excluded. In other words, we hope for the antithesis to continue diminishing even after death.[33]

It is when he turns to the ecclesiastical doctrines that Schleiermacher refers to Calvin. Like him, he has been wrestling with the evident inequality in the operations of grace; and like him he can attribute it only to the divine good-pleasure. Now he quotes Calvin directly three times, but each time with a critical comment or in a context that, in part, runs counter to Calvin's views. First, Calvin says that election could not stand unless set over against reprobation. Schleiermacher agrees, but only in the limited sense that those who at any particular time are passed over or rejected are *not yet* chosen. We have no warrant for concluding that they never will be.[34] Second, Calvin speaks of a twofold foreordination, either to blessedness or to damnation. Schleiermacher argues that there is but *one* divine foreordination—the decree to assume the human race into fellowship with Christ.[35] Third, Calvin defines predestination as the eternal decree of God by which he determined what he willed to become of each individual. Schleiermacher protests against any atomistic view of the work of redemption and understands the operations of grace on the individual strictly

---

[32]"Über die Lehre von der Erwählung," etc., reproduced in *SW*, 1, 2: 393-484. It is in this article that Schleiermacher mentions the description of him as a "bold and resolute disciple of Calvin," adding, "I do not know with what justice" (p. 399).

[33]*CG*, §§ 117-18. For the notion of a *verschwindender Gegensatz*, see § 118.1.

[34]*CG*, § 119.2. Schleiermacher recognizes that the qualification he introduces resembles the view Calvin rejects as childish: that the idea of election is unobjectionable if no one is actually condemned (*Institutes*, 3.23.1).

[35]*CG*, § 119.3.

in relation to the one eternal decree to redeem *humanity* in Christ.[36] So, was Schleiermacher a "bold and resolute disciple of Calvin" or not? I shall come back to the question in my conclusion. But first some reflections on Charles Hodge. They will need to be much briefer.

II

Hodge was not an original thinker of Schleiermacher's caliber, but he was surely the greatest American Calvinist since Jonathan Edwards (1703-1758).[37] Not a Calvin scholar, as B. B. Warfield (1851-1921) was a little later at Princeton, he was a learned advocate of the Calvinist theological legacy—or, as he often said, "the Augustinian system." He was appalled at the direction German theology had taken, partly under the lead of Schleiermacher's charismatic personality. In a way, his critical estimate of Schleiermacher anticipated Brunner's, since it ended in a perplexing conflict between the two sides of the father of modern theology: his devout faith in Christ and his allegedly pagan philosophy.[38] Hodge reached back into the seventeenth century for sounder and safer theological models. With a sigh of relief, he wrote: "After all the alleged improvements in theological research, we never feel so much disposed to take down one of the old Latin dogmatic writers of the seventeenth century, as immediately on closing a fresh work from Germany."[39]

Our question must be, then, whether by way of Francis Turretin (1623-87) and the other orthodox divines Hodge received a larger bequest from Calvin

---

[36]Ibid. (The expression *eine völlig atomistische Ansicht des Erlösungswerkes* appears later, in § 120.2.) Schleiermacher finds Calvin's "formula" logical enough, and he clearly sympathizes with his refusal to accept the attempts commonly made to soften the doctrine of predestination. If the operations of divine grace end at death, then the logical conclusion can only be that some are predestined to damnation, others to blessedness; and it does not help to argue that the former are passed over, not foreordained to damnation, or that God merely "foreknows" their fate. For Schleiermacher, however, the doctrine is made tolerable—i.e., consistent with the Christian consciousness—by denying the premise that death ends the work of grace. Hence § 119 concludes with a pointer to the eschatological doctrines he will take up later (see in particular the appendix to § 163).

[37]Concerning the relation of Edwards himself to the theological legacy of Calvin, we have his own direct testimony in the preface to his *Freedom of the Will* (1754). He accepts the party label "Calvinist" (in distinction from "Arminian") but disclaims dependence on Calvin: he neither holds his doctrines merely because Calvin taught them nor believes everything exactly as Calvin taught.

[38]See, for instance, his remarks in Charles Hodge, *Systematic Theology* (hereafter *ST*), 3 vols. (1871-72; reprint, Grand Rapids, Michigan: Wm. B. Eerdmans Publishing Company, 1981), 2:440-441. I have explored Hodge's relation to Schleiermacher more fully in a paper, "Charles Hodge and the Europeans," presented at the Hodge symposium held in Princeton, 22-24 October 1997, on the theme "Charles Hodge Revisited: A Critical Appraisal of His Life and Work." The papers still await publication.

[39]Hodge explains that the old Latin divines had the characteristic merits of "the American, or what is the same thing, the British mind." Hodge, "Neander's History," *Biblical Repertory and Princeton Review* 16 (1844):155-183; quotations on pp. 182-183.

than Schleiermacher did. Different it was certain to be. Schleiermacher held that theological progress, though it cannot be heretical, is bound to be heterodox and must include an honest critique of the official dogmas of the church.[40] Hodge, by contrast, liked to commend his opinions as biblical and orthodox—nothing more than the church had always taught.[41] Interestingly, there was at least one topic on which he had to locate Schleiermacher closer than himself to Johann Gerhard (1582-1637) and Johann Heinrich Heidegger (1633-98). He conceded that for the seventeenth-century theologians, both Lutheran and Reformed, the divine "simplicity" made it impossible to allow any real distinctions between one divine attribute and another, and he recognized that this put Schleiermacher in the succession of the orthodox divines, whereas he himself wanted to take the distinctions between God's various attributes in Scripture at face value.[42] But this odd change of dancing partners did not lead him to have second thoughts about Schleiermacher's relation to the dogmatic tradition.

When it comes to direct references to Calvin, Hodge easily out-quotes Schleiermacher. The index to the three-volume *Systematic Theology* (1871-72) directs us to twenty-eight places where Calvin is named or quoted, in one of which multiple pages in the third volume are indicated.[43] In some of the places mentioned, more than one actual citation from Calvin is given; in two, there are excursuses headed "Calvin's Doctrine" (on justification and the Lord's Supper). The total number of citations also needs to be adjusted to allow for the fact that Hodge quotes the Geneva Catechism (1545) without assigning it to Calvin's authorship and, conversely, cites the *Consensus Tigurinus* (1549; published 1551) as though Calvin were its sole author. Further, the index is not complete.[44] But I am not anxious to determine Hodge's exact "score," so to say. The point is to discern the pattern in his references to Calvin. Let me make three observations.

First, most of the references are to the 1559 *Institutes*, but not all. Hodge also quotes from Calvin's *Harmony of the Gospels* (on Matt 19:10-11); from the commentaries on Romans, 1 Timothy, and Titus ; and from the Geneva Catechism, the Scholars Confession (1559), the treatise against Tileman Heshusius (1561),

---

[40] *CG*, §§ 21, 25 (*Zusatz*), 27; cf. *KD*, §§ 60, 203-8.

[41] See, for instance, *ST*, 2:479. To preserve his claim that he presents simply what "has always been the faith of the Church," Hodge is sometimes obliged to "unchurch" not only the rationalists (as here), but even Roman Catholics, Lutherans, and (implicitly) the Eastern Orthodox (2:367, 373, 418, 450-451, 621).

[42] *ST*, 1: 394-97.

[43] *ST*, 3: 131-134 (on justification).

[44] In the long section on the Lord's Supper (*ST*, vol. 3, chap. 20, §§ 15-19), the index omits some of the pages on which Calvin is named (pp. 639, 645, 656, 676 n.3), or named and quoted (pp. 641, 646). There may well be other omissions that I have not noticed.

and two of Calvin's letters.[45] Three quotations from Calvin are given without identification of their sources.[46] Clearly, Hodge had some acquaintance with the commentaries and other "who knows what more seldom read" writings of Calvin.

Second, as we would expect, nearly all the discussions of Calvin serve as corroboration for Hodge's own views, but again not all. Aside from the place where Hodge simply notes that Calvin used the word "regeneration" more inclusively than ourselves, to denote the entire Christian life and not just its beginning,[47] he differs with Calvin on two topics: on virginity and on what he calls "the peculiar views of Calvin" on the Lord's Supper.[48] I will come back to the Lord's Supper in a moment. Hodge is surprisingly vehement in his critique of the views on virginity and marriage in book two of the *Institutes* (*Inst.*, 2.8.41-42, the only passage he refers to in the second book). He comments: "[Calvin says that] virginity is a virtue. Celibacy is a higher state than marriage. Those who cannot live in that state, should descend to the lower platform of married life. With such dregs of Manichean philosophy was the pure truth of the Bible contaminated even as held by the most illustrious Reformers."[49] Hodge does not mention that Calvin was attempting an honest interpretation of the Lord's saying about men who castrate themselves for the sake of the kingdom (Matt 19:12) and Paul's unsentimental view of marriage as a divine remedy for lust (1 Cor 7:2). Calvin's assertion that nature and the fall combine to make us "doubly subject to women's society" does make you wonder about him, but it may not be necessary to explain it by "the dregs of Manichean philosophy."

This brings me to my third observation: though he quotes Calvin often, Hodge's use of Calvin, whether approving or disapproving, is not always fair. On the whole, I think, he is honest enough. But sometimes he selects only what he wants (don't we all?), and sometimes he twists the evidence (*we* don't do that). It is remarkable that in his long argument against baptismal regeneration Hodge's only quotation from Calvin is a bland remark retrieved from his Commentary on Titus 3:5, "Partam a Christo salutem baptismus nobis obsignat."[50] Hodge says nothing of Calvin's argument in the *Institutes* that God can, and sometimes certainly does, effect the regeneration of baptized infants.[51] On

---

[45] *ST*, 3: 373; 3: 90, 369 n.1, 389, 596; 3: 487, 501, 580; 2: 209; 3: 629-30; 1: 467, 3: 631.

[46] *ST*, 2: 209.

[47] *ST*, 3: 3-5.

[48] *ST*, 3: 630.

[49] *ST*, 3: 371.

[50] *ST*, 3: 596.

[51] *Institutes*, 4.16.17-26. By the end of this segment of book 4, chapter 16, Calvin can speak confidently of "the dogma we have now established concerning the regeneration of infants." Though Hodge does not cite Calvin's teaching on infant baptism, as he does Calvin's teaching on the Lord's Supper, the conclusion to his preceding section, on baptism as a means of grace (*ST*, 3: 590), is in close agreement with Calvin.

the other evangelical sacrament, Hodge seems in one place clearly to misuse the sources. He conceded that Calvin spoke of receiving a supernatural power that flows from Christ's life-giving flesh in heaven. But he repudiated this "peculiar" notion and wanted to show that it was only a minor strand, not only in Reformed theology generally, but even in Calvin's own thoughts on the Lord's Supper. Calvin, he says, "avowed his agreement with Zwingle [sic] and Oecolampadius on all questions related to the sacraments." However, "at times" he did teach the peculiar notion of an influence from the glorified body of Christ. As evidence, Hodge quotes from Calvin's exposition of the *Consensus Tigurinus*. "Unless," he goes on, "we are willing to accuse the illustrious Calvin of inconsistency, his meaning must be made to harmonize with what he says elsewhere." And to prove his point, Hodge quotes from the *Consensus* itself.[52] But this, surely, is to get things exactly the wrong way around. Calvin wrote the *Expositio* as a fuller explanation of the *Consensus*, fearing that its brevity might leave it vulnerable to quibbling. If there is some tension between the explanation and the document itself, we should attribute it not only to the brevity of the *Consensus*, but also to its character as a compromise document, in which Calvin did not say all he liked to say about the Lord's Supper. His *Expositio* is where we must look to find out what was in *his* mind during the negotiations. An *expositio* by the coauthor of the *Consensus*, Heinrich Bullinger (1504-75), would no doubt look very different.[53]

Hodge's fascinating debate on the Lord's Supper with John Williamson Nevin (1803-86) was an immensely instructive chapter in the history of Calvin's theological legacy. I have written about it elsewhere and do not want to delay too much over it here, other than to reaffirm its importance to our present topic.[54] It was a clash between two varieties of Calvinism, the one predestinarian and the other sacramental. Hodge had no antenna for Calvin's strange talk about the life-giving flesh of Christ. He could not deny that Calvin did talk that way ("at times"!), but he explained that this was an "uncongenial foreign element" in Reformed theology, partly derived from Lutheran influence, and he did not wish to be troubled with the "private authority of Calvin."[55] For his part, Nevin was convinced that Calvin's talk of Christ's life-giving flesh was all-important, not least because it excluded the Zwinglian alternative. He admitted, how-

---

[52]*ST*, 3: 646-647.

[53]The pertinent documents, including the Articles of the *Consensus* and Calvin's exposition of them (i.e., his *Defensio sanae et orthodoxae doctrinae de sacramentis*, etc., 1555), will be found in *OS*, 2:241-87. On Calvin's intention in writing the *Expositio*, see p. 267.

[54]Gerrish, *Tradition and the Modern World: Reformed Theology in the Nineteenth Century* (Chicago: University of Chicago Press, 1978), 57-65.

[55]Hodge, "Doctrine of the Reformed Church on the Lord's Supper," *Princeton Review* 20 (1848): 227-278; quotations from p. 251. Hodge also dismissed the distinction, crucial to Calvin's doctrine, between "believing" and "eating" as a "distinction without a difference" (*ST*, 3: 644-645).

ever, that much of Calvin's language was fantastic and tried to reclothe the substance of it in modern categories—leaving him open to Hodge's accusation that he had fallen victim to the dreaded German philosophy.[56] Moreover, Nevin was convinced that there is a fundamental disharmony between Calvin's predestinarianism and his sacramentalism, and that increasing obsession with the divine decrees was responsible for the decline of the authentic Calvinistic view of the Eucharist.[57] If Hodge ceded Calvin's eucharistic theology to Mercersburg, then, Nevin gladly let Princeton keep the Calvin of the "horrible decree."

Nevin was a learned adversary. James Hastings Nichols, the historian of the Mercersburg theology, suspected that Hodge's Calvin citations were actually gleaned from Nevin's copious footnotes, and he concluded that Hodge was "beyond his depth . . . . He made the mistake of challenging a man whose command of the field was vastly greater than his own."[58] Personally, I would distribute the honors a bit more evenly. Hodge rightly challenged Nevin's belief that in the Calvinistic Eucharist there is "an altogether extraordinary power," quite different from what is available in the preached word. Nevin (like Schleiermacher) understood the Calvinistic doctrine to assert a real presence of Christ's body and blood in the Supper not available anywhere else. Hodge had no difficulty showing that, as an interpretation of Calvin, this was a mistake.[59] Hodge's debate with Nevin was partly a difference over the interpretation of Calvin, partly a difference over what there is in his legacy that is worth preserving. In short, it was consciously, directly, and expressly an *argument* about the theology of Calvin: what it was and where it was sound.

I want to end my remarks on Hodge and the Calvinist tradition by commenting briefly on a paradigmatic issue of another kind, in which the question is not directly about Calvin, but about an *uncontroverted* theological concept that can be traced back to him. The schema of the *munus triplex* — Christ's three offices as prophet, priest, and king—had become an accepted resource in the theologian's equipment for interpreting the work of Christ. Calvin is

---

[56]John W. Nevin, *The Mystical Presence: A Vindication of the Reformed or Calvinistic Doctrine of the Holy Eucharist* (Philadelphia: J. B. Lippincott, 1846), 155-163. Nevin traced the difficulties under which Calvin's theory labored to a "false psychology," and he believed that his proposed revisions rested on a scientific psychology.

[57]Nevin, "Doctrine of the Reformed Church on the Lord's Supper," *Mercersburg Review* 2 (1850):421-548; see p. 523.

[58]James Hastings Nichols, *Romanticism in American Theology: Nevin and Schaff at Mercersburg* (Chicago: University of Chicago Press, 1961), 89-91.

[59]Hodge, "Doctrine of the Reformed Church," 273. It must be added, however, that if Nevin overestimated the significance of Calvin's doctrine of the Lord's Supper in this respect, Hodge's refutation of Nevin underestimates Calvin's doctrine of the preached word (see Gerrish, *Tradition and the Modern World,* 62-63). In his *Mystical Presence* (p. 75) Nevin cited Schleiermacher in his support, who understood the Calvinistic Supper to affirm *die nirgend sonst zu habende wirkliche Gegenwart seines Leibes und Blutes* (*CG,* § 140. 4).

credited with introducing it into Protestant dogmatics, though he himself did not make as much use of it as he leads us to expect.[60] In book two of the *Institutes*, the fifteenth chapter sets up the framework. We are to look at three things in Christ: his "offices" as prophet, king, and priest. Calvin takes the offices to denote not only a work of Christ accomplished *extra nos*, but also an activity into which believers are drawn along with him. But chapter 16 appears to leave the threefold office behind and to concentrate heavily, if not quite exclusively, on the priestly work of Christ on our behalf.

Similarly, Hodge begins his discussion of the work of Christ with the three-fold office of the Mediator, and he stresses its dogmatic importance:

> We as fallen men, ignorant, guilty, polluted, and helpless, need a Saviour who is a prophet to instruct us; a priest to atone and to make intercession for us; and a king to rule over and protect us. . . . This is not, therefore, simply a convenient classification of the contents of his mission and work, but it enters into its very nature, and must be retained in our theology if we would take the truth as it is revealed in the word of God.[61]

But Hodge does not develop the *munus triplex* any more than Calvin did, and his rearrangement of the sequence—now prophet, priest, and king—makes the imbalance in his treatment of the offices very obvious. The presentation of the priestly office is so long that the reader has probably forgotten the kingly office by the time it receives its short chapter. Hodge's discussion of the work of Christ runs to 184 pages. He needs but two pages to dispose of the prophetic office, and only a slightly more generous fourteen to explain the kingly office. In between he lingers for no fewer than 132 pages over Christ's priestly work, most of them on the idea of satisfaction for sin (128 pages), but with a short addition (four pages) on Christ's priestly intercession. Further, Hodge takes the work of the Mediator to be a work performed strictly *extra nos*—outside of ourselves, in our place, in our stead. Calvin's notion of a threefold work of Christ performed both *for* us and *in* us is conspicuously absent.

Now, the striking absence of balance in Hodge's treatment of the three offices and his one-sided emphasis on the work of Christ in our place could, of course, reflect a sound grasp of dogmatic priorities. It would require a move from the historical to the dogmatic mode if I wished to pronounce a *theological* verdict on what Hodge does here—or does *not* do—with the tradition. I am certainly not shy about making such a move in the proper place. But let me, for now, simply conclude my remarks on Hodge with a comparison. When Schleiermacher comes to speak of the ecclesiastical doctrine of the Redeemer's

---

[60]See J[ohn] F. Jensen, *Calvin's Doctrine of the Work of Christ* (London: James Clarke, 1956), especially pp. 51-58. For a different estimate of the role of the *munus triplex* in the 1559 *Institutes*, see Klauspeter Blaser, *Calvins Lehre von den drei Ämtern Christi*, Theologische Studien, no. 105 (Zurich: EVZ-Verlag, 1970).

[61]*ST*, 2: 461.

threefold office, he commends it precisely because it *prevents* undue emphasis on a single aspect of Christ's redeeming and reconciling activity, and he is closer than Hodge to Calvin's understanding of the entire work of Christ as, at least in part, an activity into which Christians are drawn *by and with* Christ.[62] Schleiermacher makes no reference to Calvin's treatment of the threefold office. Neither does Hodge. Had he done so, he might have had second thoughts about both his and Schleiermacher's interpretations of the work of Christ. Evidently, one of the ways in which Calvin's offspring may relate to his legacy is by way of oversight or neglect—unwitting failure to explore further what Calvin left simply in the form of hints and possibilities.

III

When a mean-spirited adversary, François Baudouin, made a joke of Calvin's childlessness, Calvin replied that he had offspring by thousands all over Christendom.[63] So he did—and still does. But his heirs have not all used his legacy in the same measure or the same way. Sometimes they seem to have drawn unconsciously on their heritage, or equally unconsciously to have neglected it. But they have also argued over what Calvin said, what he meant, and what he left that is worth preserving. From the two examples I have given it is, I think, plain that the way the legacy is used is determined in part by fundamental dogmatic principles. Hodge, on the whole, held a static view of past sources and norms. True, I was able to point to one place in which he notes that a dogmatic term, "regeneration," is differently employed by us today than in his day by Calvin. But he does not stop to ask if the change of term reflects a change of thought. In this instance, it probably does not. And in general the question did not arise at all for Hodge, who understood the language of the theological tradition, like the language of Scripture, to be immobile. Hence, when reading Calvin, he could agree with what he read, or (less often) he could disagree; there was no third option. And the criterion of "orthodoxy," by which he judged even Calvin, meant firm adherence to what the church had always believed and taught as the sense of Scripture.[64]

Schleiermacher held a quite different, developmental understanding of tradition. This is nowhere more clear than in his doctrine of election. He did not quote passages from Calvin on the subject simply in order to agree with some, disagree with others. Rather, he wrestled with the *idea* of election, thought he saw what was important in Calvin's treatment of it, and tried to formulate it

---

[62]See *CG*, §§ 100-2, especially § 102.3.

[63]*Responsio ad Balduini convicia* (1562), CO, 9:576.

[64]In *ST*, 2: 166, Hodge mentions without comment the "celebrated formula" of the semi-Pelagian Vincent of Lérins (d. ca. 450): "Quod ubique, quod semper, quod ab omnibus creditum est." Though he does not here endorse the formula, he comes close to it in his characteristic appeal to what the church has always taught (see n. 41 above).

anew. As for Calvin's actual language, he could appropriate some of his terms, limit the application of others, and quietly set still others aside. Had he persuaded his church to follow him in his admittedly heterodox moves, then the single divine decree that creates only a vanishing, temporal division in the human race would have become orthodox; for orthodoxy, as Schleiermacher understood it, was not what the church had always and everywhere taught, but what had become the prevailing doctrine in a particular church at a particular time.[65] So was Schleiermacher a "bold and resolute disciple of Calvin"? If we think of the disciple as one who simply echoes the words of the master, our answer will be "No." But an interesting fact is worth mentioning when Calvin's theological legacy is under discussion. To those who refused to move beyond the details of Martin Luther's eucharistic teaching, Calvin observed—with his customary tact— that there is a difference between a disciple and an ape.[66] To one of his correspondents he wrote: "If I was not permitted at any point to depart from the opinion of Luther, it was utterly ridiculous of me to undertake the office of interpretation (*munus interpretandi*)."[67] Similarly, when accused by Albert Pighius (c. 1490-1542) of diverging from Luther's opinions on free will, Calvin replied, "If Pighius does not know it, I want to make this plain to him: our constant endeavor, day and night, is to *form* in the manner we think will be best whatever is faithfully *handed on* by us."[68] *Fideliter tradere* is also *formare*.

There is an affinity between Schleiermacher's use of Calvin and Calvin's use of Luther. We might even venture to say that we find in them both something like the old motto *Ecclesia reformata, semper reformanda*. But it is not an easy conception of the theological task to put into practice. If the obvious difficulty with Hodge's appeal to two thirds of the Vincentian canon (*Quod semper, quod ubique*) is that it is only a pious fantasy, the idea of a developing tradition poses acutely the problem of continuity. For did Calvin leave the substance of Luther's opinions unchanged, as he believed, merely expressing them more judiciously? Ask any Lutheran. And was Schleiermacher really the champion of Calvin and his doctrine of election, or was he proposing a new doctrine? If his

---

[65] *CF*, § 131.2. Schleiermacher understood the development (*Entwicklung*) of doctrine not simply as an observable historical phenomenon, but as a theological task (see, e.g., *KD*, §§ 177-182), which, by definition, both holds the theologian responsible to authorized ecclesiastical doctrines and frees him from being *nur ein Träger der Überlieferung* (ibid., § 19). In *KD*, § 29, he speaks of "mindless tradition" (*geistlose Überlieferung*). But the implicit contrast between *Überlieferung* and *Entwicklung* does not mean that "tradition" always carried negative connotations for Schleiermacher (see, for instance, *KD*, § 47). See also the references on orthodoxy and heterodoxy in n. 40 above.

[66] See, e.g., Calvin to Martin Seidemann, 14 March 1555, CO, 15: 501-502.

[67] Calvin to Francis Burkhardt, 27 February 1555, CO, 15: 454.

[68] *Defensio sanae et orthodoxae doctrinae de servitute et liberatione humani arbitrii adversus calumnia Alberti Pighii Campensis* (1543), CO, 6: 250. See further my article, "The Pathfinder: Calvin's Image of Martin Luther" (1968), reprinted in *The Old Protestantism*, chap. 2.

doctrine of election was something new, shall we call it a development or apostasy?[69] I hope I may have taken a small step toward answering these questions by showing that traditions are not simply given but constructed, and that when we look for continuity, we need to decide what kind of continuity we seek—Hodge's or Schleiermacher's, repetition or development.

---

[69]Continuity may, of course, be located in the questions asked rather than in the answers given, and of this the doctrine of election is a prime example. Preoccupation with the divine decrees and efficacious grace has been characteristic of Reformed theology from Calvin to Barth, but it has largely taken the form of a continuing attempt to *revise* Calvin's doctrine. Elsewhere, I have suggested that continuity in Reformed theology might also be sought less in the preservation of a short list of distinctive doctrines, more in the "habit of mind" brought to the doctrinal task. See Gerrish, "Tradition in the Modern World: The Reformed Habit of Mind," in *Toward the Future of Reformed Theology: Tasks, Topics, Traditions*, ed. David Willis and Michael Welker (Grand Rapids, Michigan: William B. Eerdmans Publishing Company, 1999), 3-20.

A Response to "Constructing Tradition: Schleiermacher, Hodge and the Theological Legacy of John Calvin"

Philip W. Butin

Characteristically, Brian Gerrish has shaped his presentation on "The Theological Legacy of John Calvin" so as to raise a question that is both enduring and contemporary in a manner that is both enigmatic and intriguing. The question concerns the subtle relationship between Calvin's specific theological legacy and contemporary discussion about the meaning and boundaries of the broader Reformed theological tradition. Of course, both ideas—that of Calvin's legacy and that of a "Reformed Tradition"—must be acceptably defined before the question of their relationship can be meaningfully considered. And that is the problem that Dr. Gerrish's essay both raises and heightens.

I.

What might it mean to talk about Calvin's "theological legacy?" It is a basic question: a question that the various historical, theological, and church constituencies that identify with Calvin have typically answered in specific, diverse, and sometimes even conflicting ways. Of course, one of the more heated discussions in Calvin scholarship at present revolves around the relationship of Calvin to the self-affirmed "Calvinists." When this question dominates the center stage in discussions of Calvin's legacy, larger issues can easily be overlooked. The relationship of Calvin's 16th century, humanistically-inspired thought to its immediate offspring among the self-consciously "Calvinistic" but methodologically more scholastic and rationalistic 17th century movements is one important aspect of this issue. But it is only one. Thus Dr. Gerrish's decision to steer clear of this narrower discussion may open up the possibility of seeing the larger issues more clearly. The question he *has* placed before us is a broader and more contemporary one: a question as to whether meaningful boundaries can appropriately be placed around Calvin's legitimate "legacy," and what, if any, those boundaries might or might not be.

One not already aware of Dr. Gerrish's longstanding independent interest in Friedrich Schleiermacher might be excused for the impression that—given the myriad options—this self-confessed "Moravian of a higher order"[1] is a somewhat unlikely choice for the purpose of illustrating Calvin's theological legacy. Positively, by this choice Dr. Gerrish points out the remarkable breadth and significance of Calvin's influence. For he is convinced that "Schleiermacher was surely the greatest theologian of the Reformed church between Calvin and Barth." On the other hand, there appears to be a deeper and more subtle motive in making this choice—a motive which may also provide a clue to Dr. Gerrish's ongoing interest in the German he has called "Prince of the Church." Before we move completely into a post-modern mode, Dr. Gerrish wants contemporary Reformed Christians loyal to Calvin to come to grips—not only with Calvin—but also with modernity.

What I would like to note is the challenge to the notion of "legacy" that this choice reflects. As our colloquium comes to end, we might profitably ponder just what does and does not constitute a theological legacy in general. Surely this exercise in definition would clarify our consideration of what does and does not constitute Calvin's theological legacy in particular. How do constitutive contributions of individual figures to what we call a "Tradition" find enduring expression within that tradition? This, too, is a lively issue in [somewhat different] Reformed circles today, and the question of whether and to what extent Schleiermacher may or may not be an authentic part of Calvin's legacy poses it sharply for our consideration. Dr. Gerrish expresses the question in broader terms when, in his conclusion, he hints that it may also be a matter of properly relating the conserving phrase *"Ecclesia reformata"* to the more progressive phrase *"semper reformanda"* in the old and delicately-balanced slogan that is so widely used and misused today.

Does simple respect for Calvin's influence place one in Calvin's legacy? Do baptism and ordination in a historically "Reformed" denomination place one in Calvin's legacy? Does mere quotation of Calvin in various doctrinal discussions place one in Calvin's legacy? Does using the same theological terms that Calvin uses—albeit radically redefined—place one in Calvin's legacy? If the answer to all these questions is "yes," then this society can take heart and look forward to a bright and glorious future, because then Calvin's legacy includes almost the whole of Christian thought since the Reformation. If not, we must return to the question. Precisely what *does* constitute a theological legacy? Is any specific and publically identifiable continuity of theological method or content required?

The sharp contrast between a financial legacy and a theological legacy that begins the paper alerts the listener to Gerrish's own sympathies:

Quite different from a monetary bequest is a theological legacy. It is not only possible for Calvin's theological heirs to spend their inheritance in ways he

---

[1]Brian Gerrish, *A Prince of the Church: Schleiermacher and the Beginnings of Modern Theology* (Philadelphia: Fortress, 1984) 27, 36-37.

might not approve: even what they receive is pretty much what they decide to take. Bickering over the inheritance is likely. Not that everyone will want the same things from the treasure chest; the argument will be over the value of the things chosen.

Claims on the part of others to stand where they can adjudicate what is and is not included in a theological legacy, it seems, naively overlook the complexity of the diverse phenomena involved.

Dr. Gerrish's next sentence, however, tries to edge back towards a bit more positive understanding of what constitutes a legacy. "There are certainly limits on what one may reasonably claim as Calvin's theological legacy." It is good to hear that said, but if one begins to wonder just what those limits might conceivably be, the section of the paper that discusses Schleiermacher does not provide much tangible help. Are there specific matters of theological *method* that Calvin and Schleiermacher share in common? Here at least, Dr. Gerrish is reluctant to claim that there are (or even that there could be), given the historical distance between the two.[2] Are there specific theological *ideas* or *themes* that Schleiermacher has intentionally drawn from Calvin, embraced, and sympathetically carried forward for a new time? Dr. Gerrish offers many suggestions for consideration (use of biblical creation narratives, divine foreknowledge, the transmission of original sin, views on baptismal regeneration, and finally "election"), but even his own sympathetic discussion of how Calvin's views are used by Schleiermacher articulates a great deal more discontinuity than continuity.

Dr. Gerrish's choice of Charles Hodge as the other primary example of "Calvin's legacy" might at first seem a bit more obvious. Hodge was clearly and self-consciously, Gerrish points out, "a learned advocate of the Calvinist theological legacy." The choice becomes more interesting when it is remembered that Hodge attended Schleiermacher's church in Berlin as a graduate student there, respected and wrestled seriously with his thought throughout his life and his *Systematic Theology*, and retained a very sympathetic estimate of the latter's Christian piety and even his eternal destiny.[3] Hodge is no mere foil or straw figure in Gerrish's argument. But just what *is* Gerrish trying to say to us by pairing Schleiermacher with Hodge, again given the innumerable other possible figures who could be singled out for discussion, even among Schleiermacher's

---

[2]At the same time, Gerrish specifically points out that Schleiermacher perceived "no comparable epoch" that "separated him from the first generation of Protestants." Gerrish has elsewhere pursued the possibility that a common concern for piety governs the theological shape (method?) of both Calvin's and Schleiermacher's theological summaries . See B. A. Gerrish, *Continuing the Reformation* (Chicago: University of Chicago Press, 1993), 190ff.

[3]Charles Hodge, *Systematic Theology*, Vol. II (New York: Scribner, Armstrong, and Co., 1872), 440.

immediate contemporaries? It seems he wants us to admit that those who consciously claim Calvin's legacy are no less prone to be selective in drawing from Calvin what serves their own contemporary interests as are those, like Schleiermacher, who have often been branded as subverters of the Reformed tradition.

So did Hodge "receive a larger bequest" from Calvin than Schleiermacher did? Admittedly, the question is not as simple as it appears on the surface. Schleiermacher may brazenly substitute the "second norm" of pious experience for Calvin's primary norm of scripture, but Hodge imports the second norms of both reason and tradition into his discussions also. The difference is he does not always seem to realize he is doing it. Calvin's heirs, Gerrish points out, "have not all used his legacy in the same measure or the same way. Sometimes they seem to have drawn unconsciously on their heritage [read "Schleiermacher"] or equally unconsciously to have neglected it [read "Hodge]."

In the final analysis, Gerrish declines to offer a direct answer to his question "Was Schleiermacher a bold and resolute disciple of Calvin?" But his oblique response is that perhaps Schleiermacher's place in Calvin's legacy is not unlike Calvin's place in Luther's legacy. This is an interesting suggestion, but my thoughts are immediately drawn to a number of significant differences that call this comparison into question. As Dr. Gerrish is well aware, the particular influence of Luther's early ideas on the young Calvin has been thoroughly examined by Ganoczy and others.[4] It is clear that whatever else it may have been, it was at least an openly acknowledged and specifically theological influence. It was an influence that included Calvin's taking over many of Luther's Augustinian theological presuppositions, warmly affirming the primary authority Luther found in scripture, and retaining the specific content of many of Luther's particular theological emphases, including central issues like providence, original sin, justification, predestination, and freewill.

As near contemporaries in a post-medieval world that still shared the capacity for a common Latin discourse, Luther and Calvin were simply much closer historically, culturally, and theologically than were Calvin and Schleiermacher. This does not negate Dr. Gerrish's excellent observation that for both Calvin and Schleiermacher, "faithfully handing over" the tradition does include "forming" it in some measure. The point I am making is that the measure in the one case is incommensurate with the measure in the other. Calvin himself puts his finger on the problem with Dr. Gerrish's comparison, in the sentence just after the one Dr. Gerrish quotes from the 1555 Letter to Francis Burkhart. The quoted sentence is: "If I were not permitted at any point to depart from the opinion of Luther, it was absurd and ridiculous of me to undertake the task of

---

[4]Alexandre Ganoczy, *The Young Calvin*, tr. D. Foxgrover and W. Provo (Philadelphia: Westminster, 1987) 137-145.

interpretation at all." The next sentence continues, "This was the point at issue: whether I had eagerly sought after different meanings..." (an cupide accersam diversos sensus).5 Perhaps in deciding whether Schleiermacher or Hodge "received the larger bequest" from Calvin, we should take at least this modest cue from Calvin himself, and try to ascertain whether either of them "eagerly sought after different meanings." I will leave you to draw your own conclusions on that one.

II.

Throughout all of Dr. Gerrish's intriguing paper, his comments continue to helpfully raise the question of what constitutes a theological legacy. But that brings me to something I miss in it. I would like to have seen him address his own question more directly. Let me illustrate before I specify. Dr. Gerrish points out the different views of "past sources and norms" held by Schleiermacher and Hodge. This is the beginnings of an effort to address the question of criteria for determining a "legacy." But here he might have gone ahead to ask, "Which view of past sources and norms 'hands over' Calvin's own legacy more faithfully, while at the same time 'forming' it for a new generation?" Dr. Gerrish notes that Hodge's debate with William Nevin was "an *argument* about the theological legacy of *Calvin*: what it was and where it was sound" [emphasis mine]. In discussing Calvin's theological legacy, are not *we* who are its beneficiaries also obliged to "argue over what Calvin said, what he meant, and what he left that is worth preserving?" As committed Reformed Christians—believers who are *invested* in our tradition as those who "know" and "do" as well as "feel" our religion—are we not *obliged* to put on our "theological caps?" Surely Calvin, Hodge, and Schleiermacher— not to mention Nevin, Brunner, and Barth— would agree we must. And I would go on to submit that as we do, we need to show discernable and publically identifiable continuity of theological method and content in support of our claims for a theological legacy. Concerning Schleiermacher, Dr. Gerrish has exerted a great deal of effort to try to show this kind of continuity in various writings. I would have appreciated hearing at least a summary of the results of that effort with us here today.

One of the stronger possibilities for showing significant continuity of both theological method and content between Calvin, Schleiermacher, and Hodge, I suspect, is to follow Dr. Gerrish's lead and concentrate in some detail on their common use of the *munus triplex* as a comprehensive rubric for understanding the work of Christ. I am confused by Dr. Gerrish's comments that neither Calvin nor Hodge made as much use of the threefold office as they might have. I hope he will clarify for us what he means by these observations. His point about the relative imbalance of discussion on each aspect of the office may be telling for Hodge, but I do not believe it is for Calvin. Calvin's 16th chapter in

---

5 *CO,* 15: 454 (#2123).

Book II moves to Christ's fulfillment of the function of Redeemer, not as a corollary of his priestly office, but rather because here Calvin is moving forward in his narrative commentary on the Apostles' Creed. More broadly speaking, for Calvin, the threefold office was the crucial *conceptual* hinge between the work of the triune God *extra nos* in Christ, and the work of the triune God *in nobis*. And the *actual* connection between these two is the reality and work of God the Holy Spirit,[6] a point which Hodge seems to miss entirely.

If this is kept in mind, Dr. Gerrish is on the mark when he suggests that Schleiermacher may have actually been closer to Calvin than was Hodge in using the threefold office "to prevent undue emphasis on a single aspect of Christ's redemptive activity." Incidentally, both Brunner and Barth are also sympathetic to use of the threefold office as a comprehensive schema for organizing their discussion of the work of Christ. Perhaps a detailed examination of the *munus triplex* might reveal an interesting continuity of both method and content in all of the Reformed figures mentioned in the paper; a continuity that just might provide evidence of a shared legacy. But let us establish that point by arguing about it, with specific reference to "what *Calvin* said, what he meant, and what he left that is worth preserving."

---

[6]Compare 2. 15 with 3. 1-3 in OS; cf. Battles' English translation in *Institutes of the Christian Religion*, LCC. Also, cf. my comments in Philip W. Butin, *Reformed Ecclesiology: Trinitarian Grace According to Calvin* in Studies in Reformed Theology and History 2:1 (Princeton: Princeton Seminary, Winter, 1994), 29-35.